William Fitzgibbon

The Mine of Wealth and Guide for the Million

Containing the secret system and instructions for the manufacture of wines,

liquors, cordials, and bitters, enabling every one to manufacture for himself,

cookery in all its branches

William Fitzgibbon

The Mine of Wealth and Guide for the Million
Containing the secret system and instructions for the manufacture of wines, liquors, cordials, and bitters, enabling every one to manufacture for himself, cookery in all its branches

ISBN/EAN: 9783744785419

Printed in Europe, USA, Canada, Australia, Japan

Cover: Foto ©Lupo / pixelio.de

More available books at **www.hansebooks.com**

THE MINE OF WEALTH

AND

GUIDE FOR THE MILLION:

CONTAINING THE

SECRET SYSTEM AND INSTRUCTIONS

FOR THE MANUFACTURE OF

WINES, LIQUORS, CORDIALS, AND BITTERS,

ENABLING EVERY ONE TO MANUFACTURE FOR HIMSELF;

COOKERY IN ALL ITS BRANCHES;

THE ART OF PRODUCING BEAUTIFUL FIREWORKS

A LARGE AND VALUABLE COLLECTION OF

USEFUL MISCELLANEOUS RECEIPTS,

AND A

FAMILY MEDICAL DEPARTMENT,

BY WHICH DISEASES MAY BE TREATED WITH THE GREATEST SAFETY, AS THE INSTRUCTIONS AND PRESCRIPTIONS ARE GIVEN IN THE PLAINEST MANNER AND LANGUAGE.

We eat and drink to live,
And live to eat and drink.

BY DR. WM. FITZGIBBON.

PHILADELPHIA:
BARCLAY & CO., No 602 ARCH STREET.

Entered according to Act of Congress, in the year 1867, by
BARCLAY & CO.,
in the Clerk's Office of the District Court of the United States,
in and for the Eastern District of Pennsylvania.

PREFACE.

It has been said by a modern writer that "facts are the firmest friends of common sense." In no department of information are common sense facts, that is to say proven data, more important than in a volume of receipts. In the "Mine of Wealth," for such is the title we have given the present compend of useful knowledge, will be found such materials familiarly presented as shall justify this appellation. Like "the gems" of the poet the interior of this Mine is both "rich and rare" for not only is it valuable in regard to the secrets it divulges, but in the rarity of the information given. The costliness of some works upon this subject, and the unreliability of others made a want, that this is calculated to supply.

The publisher has long been in possession of a number of useful formulæ for which at different times he has been offered large sums of money. The present volume owes its origin to a desire to make generally known that which privately disposed of, might never meet the public eye; but as a very large sale of copies is justly anticipated the confidence of the publisher in the popular appreciation is not likely to be disappointed.

In the department of Wines and Liquors there will be found details which no one connected either with the sale or consumption of those articles should be without. In the Bread and general culinary department there are ideas that have truly been called "the *living* facts of the kitchen."

Practices based on the use of brass kettles as is generally recommended are here eschewed, and only such employment of utensils recommended as conduce to the consumer's health. Simplicity and the absence of technical or scientific terms has been made the rule of expression; and it is believed that every receipt herein published is at least worth the price of the book to every one interested in its subject. The Miscellaneous Department is necessarily an *Olla Podrida* of facts that refused other classification but possesses an importance and value little inferior to the other special departments, and without which the work would not have been complete.

W. B

PHILADELPHIA, 1867

MINE OF WEALTH,

AND

GUIDE FOR THE MILLION.

CHAPTER I.

The Manufacture of Wines, Liquors, Cordials and Bitters.

AMONG the many articles upon which increased heavy duties have been levied, in consequence of our late war, that of Foreign Wines, Liquors, Cordials and Bitters have come in for their full share, and it has therefore become a matter of great importance and economy to the distiller and to the dealer, to produce articles of a similar character and of course at a less expense than that incurred by the importation of the Foreign article. Some years ago, arising from almost similar causes British capitalists were induced to prepare this class of articles for their home consumption, and though for a long time the effort proved unsuccessful, yet at last, after the expenditure of much talent, labor and capital their efforts were crowned with success. A very excellent article of British manufacture can now be purchased in the market, at the same time some vile mixtures are sold and palmed off as genuine. Several attempts have been made to establish similar enterprises in the United States, and *now* their necessity having been experienced more than ever, it is proposed to aid and encourage overcoming this want by furnishing such important receipts for the manufacture of these articles as the skill and experience of the past has taught. The writer of this chapter here gives the formulas which he has worked over twenty years, and he can only say that, if skilful management, care, and the faithful following out of the instructions are persevered in, an article will be produced, that cannot, except by the most rigid tests, be surpassed by the original, either in quality or flavor. As large a sum as $1000 has been paid for some of the receipts here presented—the publication of this book will now, however, place them within the reach of all, and every dealer can, if he chooses, manufacture for himself a superior article and at about half the cost of an inferior and poisonously adulterated mixture, with which it is to be regretted, the country now abounds.

The French manufacturers are proverbial for the superiority of their cordials over all others, and to succeed similarly and attain to their cream-like smoothness and delicate flavor, the very purest of spirit, and sugar, and the judicious application of the flavoring ingredients must be employed. The flavoring essences should always be prepared by the manufacturer rather than purchased, and this can be done either by infusion or maceration, always in very pure spirit, and kept in a cool place, in well corked stone ware bottles. It generally occupies four or five weeks when it may be distilled or filtered—the former being preferable. Either the outer peel or fruit is used for the preparation of the essence which is obtained by carefully peeling the fruit with a knife, or by rubbing it off with a lump of hard white sugar, or pure aromatic seeds and woods by pounding them before submitting to the action of spirit for infusion. For coloring, vegetable infusions are best, agreeable to the color required.

In conclusion, let the casks, vats, and other articles used in manufacturing be always kept perfectly clean and sweet; the ingredients required for the various preparations of the first quality, and strength; the manipulation conducted with the necessary judgment and discretion, and the results will be alike satisfactory and profitable, and industry and ingenuity meet their well-merited reward.

Proportionate quantities of the articles named in the following receipts, are to be used, according as a greater or less quantity may be required.

RECEIPTS.

American Honey Wine.—Honey, twenty pounds; cider, twelve gallons; put in a forty gallon cask and let ferment. Then add—rum, half a gallon; brandy, half a gallon; red or white tartar dissolved, six ounces; bitter almonds and cloves, each one quarter of an ounce. Mix well together, let set twenty-four hours, then bottle.

Aniseed Cordial.—Bruised aniseed, sixteen pounds; proof spirits, fifty gallons; water, sixty gallons; macerate well and let stand three days: draw off one hundred gallons, and sweeten to your taste, either with clarified syrup or with white sugar, and then filter through a bag, previously putting a little magnesia in the bag.

Anti-Ferment for Wine, Beer, &c.—Sulphate of lime, one part; powdered mustard seed, two parts; mix well together—this is infallible if properly used.

Anisette.—(French.)—Sugar, twelve ounces; water, five pints; proof spirits, three pints; oil of aniseed, fifteen drops. Rub the oil with a little of the sugar before adding it to the mixture.

Brandy Bitters.—Bruised gentian root, eight ounces; bitter orange peel, five ounces; cardamons, three ounces; cassia, one ounce; cochineal, one quarter an ounce; proof spirits one gallon. Let it digest one week, and then decant the clear; pour five pints of water on the sediment and let it digest another week, then decant and mix both together. Bottle.

Brandy Bitters.—(American.)—Wild cherry, one ounce; peelings of oranges and lemons dried, two ounces each; the same of fresh, two ounces and a half each; French brandy, one gallon. Digest for twelve days, shaking frequently, then press out the liquor and strain carefully, add loaf sugar, one and a half pounds. As soon as the sugar is dissolved and mixed, bottle.

Brandy Bitters.—(Common.)—American brandy, three gallons; orange and lemon peel, each half a pound; calamus root, three and a half ounces; sugar one and a half pounds; camomile flowers, two drachms; syrup, half gallon. Water, two gallons. Digest the whole well for twelve days; draw off carefully and bottle.

Aniseed Cordial.—(British.)—Oil of aniseed, five drachms; oil of carraway, thirty drops; proof spirit two gallons. This is a very excellent cordial for lowness of spirits, flatulence, &c. By adding four pounds of loaf sugar, it is much improved.

British Brandy, No. 1.—Proof spirit, ninety-eight gallons; red tartar, five pounds; acetic ether, three pounds; wine vinegar, three gallons; bruised French plums, seven pounds; bruised bitter almonds, one ounce; water sufficient to reduce it to the strength required. Dissolve the tartar in the water, then add other ingredients; after mixing well and letting stand three days to settle, draw off one hundred and twenty gallons; add brown sugar for coloring and bottle.

2.—Clean spirit, one hundred gallons; nitric ether, two pounds; cassia buds ground, half a pound; bitter almond meal, half a pound; orris root sliced, six ounces; good vinegar, two gallons; brandy coloring, one quart. Mix well in a brandy cask, stirring occasionally for a fortnight; let settle three days and bottle.

3.—Clean spirit one hundred gallons; strong vinegar, three gallons; bitter almonds ground, quarter of a pound; cassia buds ground, half a pound; orris root ground, seven ounces; guinea pepper, six ounces; powdered cloves, one ounce; tincture of catechu four pints; nitric ether two pints; brandy coloring, one quart; put the above on the lees of a freshly emptied cognac cask; mix well and treat like No. 2.

4.—Good plain malt spirits, one hundred gallons; finely powdered catechu twelve ounces; tincture of vanilla, two ounces; brown sugar coloring, one quart or more as may be required. Mix well, let clear thoroughly and bottle.

☞ Ripe pine apples (number according to desired flavor), mashed up and added to either of the above brandies in lieu of vinegar, will produce a superior pine apple brandy. Should it show signs of fermentation after adding the pines, add the antiferment.

5.—Proof spirit, forty gallons; oil of cognac, one drachm, dropped on a little white sugar and mixed in alcohol; bruised dried prunes, six pounds; white sugar, five pounds; coloring to suit. Digest for ten days, stirring occasionally.

Brandy Flavoring.—Finely powdered charcoal, three and a half ounces; ground rice, four and a half ounces; put in a quart of malt spirits and work up for fourteen days. This is the required quantity for one hundred gallons.

British Burgundy Wine.—Good cider thirty gallons; juice of elderberries, seven gallons. Lees of old burgundy wine, four and a half gallons; brandy, two gallons. Isinglass one pound, dissolved in a gallon of warm cider; lemon juice, one quart; orange flower water half a gallon; alum, four ounces. Bury down for two months, then bottle and store away for twelve months in a cool cellar. Then use.

British Claret Wine.—Good cider and port wine, each twenty-five gallons; cream of tartar, three ounces; good juicy lemons, (the juice only), one dozen. Mix well, and at the end of five weeks fine down with the whites and shells of three eggs, then bottle. This imitation if properly attended to and made as above can scarcely be distinguished from pure Bordeaux wine.

British Madeira Wine.—Infuse in forty-four gallons of boiling water, four bushels of ground pale malt. Strain off while warm twenty-four gallons, and add fourteen pounds of sugar candy, three ounces of cream of tartar, and when dissolved, two pounds of yeast. Ferment, keep skimming off the yeast, and when the fermentation is nearly finished, add raisin wine, two and a half gallons; brandy and sherry wine each, two gallons; and rum one quart. Bury down close for six to eight months. Refine and use.

British Port Wine.—Good cider, twenty-four gallons; juice of elderberries, six gallons; port wine, four gallons; brandy, one and a half gallons; logwood, one pound; isinglass, twelve ounces, dissolved in a gallon of the cider. Bury it down and in two months it will be fit to bottle, but should not be drank for twelve months. Four ounces of alum may be added to give a rough flavor.

British Sherry Wine.—Loaf sugar, thirty-two pounds; sugar candy, ten pounds: water, sixteen gallons; boil and add six gallons of pale ale wort, similar to that used for madeira; yeast, one pound. On the third day add stoned raisins ten pounds, and in another three days, brandy, one gallon; bitter almonds grated, one drachm. Bury it down for four months, draw it off into another cask, add another gallon of brandy and in three months bottle.

☞ None of the British imitation wines are mellow enough for use under twelve months after their manufacture.

British Shrub, No. 1.—Best white sugar, one hundred and seventy-five pounds; proof spirit, twenty-two gallons; British brandy, ten gallons; bitter almonds, bruised, one ounce and a half. Orris root powder, three ounces; powdered cassia, two ounces; essence of orange, one ounce; lemons sliced, one dozen; water twenty-five gallons; put the whole into a proper sized cask, and work up well every day for one week, then add water to make up one hundred and five gallons, and one quart of coloring. Beat up lightly the whites of two dozen eggs, and with the shells finely broken up, add to refine and clear.

2.—Tartaric acid powdered, eight pounds; loaf sugar, two hundred and forty pounds; dissolve them in thirty-five gallons of water; put into a cask and then add, proof spirit, or English or American brandy, thirty-five gallons; brandy coloring, one pint; oranges sliced, two dozen; bitter almonds bruised, half an ounce; cassia bruised, half an ounce; cloves bruised, half an ounce; stir up well daily for one week, keeping the casks in the meantime well bunged, then add the yolks, whites, and shells of twenty eggs, beaten to a froth mix well again, bung close and let settle, bottle.

Bourbon Whiskey.—Proof spirit, thirty-five gallons; spirits of nitre, three ounces; fusil oil of corn, two ounces, steeped four days in a pint of alcohol; sugar, dissolved in five gallons of soft water; three pounds; half dozen mellow ripe peaches mashed up. Mix well and digest twenty-four hours.

Carraway Brandy.—Carraway seed bruised. seven pounds; proof spirits, eighty gallons; sugar, forty-two pounds; water twenty gallons. Mix well, let steep for a month; let settle three days after last mixing, and bottle.

Carraway Cordial.—Oil of carraway, three ounces; oil of cassia, one drachm; oil of lemon, fifteen drops; proof spirits, twenty-five gallons; mix well, then add, white sugar, seventy pounds; dissolved in fifteen gallons of water. Mix well, let settle, and refine with the whites and shells of eight eggs beat up.

Carraway Cordial.—(West India.)—Proof spirits, forty gallons; bruised caraway seed, three pounds; white sugar, fifty-six pounds; oil of lemon and of orange peel, and of capsicum, each thirty drops; reduce with soft water to suit the taste. Mix well and digest ten days and fine with white of four eggs,

Champagne, No. 1.—Loaf sugar, fifty-six pounds; pale brown sugar, forty-eight pounds; white tartar, four ounces; warm water, forty-five gallons; mix well and when cold add, yeast, one quart; sweet cider, five gallons; bitter almonds, bruised, eight ounces; proof spirits, one gallon; orris root powder, half an ounce. Mix well, keeping the cask closely bunged. At the end of a week draw off and bottle carefully.

2.—Take three gallons of water and nine pounds of pale raw muscovado sugar, boil half an hour; skim clear with the greatest care and then pour the boiling liquid upon one gallon of red or white currants picked from the stalk, but not bruised, and when cold work it up well for two days with half a pint of ale yeast; afterwards pour it through a flannel bag, and put it into a clean cask with half a pint of isinglass fineing. When it has done working, bung it and let it stand for a month, then bottle with care, putting into every bottle a lump of loaf sugar about the size of a pigeon's egg. This is an excellent wine, has a beautiful color, sparkles brilliantly, and has been used by thousands supposing it to be the genuine article. It must be preserved or kept packed in salt.

Claret Wine.—Cider, forty gallons; cherry brandy, six gallons; cream of tartar, five pounds; white sugar, five pounds; color with red beet juice. Digest for twelve days, with occasional stirring,

Clove Cordial.—Bruised cloves, seven pounds; pimento one pound; proof spirits, fifty gallons; mix well for fourteen days, then add white sugar, one hundred and fifty pounds, dissolved in forty-five gallons water; mix well and refine with whites and shells of twelve eggs.

Cherry Brandy, No. 1.—Best thick sugar house molasses, one hundred and twenty-five pounds; proof spirits, ninety-five gallons; bruised bitter almonds, half a pound; cloves, one ounce; cassia, one ounce; put the ingredients into a large cask, mix well and let them remain a month with occasional stirring, bottle.

2.—Bruised cherries, twenty-five gallons; sugar thirty pounds; cloves and cassia, each, half an ounce: 35 proof spirit sixty gallons; bruised bitter almonds, three ounces; dissolve the sugar in sufficent warm water to dissolve it—no more— then put the whole into a cask, mix well, let stand for three months with an occasional stirring then let settle and bottle.

Cinnamon Cordial.—Oil of cassia, one ounce; essence of lemon, thirty drops; proof spirit, fifteen gallons; sugar fifty pounds; water, ten gallons; mix the spirit with the oil and essence, then add the sugar dissolved in the water, mix well again, let settle, filter through a flannel bag and bottle.

Cognac Brandy,—Prepared whiskey, twenty-eight gallons; fourth proof brandy, three gallons; tincture of kino, four ounces; spirits of nitre, seven ounces. Digest twenty-four hours.

Common Brandy.—Whiskey, twenty-five gallons, fourth proof brandy, one gallon, spirits of nitre, five ounces; one fourth of an ounce of Russia castor, mixed in half a gallon of alcohol; loaf sugar, two and a half pounds. Mix well and let stand twenty four hours.

Common Gin.—Whiskey, thirty-five gallons; spirits of nitre, five ounces; oil of juniper, three quarters of an ounce, and oil of lavender, half an ounce, dissolved in half a gallon of alcohol; loaf sugar three pounds. Mix well, and let stand twenty four hours.

Common Rum.—Whiskey, thirty gallons; tincture of kino, and spirits of nitre, each four ounces; half an ounce of oil of carraway in half a gallon of alcohol; loaf sugar, ten pounds. Mix well, and let stand twenty four hours.

Common Wines.—The following formula will answer for any of the ordinary kinds of wine, by simply adding to it five gallons of the stock wine, for which it is named.—Worked cider, thirty gallons; good brandy, one gallon; cream of tartar one pound; milk to settle one quart, or the whites and shells of four eggs beat up well together. It should be well worked, and then add the five gallons of stock wine. Let stand for twenty-four hours, then draw off and bottle.

Common Bitters.—Without any exceptions one of the best stomachic bitters ever manufactured, and but very little known.—Prepared whiskey, or clean proof spirits, fifty gallons; coriander seed, thirteen pounds; cassia four pounds; ginger, calamus, and camomile flowers, each two pounds; orange and lemon peel, each two and a half pounds; caraway seed, five and a half pounds; Virginia snake root, half a pound; aniseed, cochineal, and cloves, each one pound; red sanders, half a dozen. The red sanders and cochineal should be ground together and put into a long woolen sack dropped through the bung hole of the cask, with a string so as to be withdrawn when necesary. The other articles should be well bruised and infused in the spirit or whiskey, mixing it well occasionally for at least fourteen days. Then draw off and add three pounds of loaf sugar and one ounce of saturated tincture of gentian root. Bottle and seal up carefully for use. If PURE Jamaica or Santa Cruz rum can be obtained add five gallons, with the sugar and gentian and it will greatly improve it.

Creme de Macasons.—Pale sugar, seven pounds; proof spirits eight pounds; water, ten pounds; white sugar, eight pounds; blanched bitter almonds bruised, half a pound; powdered cloves, fifty grains; powdered mace, fifty grains; tinge it with tincture of turnsole and cochineal to a violet color. Mix and work well for ten days, then let settle and bottle.

Creme de Noyeau d'Martinique.—White sugar, one hundred pounds; proof spirits fifteen gallons; orange flower water, half a gallon; bruised bitter almonds, three pounds; essence of lemons, one ounce;

water, twenty-five gallons; work up the almonds and the essence in the spirit for fourteen days, keeping the cask well bunged, then add the sugar dissolved in the water, let them stand for a month, then strain through a flannel bag and bottle.

Creme de Barbadoes.—Two dozen lemons sliced; six large citrons sliced; fresh balm leaves half a pound; white sugar, thirty pounds; proof spirits, three gallons; water, four gallons; put the fruit into the spirits and work up well for four days, then pour the water on the balm leaves; steep for half an hour; lastly add the spirit.

Curacoa, No. 1.—Cinnamon, two ounces; brandy or proof spirits, three quarts; white sugar, two pounds and a half; Seville oranges, two dozen; mix and work well for three weeks, then let settle and bottle.

2.—Proof spirits, ten pounds; water, five pounds; white sugar, four pounds; peelings of six Seville oranges; powdered cassia, two scruples; powdered mace, two scruples; brazil, one ounce; burned sugar to give a tint; work up well for ten days and then strain off and bottle.

3.—Highly rectified spirits, five gallons; fresh orange peel, four ounces; oil of bitter almonds, one drachm; oil of cassia, one drachm; pulverized brazil wood, two ounces; clarified syrup, two quarts; let the ingredients be well stirred up every day for a fortnight, then add one gallon of water and color it with caramel, or burned sugar, and let it stand to clear; and if not quite clear in three days pass it through a filtering bag. Bottle.

Essence of Peppermint.—Oil of peppermint, one pound; rectified spirits, two gallons; green peppermint to color; mix well, settle and bottle.

English Gin.—Clear rectified spirits, one hundred gallons; English juniper oil, one and a half ounce; angelica essence, half an ounce; bitter almond oil, half an ounce; oil coriander, half an ounce; oil of carraway, half an ounce; put these into the rectified spirit and mix well during three days, then add forty-five pounds best loaf sugar, dissolved in a small quantity of rain or distilled water, again mix well and add four ounces of roche alum, and two ounces of salts of tartar. Work the whole up well for a day, let settle and bottle.

English Imitation Holland Gin.—Juniper berries, two pounds; proof spirit, eighty-three gallons; water sufficient to draw off one hundred gallons; mix and work up well for ten days, let settle and bottle.

Essence of Ginger.—Capsicum, one drachm; bruised ginger, three ounces; alcohol, **one** pound; mix and work well for **ten days.** Bottle.

Flask.—Thick sugar coloring, nine parts; extract of capsicum, three parts; mix. This is used to color and give false strength to weak brandies, &c. Sugar coloring is made by roasting coarse brown sugar to a dark color and then burning it with any hot iron instrument; or loaf sugar burned in the same manner.

Gentian Bitters.—Bruised gentian root, four ounces; cassia bark, two ounces; fresh orange peel, five ounces; bruised cardamon seed, one ounce, Jamaica or Santa Cruz rum, one gallon. Digest for eight days, then decant the clear liquor, press out the sediment, pour on it five pints of water, digest again for two days, press out again and add the two liquors together and dissolve in them two pounds of loaf sugar.

Ginger Beer, No. 1.—Bruised ginger, two ounces; water five gallons; boil for an hour, then add when sufficiently cool, loaf sugar, three pounds; cream of tartar, one and a half ounce; essence of lemon, one drachm; yeast, half a pint; mix, then strain, bottle and cork down with cord if for immediate use, but if to be kept for a time then secure with wire.

If the beer is liked stronger make in the proportion of two pounds of sugar and one ounce of ginger to each gallon of water.

2.—One and a half ounces of well sliced ginger; one ounce of cream of tartar; one lemon sliced; one pound of white sugar; put the above into an earthen vessel and pour on them one gallon of boiling water. When cold add a table spoonful of yeast, and let the whole stand for twenty four hours, skim, bottle and cork down well and in three days it will be fit for use.

3.—White sugar, four pounds; water, nine gallons; well sliced ginger, two pounds; citric acid, sixty grains. Pour the water hot (not boiling) on the ginger, and when cool, mash up and add two sugar loaf, or sweet pine apples, well ripe, then add the sugar and citric acid. Clear the whole with the whites and shells of two eggs well beat up—let stand four days and bottle carefully.

☞ The above ginger beer stands unrivalled and this receipt has been sold as high as one hundred dollars.

Ginger Pop, No. 1.—Cream of tartar, one pound; ginger, one and a half ounces; white sugar, seven pounds; essence of lemon, one drachm; water, six gallons; yeast, half a pint; mix and work well, let settle, strain, bottle and cork down with cord.

2.—Cream of tartar, one and a half ounces; sliced ginger, one ounce; white sugar, twelve ounces; oranges sliced, three; boiling water, one gallon; work well, let settle until clear, add a little yeast, draw off and bottle.

Ginger Wine.—Water ten gallons; white sugar, thirty pounds; bruised ginger, fifteen ounces; four eggs beat up; boil well and skim, then pour the liquid hot on six lemons cut up in thin slices, work up well, rack and ferment, then add two quarts of proof spirits and one pint of finings of isinglass to clear up—bottle.

Jamaica Rum.—Brown oil of rum, six ounces; oil of pimento, half an ounce; dissolved on sugar and mixed in a quart of ninety-five per cent. alcohol; proof spirit, thirty-five gallons. Mix well and re-cask after twenty-four hours.

Lemon Brandy.—Proof spirit, seventy gallons; essence of lemon, three ounces; sugar, fifty pounds; dissolved in twenty gallons of water; mix and work well for fourteen days, let settle and bottle.

Lemon Cordial.—Essence of lemons, two ounces; proof spirit, twenty-five gallons; mix and work up well; then add fifty pounds sugar, dissolved in twenty gallons of water; mix well, work up for twelve days, clear with the whites and shells of eight eggs beat up to a froth, and bottle.

Lemon Peel, Essence of—Oil of lemons, six drachms; proof spirit, one pound; mix well.

Liquodilla.—Take the fresh peelings of one dozen each of oranges and lemons, and steep them for three days in three gallons of brandy or rum; then add, water two gallons; sugar, eight pounds; mix, filter and bottle.

Madeira Wine.—Cider, forty gallons; cherry brandy, six gallons; proof spirit, two gallons; tartaric acid, one quarter of a pound; oil of bitter almonds, half an ounce infused in ninety-five per cent. alcohol; raisins, five pounds. Digest and mix well for ten days.

Mixed Bitters.—Fresh orange and lemon peel, wild cherry, colomba root, quassia and camomile flowers each one ounce; proof spirit, half a gallon. Digest for eight days, strain and express all the liquor, and add half a pound of loaf sugar and a little tincture of cochineal for coloring.

New England Rum.—Whiskey, twenty-seven gallons; New England rum, three gallons; ninety-five per cent. alcohol, half a gallon; liquorice root, three ounces; orris root, two ounces; spirits of nitre, one ounce; mix well and digest for twenty-four hours.

Noyeau.—Bruised bitter almonds, four ounces; cassia and cloves bruised, each one quarter of an ounce; essence of orange peel, one drachm; essence of lemon peel, one drachm; proof spirit, twenty gallons; mix and work well, and then add sugar, thirty pounds, dissolved in five gallons of water. Mix, let settle and bottle.

Orangeade.—Sugar, one pound; tartaric acid, one quarter of an ounce; essence of oranges, thirty-five drops; rub well together then add three quarts of water. This is a most refreshing drink.

Orange Peel, Essence of—Orange peel, one pound; proof spirit, one gallon; work well for ten days, let settle and bottle.

Another.—Orange peel, one pound; proof spirit, one pound; work well, for two days, then add six pints of white wine, work for one day, draw off the clear and bottle.

Orange Wine.—Take two hundred of the finest ripe and juicy oranges and forty lemons, or Seville oranges instead of the lemons, peel them as thin as possible, then pour eleven gallons of boiling soft water upon the peelings; let stand ten or twelve hours then strain and add the expressed juice of the oranges and lemons and thirty pounds of white sugar, work the whole well and ferment with half a pint of yeast for four or five days. Now cask and add one a half gallons of French brandy. Bury the cask closely and let stand six months to ripen, when it will be found perfectly clear and ready for bottling. The whites of two dozen eggs boiled in the water before pouring on the peelings is found to be a great improvement.

Peach Brandy.—Bruised bitter almonds, three pounds; proof spirit, one hundred gallons; sugar, sixty pounds; dissolved in thirty gallons of water; mix and work well for fourteen days, color with brandy coloring if required, let settle and bottle.

Peach Wine.—Full ripe peaches, one hundred pounds; water, twenty gallons; white sugar eighty pounds; cream of tartar dissolved in boiling water, one and a half pounds. Digest the whole well for fifteen days occasionally stirring up well, then add one quart of best brandy and let stand bunged close for six months. Draw off and bottle.

Peppermint Cordial.—White sugar, one hundred and ninety-six pounds; water, fifteen gallons; break up the sugar and put into a one hundred and twenty gallon cask, and pour the water on it, then work it up well until all the sugar is dissolved; and add English oil of peppermint, two ounces; proof spirit forty gallons; mix well, then add sufficient water to make one hundred and six gallons. Let it stand until clear, then bottle.

Pine Apple Cordial.—Proof spirits, ten gallons; white sugar, eighty pounds, in as much water as is necessary to dissolve it; ten sugar loaf pine apples, soft, ripe and in the rind, well mashed; mix well and work for ten days, then add four drachms otto of roses; let settle and bottle.

Port Wine, No. 1.—Burgundy port wine, five gallons; elderberry wine, fifteen gallons; brandy half a gallon; white sugar, three pounds; alum, three ounces. Mix well and digest for about two months stirring occasionally; then put in a fresh cask, bung close and let stand at least twelve months before using.

2.—Cider, twenty-seven gallons; cherry brandy, six gallons; proof spirit, five gallons; sugar syrup, two gallons; alcanet root, four pounds; tartaric acid, half a pound; alum, four ounces. Mix and treat as above.

3.—Cider, twenty-four gallons; juice of elderberries, six gallons; port wine, four gallons; brandy, one and a half gallons; isinglass, four ounces; dissolved in one gallon of cider. Bung down and treat as above.

Prepared Whiskey.—Common whiskey, twenty-eight gallons; unslacked lime, one pound; alum, half a pound; sweet spirits of nitre, one pint. Mix well and digest twenty-four hour.

Raisin Wine.—To every eight pounds of good raisins add one gallon of cold soft water. Put the whole into a vat or large tub, and keep well worked up every twenty-four hours until thoroughly sweet and fit to draw off. The vat or tub must be kept well covered with a mat or cloth. If the weather is warm the wine is fit to draw off generally in four or five weeks—if cool seven or eight weeks. Cask but simply cover the bunghole with a piece of cloth to keep out the dust. Let stand about five months, then draw off into a fresh cask, carefully filtering the lees. If not clear and bright, refine with isinglass dissolved in some of the wine, putting it in quite cold, and let rest a few days. Now add one gallon of the best brandy to each fourteen gallons of the wine, and let stand for about three months when it will be fit for use.

Ratafia.—(British.)—Bruised bitter almonds, five pounds; well bruised nutmegs, ten ounces; white sugar, ten pounds; ambergris, ten grains; strong French brandy, six gallons; mix and work well, keeping closely bunged, for a fortnight, then filter and bottle.

Ratafia de Curacoa.—Very superior proof spirit, two gallons and a half; peelings of one dozen fine quality sweet oranges; infused for fifteen days then add ten pounds of white sugar, dissolved in one gallon of water; mace and cinnamon, each, well bruised, one quarter of an ounce; ground Brazil wood, one ounce; bitter almonds, well bruised two pounds. Infuse the whole for ten days more, bring up the color, with brandy coloring, filter and bottle.

Ratafia des Dames.—Stoned and bruised black currants, four pounds; cloves, one and a half drachms; cinnamon, two and a half drachms; proof spirit, one gallon and a quarter; white sugar, three pounds; digest well for fifteen days, in a close vessel, occasionally shaking it—let settle three days after last shaking, strain and bottle.

Ratafia de Noyeau.—Bruised bitter almonds, two ounces; proof spirit, one gallon; two pounds of sugar dissolved in three pints of water; cassia bruised, one quarter of an ounce; cloves, one quarter of an ounce; mix and work well for twenty days, then filter and bottle.

Rhubarb Wine.—(Champagne.)—To every gallon of soft water, add five pounds of ripe rhubarb, cut into thin slices and well bruised; let stand nine days stirring well three times a-day; keep the tub or vat in which it is well covered with a cloth; strain, and to every gallon of the liquor add four pounds of white sugar, two lemons sliced with peeling, and refine with one ounce of isinglass to every nine gallons; let ferment three weeks, add one pint of brandy to each ten gallons and bring up. Make it in July and bottle in October, and put one tablespoonful of brandy and a teaspoonful of white sugar in each bottle when corking.

Rum Shrub, No. 1.—Oranges and lemons four dozen each; loaf sugar, twenty-five pounds; rub the sugar on the fruit until the whole of the rind is off, then add twelve gallons of rum and allow the sugar to dissolve in the spirit; mix and add of lemon juice and orange juice each one gallon and a half and six gallons of water that has boiled and cooled again. Mix well, digest three days.

2.—Tartaric acid, five pounds; white sugar, one hundred and twelve pounds; oil of lemons, four drachms; oil of oranges, four drachms; put them into an eighty gallon (or larger) cask, and add ten gallons of water. Work well until the sugar is dissolved, then add rum proof twenty-five gallons, and water to make up the whole to fifty-five gallons; coloring one quart; clear with twelve entire eggs, well beat up; add now one dozen Seville oranges finely sliced, and three quarters of an ounce of bruised bitter almonds. Mix the whole well, let stand until clear and bottle.

Rye Whiskey.—Good corn whiskey, thirty-eight gallons; high wines, three gallons; peaches bruised up, two pounds; sugar, two pounds. Digest and mix well up for eight days.

Santa Cruz Rum.—Prepared whiskey, twenty-five gallons; Santa Cruz rum, three gallons; oil of carraway seed, one ounce; spirits of nitre, four ounces; tincture of kino, half an ounce. Digest twenty-four hours.

Sherry Wine.—Soft old racked cider, forty gallons; proof spirit, two gallons; raisins, five pounds; sherry wine, six gallons; bitter almond oil, half an ounce dissolved in alcohol. Let stand ten days, fine down and re-cask.

Sighs of Love.—Proof spirit, three gallons; white sugar, dissolved in one and a half gallons of common rose water, eight pounds; mix and add tincture of cochineal, to color. A fashionable cordial.

Tomato Wine.—The following recipe for the making of tomato wine, will retain all the well known medicinal properties of the fruit, and good judges unaware of its nature have pronounced it excellent catawba wine. Express the juice of fully ripe tomatoes, but perfectly sound, and add one pound of loaf sugar, to each quart of the juice and bottle. In a few weeks it will have the appearance and flavor of wine of the best quality. No alcohol is needed to preserve it. Mixed with water it is a delightful and refreshing beverage for the sick.

White Elder Flower Wine.—(IMITATION FRONTINAC)—Boil eighteen pounds of white sugar in six gallons of water, and the whites of two eggs, well beaten up; then skim repeatedly until no more rises, then add a quarter of a peck of elder flowers from the tree. Do not keep them on the fire. When nearly cold stir in four or five spoonsful of good yeast and the juice of four lemons and work well into the liquor, and keep well stirred daily for eight days, then add six pounds of the best raisins stoned. Bung the cask close and let stand six months then bottle.

Whiskey Cordial.—Bruised cassia, one ounce; bruised ginger, one ounce; coriander seed, one ounce; mace, cloves, and black pepper, each half an ounce; saffron, one ounce and a half; steep for five days in four gallons of whiskey, then add twelve pounds of sugar dissolved in five gallons of water. Clear with six eggs beat up. Work well for ten days then let settle and bottle.

Wine Bitters, No. 1.—Any good wine will answer the purpose. Bruised gentian root, lemon peel, juniper berries and white camelia, each one ounce and a half; bruised chinchona bark, eight ounces; carbonate of soda, one ounce; wine, one gallon. Digest for twelve days, strain, press out the liquor and add half a pound of loaf sugar,

2.—For Restoring a Jaded Stomach.—Chamomile, bitter orange-peel, caraway seed, juniper berries—an ounce of each. Simmer slowly in a pint and a half of water till reduced to a pint. Strain and bottle. Take half a wine-glassful in an equal quantity of wine, say an hour before dinner, daily. Unequalled in convalescence when bitter medicines have not been much taken previously.

Wines.—How to Detect Adulteration of.—Champagne wine, if pure from any mixture not belonging to it forms a star in the centre of the effervescing froth, when poured into a glass standing on a table. Poor and adulterated wine named champagne is thus easily detected, as are also home made imitations from any fruit whatever, many of which owing to their sparkling qualities and close approach to real champagne have deceived some of the best judges of the wine. All other wines may easily be tried by slaking a piece of quick lime in water and bottling for use when perfectly clear and transparent. To test the suspected wine half fill a wine glass with the lime water and fill up with the wine; if it turns black or muddy it is impure and adulterated if not the liquid will remain clear.

Wooden Casks.—Wine and other liquors are subject to considerable loss and even to changes which deteriorate them in consequence of the porosity of the wooden casks in which they are kept. These evils may be prevented by drying and warming the casks, and then causing their interior to imbibe pure fused paraffine.

Note on Essential Oils.—All the essential oils mentioned in the preceding receipts must be thoroughly killed in spirits of wine before being added to the other ingredients. By killing is meant that they mix thorougly with the spirits of wine without appearing oily. The quantity of spirits of wine cannot be determined upon, but by beginning with double the quantity that there is of oil, if not enough more can be added, until it is thoroughly mixed.

Black and Red Bottle Wax.—As the bottling of wines and liquors properly is of the last importance, the following preparations will be found of great utility for corking.

Red Wax.—Common resin, twenty pounds; tallow, five pounds; lampblack, four pounds; melt and mix with a gentle heat.

Common Wax.—Resin, pitch and ivory black in equal parts. Prepare as above.

GUIDE FOR THE MILLION. 21

To make this Chapter as complete as possible, and at the same time give varied information, we annex the following highly valuable and important receipts for Summer and Winter Drinks and beverages:—

RECEIPTS.

Summer Drinks, and Beverages.

Appleade.—Cut two large apples in slices, and pour a quart of boiling water on them, strain well, and sweeten. To be drank when cold, or iced.

Apricot Effervescing Drink.—Take a pint of the juice of bruised apricots, filter until clear, and make into a syrup with half a pound of sugar, then add one ounce of tartaric acid, bottle, and cork well. For a tumbler three parts full of water, add two tablespoonfuls of the syrup, and a scruple of carbonate of soda, stir well, and drink while effervescing.

Barley Water.—1. Pick clean, and wash well a handful of common barley, then simmer gently in three pints of water with a bit of lemon-peel. Prepared thus, it does not nauseate like pearl barley water.

2.—Take two ounces and a half of pearl barley: wash well, then add half a pint of water, and boil for a little time, throw away the liquor, pour four imperial pints of boiling water on the barley, boil down to two pints, strain, flavor with sugar, and lemon-peel if wished.

Barley Water, Compound.—Boil two pints of barley water, and a pint of water together, with two ounces and a half of sliced figs, half an ounce of licquorice root sliced and bruised, and two ounces and a half of raisins. Reduce to two pints, and strain.

Beer, Treacle.—Take a pound and a half of hops, and boil in thirty-six gallons of water for an hour, then add fourteen pounds of treacle, and a little yeast to work it; ferment, and bottle.

Brown Spruce Beer.—Pour four gallons of cold water into a nine-gallon barrel, then add four gallons more, quite boiling, and six pounds of molasses, with about eight or nine table-spoofuls of the essence of spruce, and on its getting a little cooler, the same quantity of good ale yeast. Shake the barrel well, then leave with bung out for three days; bottle in stone bottles, cork well, wire carefully, pack in sand, and it will be fit to drink in two weeks.

Capillaire Mock, No. 1.—Take three pounds and a half of loaf sugar, three quarters of a pound of coarse sugar, two whites of eggs well beaten with the shells, boil together in a pint and a half of water, and skim carefully. Then add an ounce of orange-flower water, strain, and put into perfectly dry bottles. When cold, mix a tablespoonful or two of this syrup in a little warm or cold water.

2.—Mix two teaspoonsful of curacoa with a pint of syrup.

3.—Boil a quart of water well, add three pounds of white sugar, the white of an egg; skim, and boil to a syrup; then add while warm, four tablespoonsful of orange-flower water, strain, and use the same as the others.

Capillaire, True.—Take forty-eight grains of Canadian maiden-hair, (*adiantum pedatum*), six drams of boiling water, and an ounce and twenty grains of white sugar. Infuse two-thirds of the maiden-hair in the water, strain, dissolve the sugar in the infusion. Clarify with the white of an egg, pour it over the remainder of the maiden-hair, placed in a water-bath, digest for two hours, and strain the syrup. For large quantities the proportions are:—maiden-hair, one hundred ninety-two parts. Boiling water, one thousand five hundred parts. White sugar, two thousand parts.

Cherry Drink.—Prepare the same as apricot, substituting the cherry juice for the other fruit.

Cobbler, Sherry.—Take some very fine and clean ice, break into small pieces, fill a tumbler to within an inch of the top with it, put a tablespoonful of plain syrup, capillaire, or any other flavor—some prefer strawberry—add the quarter of the zest of a lemon, and a few drops of the juice. Fill with sherry, stir it up, and let it stand for five or six minutes. Sip it gently through a straw.

Cool Tankard.—Put into a quart of mild ale, a wine-glassful of white wine, the same of brandy, and capillaire, the juice of a lemon, and a little piece of the rind. Add a sprig of borage or balm, a bit of toasted bread and nutmeg grated on the top.

Cranberry Drink.—Put a teacupful of cranberries into a cup of water, and mash them. Boil, in the meantime, two quarts of water with one large spoonful of oatmeal, and a bit of lemon-peel; add cranberries, and sugar, (but not too much, otherwise the fine sharpness of the fruit will be destroyed) a quarter of a pint of white wine, or less, according to taste; boil for half an hour, and strain.

Curds and Whey—Cheap Method.—Add six grains of citric acid to a wineglassful of milk, and the result will be a pleasant acidulous whey, and a fine curd.

Curds and Whey—Italian Method.—Take several of the rough coats that line the gizzards of turkeys and fowls, cleanse from the dirt, rub well with salt, and hang them up to dry; when required for use, break off some of the skin, pour boiling water on, digest for eight or nine hours, and use the same as rennet.

Currant Water.—Take a pound of currants, and squeeze into a quart of water; put in four or five ounces of pounded sugar. Mix well, strain, and ice, or allow to get cold.

Drink, Divine.—Mix a bottle of cider, half a bottle of perry, and the same of sherry, with half a gill of brandy, then add a sliced lemon, the rind pared as thin as possible, and a toasted biscuit, which is to be added to the liquor as hot as possible. Drink iced or cooled.

Effervescing Lemonade.—Boil two pounds of white sugar with a pint of lemon-juice, bottle and cork. Put a tablespoonful of the syrup into a tumbler about three parts full of cold water, add twenty grains of carbonate of soda, and drink quickly.

Ginger Beer, Indian.—To ten quarts of boiling water, add two ounces of pounded ginger, one ounce of cream of tartar, two limes, and two pounds of sugar. Stir until cold, then strain through flannel until quite clear, adding a pint of beer, and four wineglassesful of good toddy. Bottle, tie down the corks, shake each bottle well for some time, place them upright, and they will be fit to drink the next day. This does not keep long.

Ginger Lemonade.—Boil twelve pounds and a half of lump sugar for twenty minutes in ten gallons of water; clear it with the whites of six eggs. Bruise half a pound of common ginger, boil with the liquor, and then pour it upon ten lemons pared. When quite cold, put it in a cask, with two tablespoonsful of yeast, the lemons sliced, and half an ounce of isinglass. Bung up the cask the next day; it will be ready to bottle in three weeks, and to drink in another three weeks.

Hippocras.—Digest for three days half a drachm of mace, ginger, cloves, nutmegs, and gatingale, in three quarts of Lisbon wine, and also carraway, add an ounce of cinnamon. Strain, and mix twenty ounces of white sugar with the liquor.

Imperial, Bottled.—Pour a pint of boiling water on a drachm of cream of tartar, flavor with lemon-peel and sugar, and bottle.

Imperial Drink.—Put half an ounce of cream of tartar, four ounces of white sugar, and three ounces of orange-peel, into a pan; pour three pints of boiling water on, strain, and cool.

Imperial Pop.—Take three ounces of cream of tartar, an ounce of bruised ginger, a pound and a half of white sugar, an ounce of lemon-juice, and pour a gallon and a half of boiling water on them, add two tablespoonsful of yeast. Mix, bottle, and tie down the corks as usual.

King Cup.—Take the rind and juice of a lemon, a lump of sugar, a small piece of bruised ginger, and pour on them about one pint and a half of boiling water; when cold, strain, add a wineglassful of sherry, and ice.

Lemonade.—Take sixteen lemons, pare thin, cut in halves, squeeze well, and throw all into a pan; add a pound and a half of white sugar, a gallon of boiling water, and five tablespoonsful of white wine (four if sherry), mix, strain, and cool.

Mint Julep.—Put about a dozen of the young sprigs of mint into a tumbler, add a tablespoonful of white sugar, and half a wineglassful of peach, and the same of common brandy, then fill up the tumbler with pounded ice.

Orange Drink, Effervescing.—Put the juice of six or eight oranges, two quarts of boiling water, and two drachms of tartaric acid into a bottle. When required for use, pour out a tumblerful, and add thirty grains of carbonate of soda.

Poor Man's Champagne.—Put a pint of Scotch ale into a jug, and add a bottle of good ginger beer.

Quince Syrup.—Grate quinces, pass the pulp through a sieve, then set before the fire for the juice to settle and clarify; strain and add a pound of sugar (boiled down) to every four ounces of juice; remove from the fire, and when cold, bottle for use. A tablespoonful of this syrup will flavor a pint of water.

Royal Lemonade.—Pare two Seville oranges and six lemons as thin as possible, and steep them four hours in a quart of hot water; boil a pound and a quarter of loaf sugar in three pints of hot water, skim it, and add the two liquors to the juice of six China oranges and a dozen lemons; stir well, strain through a jelly-bag, and ice.

Raspberry Sherbet.—Add half an ounce of raspberry vinegar to half a pint of iced water.

Raspberry Vinegar.—Put a pound of fine fruit into a bowl, pour upon it a quart of the best white wine vinegar, next day strain the liquor on a pound of fresh raspberries; the following day do the same, but do not squeeze the fruit only drain the liquor as dry as you can. Bottle, and cork well, then cover the corks with bottle cement.

Sangaree.—Mix a bottle of Marsela wine with a bottle and a half of iced water, sweeten with loaf sugar, and flavor with lemon-juice, and grated nutmeg.

Sherbet, Lemon.—Mix half a dram of tartaric acid, an ounce and a half of white sugar, with half a pint of water, and flavor with essence of lemons.

Supreme Nectar.—Put in a nine gallon cask six pounds of moist sugar, five ounces of bruised ginger, four ounces of cream of tartar, four lemons, eight ounces of yeast, and seven gallons of boiling water. Work two or three days, strain, add brandy one pint, bung very close, and in fourteen days bottle, and wire down.

Tamarind Drink.—Boil three pints of water with an ounce and a half of tamarinds, three ounces of currants, and two ounces of stoned raisins, till about a third has evaporated. Strain, add a bit of lemon-peel, which is to be removed in half an hour, then cool.

White Spruce Beer.—Take six pounds of white sugar, four ounces of essence of spruce, ten gallons of boiling water, and an ounce of yeast. Work the same as in making ginger beer, and bottle immediately in half pints. Brown spruce beer is made with treacle instead of sugar.

Winter Drinks, and Beverages.

Aleberry.—Mix two large spoonsful of fine oatmeal in sufficient sweet small beer, two hours previous to using it; strain well, boil, and sweeten according to taste. Pour into a warm jug, add wine, lemon juice, and nutmeg to taste, serve hot with thin slips of toast or rusk.

Ale, Mulled.—Boil a pint of good sound ale with a little grated nutmeg and sugar. Beat up three eggs, and mix them with a little cold ale; then add the hot ale to it gradually, and pour backwards and forwards from one vessel to the other several times, to prevent it curdling. Warm, and stir till it thickens, then add a tablespoonful of brandy, and serve hot with toast.

Arrack, Mock.—Take a scruple (twenty grains) of benzoic acid, and add to a quart of rum. Prepare punch with it.

Athol Brose.—Add two wineglassesful of Scotch whiskey to a wineglassful of heather-honey; mix well, and then stir in a well-beaten new laid egg.

Bang.—Take a pint of cider and add to a pint of warm ale; sweeten with treacle or sugar to taste, grate in some nutmeg and ginger, and add a wineglassful of gin or whisky.

Bishop.—Take three smooth-skinned and large Seville oranges, and grill them to a pale brown color over a clear slow fire; then place in a small punch-bowl that will about hold them, and pour over them half a pint from a bottle of old Bordeaux wine, in which a pound and a quarter of loaf sugar is dissolved; then cover with a plate, and let it stand for two days. When it is to be served, cut and squeeze the oranges into a small sieve placed above a jug containing the remainder of the bottle of sweetened Bordeaux, previously made very hot, and if when mixed it is not sweet enough, add more sugar. Serve hot in tumblers.

Some persons make Bishop with raisins or Lisbon wine, and mace, cloves, and nutmegs, but it is not the proper way.

Cardinal is made the same way as Bishop, substituting old Rhenish wine for the Bordeaux.

Clary, Mock.—Warm a bottle of claret, sweeten with honey, and add allspice and cloves to taste. Serve hot.

Crambambull.—Take two bottles of light porter or ale, and boil them in a pan. Then put into the liquor half a pint of rum, and from half a pound to a pound of loaf sugar. After this has been boiling for a few minutes, take the whole from the fire, and put into the mixture the whites and yolks of from six to eight eggs, previously well whisked; stir the whole for a minute or two, and pour it into a punch-bowl, to be drunk out of tumblers. It tastes well hot or cold.

Caudle, No. 1.—Make half a pint of fine gruel with very fine groats or oatmeal; add a piece of butter the size of a large nutmeg, a tablespoonful of brandy, the same of white wine, a little grated nutmeg and lemon-peel, and serve hot.

2.—Put three quarts of water into a pot, set over the fire to boil; mix smooth as much oatmeal as will thicken the whole with a pint of cold water, and when the water boils, pour in the thickening, and add about twenty peppercorns finely powdered. Boil till pretty thick, then add sugar to taste, half a pint of good ale, and a wineglassful of gin, all warmed up together. Serve hot.

Caudle, Brown.—Take a quart of water, mix in three tablespoonsful of oatmeal, a blade of mace, and a small piece of lemon-peel; let it boil about a quarter of an hour, skimming and stirring it well, but taking care that it does not boil over. When done, strain through a coarse sieve, sweeten to taste, add a little grated nutmeg, a pint of good, sweet ale, and half pint of white wine; then serve hot.

Caudle, Cold.—Boil a quart of spring water, when cold, add the yolk of an egg, the juice of a small lemon, six tablespoonsful of raisin wine, and sugar to taste.

Caudle, Flour.—Take a dessertspoonful of fine flour, and rub it into a smooth batter, with five tablespoonsful of spring water. Put a quarter of a pint of new milk into a saucepan, set over the fire, with two lumps of sugar, and when it boils, stir the flour and water gradually into it, and keep stirring for twenty minutes over a slow fire. Nutmeg or ginger may be grated in, if thought proper.

Caudle, Flummery.—Put half a pint of fine oatmeal into a quart of spring water, and let it stand all night. In the morning stir it well, and strain through a coarse sieve into a skillet or saucepan, then add two blades of mace and some grated nutmeg; set on the fire, keep stirring and let boil for a quarter of an hour, when if too thick, add a little more water, and let it boil a few minutes longer; then add half a pint of white wine, a tablespoonful of orange-flower water, the juice of a lemon, the same of an orange, sugar to taste, and a piece of butter about the size of a walnut; warm the whole together, thicken with the yolk of a well-beaten egg, and drink hot.

Caudle, Oatmeal.—Take a quart of ale, a pint of stale beer, and a quart of water; mix all together, and add a handful of fine oatmeal, six cloves, two blades of mace, some nutmeg, and eight allspice berries bruised. Set over a slow fire, and let it boil for half an hour, stirring it well all the time; then strain through a coarse sieve, add half a pound of sugar, or to taste, a piece of lemon-peel. Pour into a pan, cover close, and warm before serving.

Caudle, Rice.—Make the same as flour caudle, using ground rice instead of flour, and when done add cinnamon and sugar to taste, and a wineglassful of brandy.

Caudle, Tea.—Make a pint of strong green tea, pour it into a saucepan, and set over a slow fire. Beat the yolks of two eggs well, and mix with half a pint of white wine, some grated nutmeg, and sugar to taste; then pour into the saucpan, stir well until hot, and serve.

Caudle, White.—Mix two tablespoonsful of fine oatmeal in a quart of water, two hours before using it, strain through a sieve and boil it, then sweeten with sugar, and season with lemon-juice and nutmeg

Devilled Ale.—Cut a slice of bread about an inch thick, toast and butter it, then sprinkle with cayenne pepper and ginger, and place in the bottom of a jug, add a pint of warm ale, and sugar to taste.

Egg Flip.—To mix a quart of flip put the ale on the fire to warm, and beat up three or four eggs with four ounces of moist sugar; remove the froth of the ale, while on the fire, until it begins to boil, mix the froth with the sugar and eggs, add grated nutmeg or ginger to taste, and a girl of rum. When the ale boils, stir it gradually into the eggs and rum, until quite smooth, then serve.

Egg Wine.—Beat up an egg and mix it with a tablespoonful of spring water. Put a wineglassful of white wine, half a glass of spring water, and sugar and nutmeg to taste, into a small saucepan, place over a slow fire, and when it boils add it gradually to the egg, stirring well; then return the whole to the saucepan, and place over the fire again, stir for a minute, remove, and serve with toast.

If it boils when placed on the fire a second time, it will curdle.

Elder Wine, Mulled.—Put sufficient wine into a saucepan, warm over the fire, and if requisite add sugar, spice, or water. When warmed, serve with thin slips of toast or rusks.

Fun.—Take half a dozen or more lemons, as may be desired, and extract the juice, adding half the bulk of water; saturate with loaf sugar, then heat to boiling point and add an equal quantity of best gin, brandy or whisky according to taste, grate a little nutmeg on it, serve thus hot in tumblers and you have a "night-cap" for a winter's night that cannot be equalled. A strong solution of citric acid will answer instead of lemons, if they cannot be obtained.

Hot Purl.—Put a quart of mild ale into a saucepan, add a tablespoonful of nutmeg, and place over a slow fire until it nearly boils. Mix a little cold ale with sugar to taste, and, gradually, two eggs well beaten; then add the hot ale, stirring one way to prevent curdling—and a quarter of a pint of whisky. Warm the whole again, and then pour from one vessel into another till it becomes smooth.

Jingle.—Roast three apples, grate some nutmeg over them, add sugar to taste, and place in a quart jug, with some slices of toasted plum cake; make some hot ale, and fill up the jug, then serve

Oxford Nightcap.—Take half a tumbler of tea made as usual with sugar and milk, add a slice of lemon, a wineglassful of new milk, and the same of rum or brandy; beat up a new-laid egg, and add to the whole while warm.

Poor Man's Drink.—Take two quarts of water, and place in a saucepan with four ounces of pearl barley, two ounces of figs split, two ounces of stoned raisins, and an ounce of root-liquorice sliced; boil all together till only a quart remains; then strain, and use as a drink.

Posset Ale.—Boil a pint of new milk with a slice of toasted bread, sweeten a bottle of mild ale, and pour it into a basin with nutmeg or other spice, add the boiling milk to it, and when the head rises, serve.

Posset, Cold.—Take a pint of cream, half a pint of white wine, the juice of half a lemon, and the peel rasped into it. Sweeten the cream and wine, put the latter into a basin, and then pour the cream from a height into the basin, stirring both well all the time; remove the froth, let it remain for a day in lukewarm water if the weather is cold, and then serve.

Posset, Jelly. Take eight eggs, leave out the whites of four, and beat all the remainder well together in a basin; then add half a pint of white wine, a little strong ale (to taste), and sugar; put into a saucepan, and set over a slow fire, stirring all the time. Boil a pint of milk with a little nutmeg and cinnamon, just enough to flavor it, and, when the eggs and wine are hot, add the boiling milk to it; then remove from the fire, pour into a punch-bowl, cover with a plate for half an hour, then sprinkle the top with pounded sugar, and serve.

Posset, Lemon.—Steep the rind of a lemon pared thin, in a pint of sweet white wine two hours before required, add the juice of one lemon, and sugar to taste; put it in a bowl with a quart of milk or cream, and whisk one way until very thick. This will fill twenty glasses, which may be filled the day before required.

Posset, Orange.—Take the crumb of a penny loaf grated fine, and put it into a pint of water, with half the peel of a Seville orange grated, or sugar rubbed upon it. Boil all together till it looks thick and clear; then take the juice of one half a Seville orange, three ounces of sweet, and one ounce of bitter almonds, beat well with a tablespoonful of brandy, add sugar to taste, and a pint of white or raisin wine; mix well, add to the posset, and serve.

Posset, Pope's.—Blanch and pound four ounces of sweet almonds, and half an ounce of bitter ones; add boiling water, and strain, sweeten, and make hot half a bottle of white wine; mix.

Planter's Punch.—Infuse two ounces of good green tea in a pint of boiling water, and when well drawn, draw off without sediment; dissolve in it about half a pound of best white lump sugar; take three large full lemons and rub off the rind with a second half pound of lump sugar to impregnate with the essential oil, then cut up the lemons in small slices and bruise; add a small pot of pure guava jelly, and mix the whole thoroughly; next add six wineglasses of best cognac brandy, two of madeira wine, one bottle of old rum and about a quart of boiling water. Work up and mix thorougly, add a little grated nutmeg, and you have a punch that cannot be surpassed, if equalled by any other compounded.

Posset, Royal.—Take a pint of ale, mix a pint of cream with it; then add the yolks of four and the whites of two eggs well beaten, sweeten to taste and flavor with nutmeg. Pour into a saucepan, set over the fire, stir well until thick, and before it boils; pour into a basin and serve hot.

Posset, Rack.—Put a quart of new milk into a saucepan, and place it over a slow clear fire. When it boils, crumble four Damascus biscuits into it; give it one boil, remove from the fire, add grated nutmeg and sugar to taste, stir in half a pint of sack, (canary wine,) and serve. French roll will answer instead of the biscuit.

Posset, Snow.—Boil a stick of cinnamon, and a quarter of a nutmeg, with a quart of new milk, and when it boils remove the spice. Beat the yolks of ten eggs well, and mix gradually with the milk until thick; then beat the whites of the eggs with sugar and canary wine into snow. Put a pint of canary (sack) into a saucepan, sweeten to taste; set over a slow fire, and pour the milk and snow into the saucepan, stirring all the time it is over the fire; when warm, remove from the fire, cover close, and set aside for a little time before being used.

Posset, Treacle.—Boil a pint of milk, add sufficient treacle to curdle it; allow the curd to settle, strain off the liquid, and drink it as hot as possible.

Posset, Wine.—Boil some slices of white bread in a quart of milk; when quite soft take it off the fire, add sugar and grated nutmeg to taste. Pour it into a basin, add a pint of raisin or sweet wine by degrees, and serve with toasted bread.

Punch, Cold.—Pour half a pint of gin on the rind of a lemon; add a tablespoonful of lemon-juice, a wineglassful of maraschino, a pint and a half of water, and two bottles of iced water.

Punch, Common.—Take two large fresh lemons with rough skins and full of juice. Rub some large lumps of white sugar over the lemons till they have acquired the oil from the rind, then put them into a bowl with as much more as is necessary to sweeten the punch to taste; then squeeze the lemon-juice upon the sugar, and bruise the sugar in the juice, add a quart of boiling water and mix well; then strain through a fine sieve, and add a quart of rum or a pint of rum and brandy, or a pint and a half of rum and half a pint of porter; then add three quarts more water, and mix well.

About half a pound of sugar is usually required, but it is impossible to fix a limit to sugar, spirits, or lemon-juice, as they depend upon taste.

Punch Milk—FOR CHRISTMAS-DAY.—Add the peel and juice of twenty-four lemons, and three pounds and a half of loaf sugar, to five bottles of cold water, and four bottles of rum; when these are well mixed, add two bottles of boiling milk, and mix the whole well. Let it stand for twenty-four hours, strain well, bottle, and cork tight; it is then ready for use. N. B. The finer the strainer is, the better the punch. This is the best receipt we have ever seen or used.

Punch, Milk, Ordinary.—Pare six oranges and six lemons as thin as you can; grate them over with sugar to get the flavor. Steep the peels in a bottle of rum or brandy stopped close twenty-four hours. Squeeze the fruit on two pounds of sugar, add to it four quarts of water and one of new milk boiling hot; stir the rum into the whole, run through a jelly-bag till clear, bottle and cork close immediately.

Punch, Regent.—Take a bottle of Champagne, a quarter of a pint of brandy, the juice of a lemon, a Seville orange, and a wineglassful of Martinique, with this mix a pint or more of a strong infusion of the best green tea strained, and syrup or sugar to taste.

Punch a la Romaine.—Take a quart of lemon ice, add the whites of three eggs well beaten, with rum and brandy, till the ice liquefies, in the proportion of three parts of rum to one of brandy, and water to taste. Then add a teacupful of strong green tea infusion, strained, and a little champagne.

Punch, Tea.—Infuse two ounces of hyson tea, and an ounce of black tea, in three quarts of boiling water; then add four pounds of loaf sugar, citric acid and spirit of citron, of each six drachms; rum one pint, and five pints of brandy; mix well, and serve.

Toddy, Buttered.—Mix a glass of rum-grog pretty strong and hot, sweeten to taste with honey, flavor with nutmeg and lemon-juice, and add a piece of fresh butter about the size of a walnut.

Wine Mulled, No. 1.—Boil some cloves, mace, cinnamon, and nutmeg, in about a quarter of a pint of water till well flavored with spice, then add to a pint of port or home-made wine; sweeten to taste, and serve hot with thin toast or rusks.

2. Boil a small stick of cinnamon, a blade of mace, and three cloves, in a breakfast cupful of water for a few minutes; add some grated nutmeg, and a pint of home-made or port wine, sweeten to taste, boil for one minute, and serve hot.

3. Put a bottle of port wine, half a bottle of water, and sugar to taste, into a saucepan; then add allspice, cloves, and a blade of mace; boil all together, serve in a jug with grated nutmeg, and rusks or slips of thin toast. Some persons add lemon-juice to the mull, but it does not generally please.

Wine Whey.—Put half a pint of new milk in a saucepan, set on the fire, and when it boils add as much raisin wine as will turn it; let it boil up, then set the saucepan aside till the curd subsides, but do not stir it. Pour off the whey, then add half a pint of boiling water, and white sugar to taste.

To Preserve Liquors Colorless.—Oaken barrels may be prevented from coloring spirit by dissolving one part of ammonia alum, and two parts of sulphate of iron in one hundred parts. Well wash the casks with this solution, boiling hot, and allow them to stand twenty-four hours. Then rinse out the casks well, dry them, and finally give them a washing with a thin solution of silicate of soda.

Brewing.

GENERAL NOTICE—Before entering on a description of the process of brewing, it will be necessary to notice the apparatus and materials required for its conduct.

A copper or boiler capable of holding fully two-thirds of the quantity proposed to be brewed; with a gauge-stick to determine the number of gallons of fluid at given depth therein. A copper holding about 140 gallons is a convenient size for brewing a quarter of malt.

A mash-tub, or tun, capable of containing rather more than the copper.

One or more tuns, or vessels, to ferment the beer in.

Three or four shallow coolers to reduce the wort as rapidly as possible to a proper temperature for fermenting.

One or two copper or wooden bowls, for bailing, &c.

A thermometer with a scale reaching from zero to above the boiling point of water.

A suitable number of casks [clean] to contain the beer.

One or more large funnels, or tunners.

Two or more clean pails.

A hand-pump of a size proportionate to the brewing.

The materials necessary to brew beer are, good malt, hops, and water, and a little yeast.

The malt is bruised or crushed in a mill before brewing, that it may be acted on the more readily by the water. It should not be ground too small, as it would then make the wort thick; the crushed malt may advantageously lie for a few days in a cool situation, by which it will attract a considerable quantity of moisture from the air, and consequently its soluble portion will be the more easily dissolved out by the water used in mashing. Pale malt may be used coarser than amber or brown malt. A bushel of malt should make a bushel and a quarter when ground, and a quarter should yield between 9 and 10 bushels, the quantity slightly varying according to the degree of bruising it has undergone. On the large scale, malt is ground in crushing mills, furnished with iron rollers; and on a small scale, by wooden rollers or small mills worked by hand. For private brewing, the malt is generally bought ready ground, for convenience sake. The hops should be those of the previous season.

The quantity of hops required to a given measure of malt varies from 2 lbs. to 8 lbs of the former, to 1 quarter of the latter, according to the nature of the brewing. For good strong beer, 4 lbs. or 4 1-2 lbs. is usually sufficient, but when the liquor is very strong, and it is intended to be highly aromatic, and to be kept for a long period, 1 lb. of hops may be used to every bushel of malt, or 8 lbs. to the quarter. Mild porter has about 3 lbs. to the quarter, and weak common beer has frequently only about 1-2 lb. of hops to the bushel of malt.

The water should be soft and clear, the yeast sweet and good, and all the vessels and casks both sweet and clean. If this be not the case, with the latter especially, the best brewing in the world will be useless.

PROCESS OF BREWING. This may be divided into

THE MASHING.—This operation consists in placing the ground or bruised malt in a large tub or "tun," known by the name of the "mash-tun," macerating it for some time in hot water, and lastly drawing off the wort from a hole in the bottom, over which a bunch of straw, or a strainer, or false bottom, is placed, to prevent the malt passing out along with the liquor. During the process of mashing, a peculiar principle, called by chemists diastase, reacts upon the starch also contained in the malt, and converts it first into a species of gum, called by the French chemists "dextrine," and then into a species of sugar resembling that produced by the action of sulphuric acid. The greater the quantity of starch converted into sugar in this way, the stronger and finer will be the wort. It therefore becomes a desideratum with the brewer to mash at a temperature that will most fully promote this object.

The action of the first mash is merely to extract the sugar contained in the malt already formed; that of the second to convert the starch into sugar by the action of the diastase; the third to fully complete this object, as well as to carry away the remaining portion of extract.

The mashing is usually performed by filling the copper with water, and as soon as it acquires the temperature of 145° in summer, or 167° in winter, 45 gallons are run off into the mash-tun, and 1 quarter of crushed malt gradually thrown in and well mixed by laborious working, until it becomes throughly incorporated and no lumps remain; the agitation is then continued for 30 or 40 minutes, when 36 gallons of water from the boiler, at a temperature of 200° are added, and the whole again well agitated until thoroughly mixed. The mash-tun is now closely covered up, and allowed to stand for an hour or an hour and a half. At the end of this time the tap is set, and the wort is drawn off into the "underback," and generally amounts to about 50 to 52 gallons: 60 gallons of water, at a temperature of 200°, are next added to the mash-tun, previously drained well, and after being well worked, the whole is covered up as before. This mash is allowed to remain for an hour, when it is drawn off, and the malt again drained ready for the third mash. This time only 35 gallons of water are added at 200°, and allowed to stand for 1-2 an hour, when it is run off in the same manner as before, and the malt allowed to drain. The worts are now ready for boiling,

II. BOILING.—The wort is next transferred to the copper, and heated to the boiling point as soon as possible. In large breweries where several coppers are employed, the first mash is no sooner run into the underback, than it is transferred to the wort copper, and immediately boiled, and the successive mashings added as soon as drawn off; but in private houses, where there is only one copper, the boiling cannot be commenced until the water for the last mashing is removed. In some cases the worts are brewed separately, thus producing 2 or 3 qualities of beer, viz, strong ale or stout, beer and table beer. No sooner has the boiling commenced than the hops may be added, and the boiling continued for 2 or 3 hours or more.

In general, two hours good boiling will be found sufficient. In small brewings the first wort should be sharply boiled for 1 hour, and the second for 2 hours. But if intended for beer of long keeping, the time should be extended half an hour. The hops should be strained from each preceding wort, and returned into the copper with the succeeding one. Between the boilings the fire should be damped with wet cinders, and the copper door set open.

III. COOLING.—The boiling being finished, the wort is run off from the copper into the hopback, which is furnished with a strainer to keep back the hops. It is then pumped into large square shallow vessels called "coolers," where it is exposed to a good current of air to cool it down to a proper fermenting temperature as quickly as possible. This is of the utmost importance for the success of the brewing. The wort should be laid so shallow as to cool within 6 or 7 hours to the temperature of about 60°. In warm weather, the depth should not exceed 3 or 4 inches; but in cold weather it may be 5 or 6 inches. As soon as the heat has fallen to about 60°, it should be instantly tunned and yeasted.

IV. FERMENTATION.—When the wort is sufficiently cool, it is run into the fermenting tuns or vessels, which in small brewings may be casks, with one of their heads removed. These are called "gyle tuns," and should not be more than two-thirds full. The yeast, previously mixed with a little wort, and kept until this latter has begun to ferment, may now be added, and the whole agitated well; the tun should then be covered up, until the fermentation is well established. During this process the temperature rises from 9° to 15°.

V. CLEANSING.—When the fermentation has proceeded to a certain extent, the liquor undergoes the operation called "cleansing." This consists in drawing it of from the gyle tun into other vessels, or casks, set sloping, so that the yeast, as it forms, may work off the one side of the top, and fall into the vessel placed below to receive it. In small brewings, the beer is often at once transferred from the gyle tun to the store casks, which are sloped a little until the fermentation is over, when they are skimmed, filled, and bunged up. When the operation of cleansing is not employed, the yeast is removed from the surface of the gyle tun with a skimmer, and the clear liquor drawn off into the store casks.

VI. STORING.—As soon as the fermentation is concluded, which generally takes from 6 to 8 days, or more, the clear liquor is drawn off into the store casks, or vats, which are then closely bunged down, and deposited in a cool cellar.

VII. RIPENING.—After a period, varying from 1 to 12 months, or more, according to the nature of the brewing, the liquor will have become fine, and sufficiently ripe for use.

VIII. FINING.—It frequently happens that malt liquor, especially porter, with all the care bestowed upon it in brewing, will not turn out sufficiently fine to meet the taste and eye of the consumer, in which case it is usually subjected to the operation of "clarifying." For this purpose 1 oz. of isinglass is put into 1 quart of weak vinegar, or still better, hard beer, and when dissolved, a sufficient quantity of good beer may be added to make it measure 1 gallon. This mixture is called "finings;" 1 to 2 pints of which is the proper quantity for a barrel. The method of using it, is to put the finings into a bucket, and to gradually add some of the beer, until the bucket is three parts full, during which time it is violently agitated with a whisk, and this is continued until a good frothy head is raised upon it, when it is thrown into the barrel of beer, and the whole well rummaged up, by means of a large stick shoved in at the bunghole. In a few days the beer will usually become fine.

CHAPTER II.

Wheat—Flour, and the various Preparations of Bread, and Crackers.

It is by understanding the constituents of our food we are enabled to make proper selections. We have to determine whether it is "flesh and blood" we aim at that is to say nutrition, or the part only that maintains the lamp of life. These are said to be nitrogenous, or non-nitrogenous, as they are capable of supporting life, or only in warming the body.

In the first list we will mention wheat, oats, barley, Indian corn and rice; in the second all pure starches, arrowroot, tapioca, corn starch and the like—but wheat is the principal; it is foremost of them all in nitrogenous value, and it is this also that principally concerns us in our varieties of pastry and BREAD which we will speak of more at large.

Wheat ground and separated by sifting yields us much that nourishes and much that only warms. The outside of a kernel of wheat is richest in nutritive qualities, the inside in warming qualities; hence the coarser the flour the more wholesome, the finer the less power of sustaining life; and as the starch, or non-nitrogenous parts of wheat are more subdivisible than the outer or nitrogenous parts, so only the fine particles of starch are able to pass the fine bolting cloths that are used for the manufacture of the finest flour—finest in point of minuteness but by no means the finest or most desirable for wholesome bread. Yet flour preparations are said, or thought not to look well except it be thus compounded principally of wheaten starch. Let it be remembered that in making any mixture of flour there are certain conditions of success that cannot with impunity be neglected; and it is known to be due to a just consideration of these that some housewives have made themselves famous not only in the eyes of their own families, whose sound health indicate their excellent judgement and management, but before the world as teachers of the important art of making those popular articles of the table, which though graced with a hundred names and made in a thousand ways are after all but pastries led off by the "staff of life,"— EVEN BREAD.

Perhaps no article of daily consumption comes less uniformly good to the consumer's hand; not only is the flour subject to a difference of quality, for all wheats do not yield the same proportions, but it may be adulterated with gypsum, or spoiled in the harvesting, or in the cleaning by leaving in wild garlic, or in the grinding by heat, or in the storage by damp, or even in the packing, in barrels by sourness. Again, supposing the best flour, in the best condition to be in the best barrels; still almost as many mishaps follow the baum or yeast or rising, or whatever name you may give the fermenting agent, and not a few mistakes arise, after all other difficulties and uncertainties have been overcome, in the character of the oven and the nature of the fire.

The surface yeast of beer is a powerful alcohol ferment, and by its means the sugar contained in meal is thereby resolved into alcohol and carbonic acid the efforts of which to escape causes the cellular texture or rising with the dough; and thus gives to the toughness that lightness and porousness which the baking retains in the bread. If the heat of the oven is insufficient, or the dough too watery, the partitions of these cells harden too slowly and on the escape of the carbonic acid, collapse or "fall," or in other words get heavy by slack baking.

It is unnecessary here to enter into explanations of the various modes of different nations of making bread. The French, English, and Germans all aim at results adapted to the wants and tastes of their customers. The principle is one and the same;—BREAD—whatever its color, flavor, shape, or consistency, has to be leavened to become light, or what is better to call it, digestible. Raising bread, then, is simply a process of adaptation to the digestive powers of the stomach. Modern science and the tendency of man to economise labor have marked this subject out for improvement, and many are the substitutes for brewer's yeast which have found their way into use. Experiments have been made both chemically and mechancially. The chemist has combined certain carbonates and acids, as for instance carbonate of potassium or saleratus, carbonate of soda, cream of tartar, tartaric acid and lactic acid (sour milk) but the universal difficulty has been in perfect incorporation, and uniform and reliable results. Baking powders, self raising flour and a dozen marketable substitutes are offered for use, for the chemical action in the dough which renders it light and porous all of them used according to directions are more or less successes; but the question that the people want solved is to increase the nutritious properties of flour, and not destroy or impair them, by injudicious additions. The mechanically produced lightness is where such agents as ammonia in the form of a carbonate and carbonic acid gas, are used; but all these fail except in the hands of persons who understand the subject. The general housekeeper wants good bread, and cares little who makes it, or what it is made from. This being the case some advice is necessary.

If you use any of the substitutes for yeast, study the directions on the packet and follow them, for the manufacturer has there given you the result of his experience. The important points to be striven after are the greatest volume of well raised bread for a given quantity of flour. The employment of no articles that act injuriously on the digestive organs; and in whatever form or manner the bread may be manipulated, to add to rather than take from its nutritive qualities.

There is no doubt but that what is called "SELF-RAISING FLOUR" is a desideratum to a vast number of persons. Time is saved, fewer vessels of preparation are needed, less skill is required, and altogether labor is much diminished. The summer and winter make no difference in the results, and have not to be provided for, and what is of more importance than all is, that any one with clean hands and a clear head, may manufacture palatable, nutritious, and wholesome bread, light pastry, or any other of the numerous items of the table in which flour is the principal ingredient, out of it; and we are glad to see so much desire in the public mind to HAVE the RIGHT article, and among the philanthrophic discoverers of the day TO GIVE IT.

But there is yet room for improvement, and we are of opinion that before long there will be discovered greater secrets in regard to bread making, than any now in use.

We cannot however overlook the fact that Professor Horsford in Harvard University, Cambridge, has recently given the public a most interesting little work on the "Theory and art of Bread Making without the use of ferment" which cannot fail to be interesting to all who desire a fine, palatable and healthy article and among the advantages of which he enumerates the following;—

"1. Its saving of the nutritious constituents of the flour from consumption in the process of raising the bread.

"2. Its restoration of the phosphates, which are in a larger or lesser measure removed with the bran in the preparation of the fine qualities of flour.

"3. Its saving of time. While ordinary fermented bread involves as a general thing preparation over night, care for several hours before baking, and dependence on a variable supply of leaven or yeast, the phosphatic bread is prepared from the flour for the oven in a few minutes.

"4. It secures a uniformly excellent result, while the result with the process of fermentation is of doubtful issue, and in household production is more frequently indifferent than good—after a failure.

"5. It furnishes a bread that retains its moisture much longer than equally porous fermented bread, and does not mould as readily as fermented bread does.

"6. It provides a bread, from the use of which, even by persons of delicate digestive apparatus, none of the ills peculiar to fermented bread follow. It may be eaten warm with impunity, while with most persons it is necessary that fermented bread should lose its freshness, or become stale, in order to the destruction of some objectionable qualities, before it may be eaten with safety.

"7. It is a method which, by providing agents of known qualities and strength, reduce the measure of skill required to a minimum; and secures, with a very small degree of care and moderate expenditure of time, uniformly excellent bread."

And the method of preparation and use is thus described:—

"Self-raising flour is prepared, in which the phosphoric acid, bi-carbonate of soda, and common salt are present in the required proportions. With this flour, it is only necessary thoroughly to knead in sufficient water to make a slightly sticky dough, and bake in covered tins, in a quick oven. The time required for a single person to prepare four loaves of a pound each, does not exceed five minutes, and the baking takes from thirty to forty-five more.

"The acid is prepared by itself, and may be mixed with the flour and bicarbonate of soda at the same time; the equivalent quantities having been put up in separate parcels, and with them the measure for each.

"Lastly, the dry acid and dry bicarbonate of soda, mixed in equivalent quantities, may be added to the flour directly. This is the most convenient form for household use. The method applied to making a quart of flour into one loaf of bread for family use is as follows:—

"1. Provide a quick oven. [This requires a temperature of from 350 to 450 degrees Fahr.]

"2. Stir a measure [the acid measure should contain 140 grains and the soda measure 92 grains, for one pound of flour,] each of acid and soda into a quart of sifted dry flour, to which a teaspoonful of salt has been added. Mix intimately with the hands. Then add from time to time *cold* water from a pint cup, stirring and kneading meanwhile, until just a pint of water has been most thoroughly incorporated with the flour.

"3. Shape the mass of dough into a loaf, place it in a deep tin bake-pan, with a cover so high as to be out of the reach of the risen dough, and set it immediately in the oven."

The wide-spread knowledge of the value and importance, therefore, of self-raising flour, has already led to the establishment of mills for its preparation in different parts of the country, amongst the most celebrated of which are the "Franklin Mills" of Messrs. C. J. Fell & Brother, 120 South Front Street, Philadelphia. This flour has been submitted by us to the necessary chemical tests, and we find it, and the bread produced from it, not only free from every impurity, but composed of the proper nutritive qualities for sustaining life and warming the body. Under the proper headings will be found the formulas for self-raising flour.

Of the numerous baking powders and other substitutes for yeast, now before the public, we find that their general properties are as before mentioned. One of these, however, has become so celebrated that we have been induced to examine it with considerable attention. It is called "*Azumea*," and was discovered by Professor Morris some ten years ago, used in his own family for some time, and finally presented to the public. Of the commendatory remarks given it by the press we cannot do better than give the following from the *Public Ledger*:—

"An article called *Azumea* has been composed by Professor Morris. The manufacturer has shown us two loaves of bread, one made with the *Azumea*, and the other with yeast. The first is much the superior article, kept moist longer, and tasted sweeter and more nutritious than the last. This is said to be the special quality of the *Azumea*. It has the following advantages over yeast or fermented bread:—It can be made and baked in one hour from the time of first handling the flour; it will be moist and pleasant to eat for at least four days after baking; it is easy of digestion; excellent for persons suffering from dyspepsia; retains all the gluten, starch and sugar in the flour, and therefore produces 1 lb. 12 oz. of bread from 1 lb. 4 oz. of flour, while yeast produces only 1 lb. 9 oz. from 1 lb. 4 oz. of flour; thus obtaining about 27 lbs. more of bread from a barrel of flour."

And the *Press* says:—

"Of all the scientific accessions to the *culinary* department of domestic economy, we know none of more merit than *Azumea*. The merits of this simple and wholesome preparation have been established by scientific analysis, and practical demonstrations in thousands of families. The bread produced is easy of digestion, and excellent for persons suffering from dyspepsia."

The *Monthly Guardian* speaking of it has the following:—

"No other article of diet is, with the people of the United States, of such direct importance, as bread. We are more indebted to our bread makers—for just about seven-tenths of all our fashionable complaints; as indigestion, headaches, heart-burns, dyspepsia, flatulency, acidity, delicacy, and debility, than to all other causes combined. All fermented bread, must show similar results. Therefore, all leavened bread is unwholesome;—in degree, poisonous. A very large per cent. of its best life-giving properties are poisoned by impure carbonic gas—changed by fermentation into noxious *fungi*. What is to be done? Feed on unleavened gutta percha bread? No: that does not necessarily follow. The best thing we can do for making bread of all kinds of grain, cakes, pastry, pie-crust,—whatever we would make light and wholesome, will be to resort to *Azumea*, the invention of Prof. Morris, of Philadelphia. By using this material, the tedious waiting for the 'batch' to get light enough to bake is dispensed with, and good, sweet bread the result."

And the *Saturday Evening Post* makes the annexed comments:—

"By all means let us have daily the very best bread that is to be made—not that which is leavened and made light by any process of fermentation. We have bidden our last good-bye to that kind of material, after applying a microscopic test of twelve hundred diameters power to a loaf of our nicest, newest yeast baking, and finding a large per cent. of good food material metamorphosed into *fungi*—in plain English, "toad stools," by fermentation, and thus rendered not only unfit for food, but in so far absolutely, poisonous. We are particularly attached to good, pure mushrooms, but always detested toad stools, and finding a large per cent. of the very best fermented bread we could make presented in this form, we were in a dilemma. Perhaps we should have discarded bread entirely, but for the timely suggestion of our friend, Dr. G., who simply said, '*Azumea.*' We had no definite idea what *Azumea* was, and have not yet, beyond the fact that it produces the very best bread, cakes, pie crusts, puddings, and all sorts of pastry without fermentation, that we have ever seen. Our honest conviction is that the public ought to be advised where to get, and how to use, the material, the value of which we can fully endorse."

Another article of recent introduction is called *Ærated Bread*. It has its advocates and opponents, the latter asserting that it is not as wholesome as ordinary bread and the former insisting that it is superior to any now made. Time alone and its use can settle this question. It is produced, as we are informed, by forcing carbonic acid gas (or some other) into the dough whilst being mixed, and thus the necessary cellular condition of raising is produced. Should this be the case, then it can hardly ever be made available for general *family* use. It may and will suit the baker—but not the housekeeper. We have tried the bread and found it palatable, —and others can try it and judge for themselves.

We cannot conclude our remarks upon the subject of BREAD, without urging upon all who desire a *healthy* and *nutritious* article to abandon the use of yeast, as fermentation decomposes the gluten and starch contained in the flour, disengages much carbonic acid gas, causes dyspepsia and flatulence, and has a tendency to produce a fibrous, woody substance, which although it may allay the appetite, is neither calculated to nourish life, nor benefit the health.

BISCUIT AND CRACKER.—The popular mind has long been disturbed on the subject of pure bread in the form known as Biscuit across the Atlantic and Crackers on this side. There is probably no greater temptation to economize materials than in the manufacture of these essential articles of food, and no where else in the vast catalogue of productions in which flour is the base, is there so much admixture of economizing ingredients. But on the other hand it may be safely stated, that it is almost unknown that at any manufactory positively injurious adulterations of wheat flour have been employed. The mistake has been the call for cheap articles on the part of consumers and the effort to make cheapness remunerative on the part of manufacturers.

The popular mind has also been deceived in this wise, willing to pay for the best when means were sufficient, the best has been asked for, and the best sold—but what kind of "best"—why the best the shopkeeper has on hand, not the best he might have supplied, if this class of customers was more numerous. Bakers like to make what they can sell most of—and the storekeeper likes to sell what he disposes most of—and so it has generally prevailed as a settled popular conviction—that Crackers are Crackers—nothing more. Yet there is as much difference in the quality of different makes, as in the grades of flour in the meal market—and it is our opinion that the best is always the cheapest taking into account its sanitary effect, and not its simple bulk. The term Biscuit, means *twice baked*, hence such articles as are of the rusk character, are nearer the original idea; but the Cracker is a different article altogether. It is so made (or ought to be) that it splits in two easily and hence the name of Cracker—but only the best materials made in the best manner by the best workmen, turn out CRACKERS to perfection.

In our endeavors to realize our ideal of a perfect article, we have tried, we believe, every kind the cities of Philadelphia and New York have for sale, and without any disparagement to others, candor and truth alike render it obligatory upon us to say, that we have found none manufactured superior to those made by Mr. Robert Pearce, Ninth street below Dickerson,—the which we have found to possess all the requisites and properties so essentially necessary to nutrition and health.

In the meantime, however, and until such further improvements are made in every department of "Flour preparations" we must rest satisfied and be grateful for what we have; and the millions of cooks, housekeepers, bakers, and all others interested, who will make THE MINE OF WEALTH their guide, are referred to the necessary, but simple instructions for the use of "Yeast," "Self-Raising Flour," and "Baking Powders," which will be found under their appropriate heads.

RECEIPTS.

Bread, French.—Mix together three quarts of water and one pint of milk; for summer use let it be milk warm, but in winter scalding hot, adding a sufficiency of salt. Take one and a half pints of good ale yeast, free from bitterness, and lay it in one gallon of water the night before. Pour off the yeast into the milk and water and then break in rather more than a quarter of a pound of butter. Work it well until it is all dissolved; then beat up two eggs in a basin, and stir them in. Mix about one and a half pecks of flour with the liquor, and in winter make the dough pretty stiff, but in summer more slack; mix it well, but the less it is worked the better. Stir the liquor into the flour as for pie-crust, and after the dough is made cover it with a cloth, and let it lie to rise, while the oven is heating. When the rolls or loaves have lain in a quick oven about a quarter of an hour, turn them on the other side for about a quarter of an hour longer. Then take them out and chip them with a knife, which will make them look spongy, and of a fine yellow, whereas washing takes off this fine color, and renders their looks less inviting.

Bread, Family.—Boil five pounds of the flake of bran in four gallons of water, until the water is reduced to three and a half gallons, then strain it and knead in fifty-six pounds of flour, adding salt and yeast as for bread. A quarter of an ounce of carbonate of magnesia, (a perfectly innocent article) added to every four pounds of flour materially improves the quality of the bread, even when made from the worst new second flour.

Bread, Leavened.—Take about two pounds of dough of the last making which has been raised by barm; keep it in a wooden vessel, covered with flour. When sufficiently sour it will become leavened. Work this quantity with warm water into a peck of flour. Cover the dough close with a cloth, or flannel, and keep it in a warm place; mix it next morning with two or three bushels of flour, mixed up with warm water and a little salt. When the dough is thoroughly made, cover it as before. As soon as it rises well, knead it into loaves. Observe in this process, that the more leaven is put to the flour, the lighter the loaves will be, and the fresher the leaven, the less sour it will taste.

Bread, Extemporaneous and Wholesome.—Take eight pounds of flour and divide into two parts; mix one part, four pounds, in water in which two ounces of bicarbonate of soda has been dissolved, and the other part with water to which one ounce of muriatic acid has been added. Knead both parts well, but separately until perfectly kneaded, then work both together thoroughly as rapidly as possible, make into such sized loaves as may be required and bake immediately.

Bread or Biscuit.—(SELF-RAISING FLOUR).—Take in the proportion of one quart of milk or cold water to three pounds of flour—mix as little as possible—just enough to wet through and form a slack dough. Immediately bake in a deep pan, about half full, in an oven well heated, to be ready when you commence mixing. If a shallow pan be used, cover it, but not so as to press on the dough and injure its rising. Thus protecting the bread from being burned or crust-bound which would deter its full expansion. Use no salt. Weigh the flour, and measure the water to secure accuracy, which is very important.

Flour Pudding.—A superior pudding can be made by simply mixing Self-Raising Flour and water together, boiling it in a cloth, or steaming it, leaving it room to expand, and using a little sauce made from melted butter and sugar.

Azumea Bread.—The Azumea makes the finest wheat bread possible; it is made in the simplest manner, as follows:—Get one quart, equal to one and a quarter of a pound of flour; mix into it, quite dry, three ordinary-sized teaspoonsful of Azumea; add cold water, with a little salt dissolved in it, sufficient to make a dough as soft as can be conveniently handled, which is generally a little less than one pint of water to one quart of flour; do not knead it, shape it very lightly and immediately bake in a quick oven, which must be quite hot before you begin to mix. It has the following advantages over yeast or fermented bread:—It can be made and baked in one hour from the time of first handling the flour; it will be moist and pleasant to eat for at least four days after baking; it is easy of digestion; excellent for persons suffering from dispepsia; retains all the gluten, starch and sugar contained in the flour, and therefore produces one pound and twelve ounces, of bread from one pound and four ounces, of flour; whilst yeast produces only one pound and nine ounces, of bread from one pound and four ounces, of flour; thus obtaining about twenty-seven pounds more of bread from a barrel of flour, which, with the saving of yeast, will about balance the cost of the Azumea.

Azumea Corn Bread.—It makes delightful Egg Bread with white corn meal. Beat the eggs; put in old or new milk—even if it is not perfectly sweet—and mix the meal with the Azumea well; dissolve the salt in a little water; and, after stirring all well together, grease your baker or pan, and bake with a moderately quick fire. When done, add butter, and you cannot wish for a greater treat.

Azumea Brown Bread.—One quart of yellow corn meal, one pint of flour, three tablespoonsful of Azumea, all sifted together; add one gill of molasses, two beaten eggs, make a thin paste with milk, and bake slowly.

Azumea Biscuit.—One quart of flour, three teaspoonsful of Azumea, one heaping tablespoonful of butter or lard; rub the shortening into the flour, add the Azumea and mix well; dissolve a little salt in enough cold water or sweet milk (a coffee cupful is about the quantity) to make a dough as soft as can be conviently handled; flour the hands and make into smooth round balls, or roll out and cut; place in a greased pan, and immediately bake.

Azumea Rolls.—Three teaspoonsful of Azumea to one quart of flour; mix thoroughly by passing two or three times through a sieve; rub in a piece of butter half the size of an egg, with salt as usual, and make the paste with cold milk or water—milk is best—barely stiff enough to permit rolling out; do not knead the dough; cut in any desired form; place immediately in a hot oven, and bake quickly.

CHAPTER III.

Cookery in its various Departments.—Boiling, Baking, Roasting, Frying, and Grilling.

MAGENDIE the great Chemist once made some experiments on geese—His object was to find out what may be called the carbon doctrine of aliment. It is said that every thing eaten can, with the exception of salt be turned into charcoal—but this has not precision of statement enough to be perfectly intelligible—we prefer to say that Carbon being the one solid of the four organic elements, the others may be driven off by heat leaving the carbon behind in the form of charcoal. And here we have a valuable hint in cookery.— Persons cannot be efficient cooks without a knowledge of the laws by which food is carbonized by Caloric. Magendie fed some geese on gum only, and they all died on the 16th day, others on starch and they all died on the 24th day, again others on boiled albumen (the whites of eggs) and they died on the 46th day—again he fed others on all three articles together and they lived and throve and fattened. By this he demonstrated the necessity of a variety of food, so that every tissue may have a due supply of its proper components —we must *vary* our food as much as possible in order to supply the waste of every part of the system—but there are two pre-requisites to be considered, the one is the selection of proper articles of food, and the other is in their proper preparation for the table. Things must be right from the beginning, or they will be wrong in the end, is an old but sound axiom. Food requires to be judiciously chosen, judiciously prepared, and judiciously eaten. When this trinitarian duty is performed, the result is the very acmè of human desire—a sound mind in a sound body—provided no constitutional disqualification chronically exist. The products of the "land we live in" are invariably more beneficial than importations. How unnatural it would be to a visitor of the icy zones, to crave the highly seasoned articles of the tropics—or he who witnesses the thin spare character of the inhabitants of the warmer latitudes, to fancy they only needed fat. Yet such a theory would only end practically in disease and death. The Laplander must have fat, the West Indian his cayenne. Why? because it is a law of Nature's Harmony to live *off* the land we live *in*. But we must not wander from the subject matter in hand, and therefore return from our digression.

"To keep the pot boiling" is a saying that has extended itself into every department of life—it is almost a synonyme for PERSE- VERANCE—but be this as it may, it is quite certain that when by proper attention to the cleanliness and proper draught of the cook- stove, the pot boils, it must be perseveringly kept boiling until the contents are cooked.

Some cooks, or rather some miserable apologies for cooks, place the dinner on the fire and leave it to take care of itself, and then when dinner time arrives, turn out of the pot probably as tough a piece of meat as ever a poor butcher was blamed for supplying, and never think that such "pot-luck" is an unworthy waste of the money expended in market, for the fault always lies with the cook, not the meat. There is probably not a piece of sound meat sold in any market in the world, that may not be by judicious boiling ren- dered tender, palatable and digestible—but if cooks trifle with or neglect to keep "the pot boiling," in harmony with the conditions with the joint and the purpose in view, the most succulent flesh will be spoiled.

If I want soup, I cannot get it if I do not boil the meat that makes it, as slowly as a boil can be kept up—for the reason that the virtue of the meat is wanted as an extract, and a fierce fire and rapid boiling is a sure means of retaining all the meat contains within itself. It may be well here to remark that when a joint is wanted to be tender and juicy, it should be at first, for the shortest possible time quickly boiled, so as to set the fibrine of the outside of the meat and then boil slowly for the rest of the time until done.

The commonly received idea, that what goes under the denomination of "good plain living"—that is, joints of meat, roast or boiled—is best adapted to all constitutions, has been proved to be a fallacy. Many persons can bear testimony to the truth of Dr. Kitchener's remark, that "elaborate culinary processes are frequently necessary in order to prepare food for the digestive organs." It may be truly said that many persons ruin their health by over indulgence in food rendered indigestible by being badly cooked.

It is our intention to endeavor to correct the prejudice in favor of a family joint—by showing that it is not only very often improperly cooked, but that the same quantity of meat, if dressed in different ways, still retaining a certain degree of simplicity, will be more pleasant to the palate, more healthful, and quite as economical, if brought to the table, as two or three instead of one.

In French cookery, those substances which are not intended to be broiled or roasted, are usually stewed for several hours at a temperature below the boiling point; by which means the most refractory articles, whether of animal or vegetable origin, are more or less reduced to a state of pulp, and admirably adapted for the further action of the stomach. In the common cookery of this country, on the contrary, articles are usually put at once into a large quantity of water, and submitted, without care or attention, to the boiling temperature; the consequence of which is, that most animal substances, when taken out, are harder and more indigestible than in the natural state.

It appears from Dr. Beaumont's Tables that the following articles are digested in the times indicated:—

	H.	M.
Rice, boiled soft	1	0
Apples, sweet and ripe	1	30
Sago, boiled	1	45
Tapioca, Barley, stale Bread, Cabbage with Vinegar, raw, boiled Milk and Bread, and Bread and Milk, cold	2	0
Potatoes, roasted, and Parsnips, boiled	2	35
Baked Custard	2	45
Apple Dumpling	3	0
Bread, Corn, baked, and Carrots, boiled	3	15
Potatoes and Turnips, boiled; Butter and Cheese	3	30
Tripe and Pigs' Feet	1	0
Venison	1	35
Oysters, undressed, and Eggs, raw	2	3
Turkey and Goose	2	30
Eggs, soft boiled; Beef and Mutton, roasted, or broiled	2	0
Boiled Pork, stewed Oysters, Eggs, hard boiled or fried	3	30
Domestic Fowls	4	0
Wild Fowls; Pork, salted and boiled; Suet	4	30
Veal, roasted; Pork, and salted Beef	5	30

When the powers of the stomach are weak, a hard and crude diet is sure to produce discomfort by promoting acidity; while the very same articles when divided, and well cooked upon French principles, or rather the principles of common sense, can be taken with impunity, and easily digested.

There are only a few persons—with the exception, perhaps, of those who take violent exercise, or work hard in the open air—who can dine heartily upon solid food without suffering from its effects; yet in order to escape indigestion, plain roast or boiled meat should be very sparingly consumed.

The foundation of all good cookery consists in preparing the meat so as to render it tender in substance, without extracting from it those juices which constitute its true flavor; in doing which, the main point in the art of making those soups, sauces, and made dishes of every sort, which should form so large a portion of every well-ordered dinner, as well, also, as in cooking many of the plain family joints—is boiling, or rather stewing, which ought always to be performed over a slow fire. There is, in fact, no error so common among American cooks as that of boiling meat over a strong fire, which renders large joints hard and partly tasteless; while, if simmered during nearly double the time, with less than half 'the quantity of fuel and water, and never allowed to "boil up," the meat, without being too much done, will be found both pliant to the tooth and savory to the palate.

For instance. The most common and almost universal dish throughout France, is a large piece of plainly-boiled fresh beef, from which the soup—or *"potage,"* as it is there called—has been partly made, and which is separately served up as *"bouilli,"* accompanied by strong gravy and minced vegetables, or stewed cabbage. Now this as constantly dressed in the French mode, is very delicate both in fibre and flavor; while, in the American manner of boiling it, it is almost always hard and insipid. The reason of which, as explained by Carême, is this:—"The meat, instead of being put down to boil, as in the American and English method, is in France put in the pot with the usual quantity of cold water, and placed at the corner of the fireplace, where, slowly becoming hot, the heat gradually swells the muscular fibres of the beef, dissolving the gelatinous substances therein contained, and disengaging that portion which chemists term 'osmazome,' and which imparts savor to the flesh—thus both rendering the meat tender and palatable, and the broth relishing and nutritive; whilst, on the contrary, if the pot be inconsiderately put upon too quick a fire, the boiling is precipitated, the fibre coagulates and hardens, the osmazome is hindered from disengaging itself, and thus nothing is obtained but a piece of tough meat, and a broth without taste or succulence."

Meat loses, by cooking, from one-fifth to one-third of its whole weight. More is lost by roasting than by boiling meat. In calculating for a family, one pound per day for each individual is a general allowance for dinner.

Meat that is not to be cut till cold must be well done, particularly in summer.

The use of skewers in joints should be avoided as much as possible, as they let out the gravy; twine will answer better.

In every branch of cookery much must be left to the discretion of the cook and knowledge of the family's taste; particularly in force-meats and seasonings.

SUET.—When sirloins of beef, or loins of veal or mutton, are brought in, part of the suet may be cut off for puddings, or to clarify. Chopped fine and mixed with flour, if tied down in a jar, it will keep ten days or a fortnight. If there be more suet than will be used while fresh, throw it into pickle, made in the proportion of one-quarter pound of salt to a quart of cold water, and it will be as good afterwards for any use, when soaked a little.

To remove the taint of meat, wash it several times in cold water; then put it into plenty of cold water, into which throw several pieces of red-hot charcoal. If you fear meat will not keep till the time it is wanted, par-roast or par-boil it, that is partly cook it; it will then keep two days longer, when it may be dressed as usual, but in rather less time.

When meat is frozen, it should be brought into the kitchen and laid at some distance from the fire, early in the morning; or soak the meat in cold water two or three hours before it is used: putting it near the fire, or into warm water, till thawed, should be avoided.

Meats become tenderer and more digestible, as well as better flavoured, by hanging. In summer, two days is enough for lamb and veal, and from three to four for beef and mutton. In cold weather, the latter may be kept for double that time.

Legs and shoulders should be hung knuckle downwards.

An effectual way of excluding the fly is by using a wire meat-safe, or by covering the joints with a long loose gauze or some thin cloth, and hanging them from the ceiling of an airy room. Pepper and ginger should be sprinkled on the parts likely to be washed off before the joint is put to the fire.

A larder should always be placed on the north side of the house; the window may be closed with canvass, but wire is preferable.

There should be a thorough draft of air through the room.

Articles that are likely to spoil should not be kept in or laid upon wood.

Warm, moist weather is the worst for keeping meat; the south wind is very unfavourable, and lightning very destructive; so that after their occurrence meat should be especially examined.

BOILING, or cooking with heated water, is an important branch of the kitchen duties. Some articles, as potatoes, should be above the water in a steamer; some should be in deep water, as cabbage; some should be in shallow water, as beans; some in a "spider" as smoked fish; some in nets within the water, as spinach; some in bags and basins, as puddings; some in small cloths as dumplings, and so on, making it necessary for the cook to have her wits about her and see that her fuel, fire, wood and furniture are all proper to use and properly used.

It is the most simple of all processes of cooking. Regularity and attention to time are the main secrets.

Much less heat is requisite to keep liquids boiling in copper and iron saucepans than in those made of tin.

There is frequently a great waste of fuel in cooking, which arises from making liquids boil fast, when they only require to be kept slowly boiling. Count Rumford (the inventor of the Rumford stove), states, that more than half the fuel used in kitchens is wasted in the above manner.

It is a sad waste to put fuel under a boiling pot. There is a degree of heat in water called the boiling-point; and all the coals or wood in the world cannot make water hotter in an open vessel; it can but boil. By this waste, the cook not only loses time, but spoils the cookery.

The loss by boiling varies, from 6 1-4 to 16 per cent. The average loss on boiling butcher's meat, pork, hams, and bacon, is 12; and on domestic poultry is 14 3-4.

The loss per cent. on boiling salt beef is 15; on legs of mutton, 10; hams, 12 1-2; salt pork, 13 and 1-3rd; knuckles of veal, 8 and 1-3rd; bacon, 6 1-4; turkeys, 16; chickens, 13 1-2.

The established rule as regards time, is to allow a quarter of an hour for each pound of meat if the boiling is rapid, and twenty minutes if slow: there are exceptions to this; for instance, ham and pork, which require from twenty to twenty-five minutes per pound, and bacon nearly half an hour. For solid joints allow fifteen minutes for every pound, and from ten to twenty minutes depend much on the strength of the fire, regularity in the boiling, and size of the joint. The following table will be useful as an average of the time required to boil the various articles:—

	H.	M.
A ham, 20 lbs. weight requires	6	30
A tongue, (if dry) after soaking	4	0
A tongue, out of pickle 2-12 to	3	0
A neck of mutton	1	30
A chicken	0	20
A large fowl	0	45
A capon	0	35
A pigeon	0	15

Dried or salted meats and fish require soaking in cold water before boiling.

Meat and poultry will lose their flavour and firmness, if left in the water after they are done; as will also fish, which will break to pieces.

The water in which meat, poultry, or fish has been boiled should be saved; this pot-liquor, as it is called, may be made into soup.

Slow boiling is very important for all meats, to ensure their tenderness; fast boiling always makes them hard and tough, less plump, and of darker color, than when they are boiled gradually.

Skimming the pot will alone ensure the good color and sweetness of the meat; a little cold water and salt will aid in throwing up the scum: milk put into the pot does good in few cases only; and wrapping in a cloth is unnecessary, if the scum be carefully removed.

The lid of the saucepan should only be removed for skimming; and, before taking off the lid, be careful to blow from it any dust or blacks from the fire or chimney.

The joint should always be covered with water; above this quantity, the less water the more savory will be the meat.

In some few instances, however, it may be necessary to boil the articles in a much larger quantity of water; a quart of water is mostly a good proportion to a pound of meat.

If meat be put into cold water, it should be heated gradually, so as not to cause it to boil in less than forty minutes; if it boil much sooner, the meat will shrink and be hardened, and not so freely throw up the scum.

Four skewers, or plate, inside downwards, should be laid on the bottom of the saucepan, especially for large joints and puddings; so that they may be equally done, and escape burning or adhering to the saucepan.

When a pot boils remove it nearly off the fire, but let the lid remain on; a very little heat will then keep up the boiling.

The time of boiling should be reckoned from the time bubbles begin to rise on the surface of the liquid; as the boiling continues, the water will evaporate, and in some cases it may be requisite to fill up the saucepan with boiling water.

BAKING of late years has come more into general use from the fact that it is found to be a cheap, expeditious, convenient and economical way of cooking. The flavor of meats, however, when baked is not considered equal to the same when roasted although there are many joints that are preferable from being more suitable to baking than roasting. Among such may be enumerated legs and loins of pork, legs and shoulders of mutton, fillets of veal, &c; and a baked pig if properly basted with butter and otherwise attended to is fully equal to a roast one. The same may be said of ducks and geese, and various pieces of beef, especially the buttock. A baked buttock of beef should be salted about eight days, then well washed and put into a brown earthenware pan (glazed inside) with a pint of water, tied over with three or four thicknesses of writing paper, and baked about five hours in a lightly heated oven. A baked ham is far preferable to a boiled one, not only is it more tender, but it retains its gravy and has a finer flavor. It should be soaked at least one hour in clean water, wiped thourghly dry and then covered over with a thin flour paste before being put in the oven.

ROASTING is prefered by many and no doubt for many joints it is preferable, but it is more tedious, requires more care and attention and in this day of cooking stoves and close ranges is not so much in general use as heretofore. It has one great advantage and that is that a roasted joint is exempted from a combination of flavors such as are attached to a baked one, when several have been cooked in the same oven together.

The success of every branch of cookery, however, depends upon the good management of the kitchen fire; roasting, especially, requires a brisk, clear, and steady fire; if made up close to the bars of the grate.

The spit being wiped clean, the joint to be roasted should be carefully spitted even, and tied tight; and if it will not turn round well, balance skewers, with leaden heads, should be used; for, if the meat be not evenly spitted, it will probably be burned on one side, and not done on the other. Avoid running the spit through the prime parts of joints. Cradle spits answer best.

A leg of mutton should never be spitted, as the spit lets out the gravy, and leaves an unsightly perforation just as you are cutting into the pope's eye.

Make up the roasting-fire three or four inches longer than the joint, else the ends of the meat will not be done.

In stirring the fire, be careful to remove the dripping-pan, else dust and ashes may fall in. On no account let the fire get dull and low, as a strong heat is requisite to brown the meat.

A thin joint requires a brisk fire; a large joint, a strong, sound, and even fire. When steam rises from the meat, it is done.

Large joints should be put at a moderate distance from the fire, and gradually brought nearer; else the meat will be over done half-way through the joint, and be nearly raw at the bone.

Such meat as is not very fat should have paper placed over it, to prevent it from being scorched.

Do not sprinkle the meat with salt when first put down, as the salt draws out the gravy.

Old meats require more cooking than young. The longer the meat has been killed, the less time it requires to roast it. Very fat meat requires more time than usual.

There are a variety of opinions respecting the washing of meat previous to roasting. Many old and experienced cooks declare that it destroys the flavor of the meat. Professors of the art, however, hold a contrary opinion. We are not disposed, from experience, to differ so essentially from them as to advise meat to be roasted without this operation, but should advise that the meat be not suffered to remain too long in the water, unless frost-bitten, and then it should soak an hour or two previous to cooking.

The time necessary for cooking a joint must depend, of course, upon the weight of the joint to be roasted; experience gives fifteen minutes to each pound of meat; where the quantity is very large, an extra two or three minutes must be given; but so much depends upon the state of the fire, and the attention directed to the joint while cooking, that the judgment must be exercised. Although the above calculation may be taken as a general rule, time for any drawback which may occur must be considered.

Baste the meat first with fresh dripping, and then with its own fat or dripping: and within the last hour of roasting, take off the paper, and sprinkle the meat with salt and flour, to brown and froth it; but some cooks dredge the meat with flour earlier, so that it may imbibe the gravy, a practice which should be specially avoided.

The spit should be wiped dry immediately after it is drawn from the meat, and washed and scoured every time it is used.

Perfection in roasting is very difficult, and no certain rules can be given for it, as success depends on many circumstances which are continually changing; the age and size (especially the thickness) of the pieces, the quality of the coals, the weather, the currents of air in the kitchen, the more or less attentions of the cook, and the time of serving, are, all to be considered. Hence, epicures say of a well-roasted joint, "It is done to a turn."

Roast meats should be sent to table the moment they are ready, if they are to be eaten in perfection.

BROILING OR GRILLING.—Broiling requires a brisk and clear fire, proportioned to the article to be broiled; for example; mutton chops require a clear rather than a brisk fire, else the fat will be wasted before the lean is warmed through; but for a beef steak, the fire can neither be too brisk nor clear, if the gridiron be placed at the proper distance. Fish requires a steady fire; as also does under-done meat.

Much, however, depends on the substance of the article to be broiled: if it be thick, it must be placed at a greater distance, at first, to warm it through; if thin, the fire must be brisk, else the meat will not be of a good color.

The gridiron should be wiped clean after it has been used, so that the bars may be kept bright on top; they should be allowed to get hot before the article is laid on them, but not too hot, else they will burn the meat or fish: the latter especially. To prevent this, the bars should be rubbed with fat.

A charcoal fire is best for broiling.

To prevent the fat dripping into the fire set the gridiron aslant.

For turning the broiling article, use tongs, as a fork will let out the gravy. When the article is done, it will feel firm if touched with the tongs: by no means cut the meat to ascertain if it be done, as that will let out the gravy.

FRYING is of all methods the most objectionable, from the food's being less digestible when thus prepared, as the fat employed undergoes chemical changes. Olive oil in this respect is preferable to lard or butter. The crackling noise which accompanies the process of frying meat in a pan is occasioned by the explosions of steam formed in fat, the temperature of which is much above $212°$. If the meat is very juicy it will not fry well, because it becomes sodden before the water is evaporated; and it will not brown because the temperature is too low to scorch it. To fry fish well the fat should be boiling hot ($600°$), and the fish well dried in a cloth, otherwise, owing to the generation of steam, the temperature will fall so low, that it will be boiled in its own steam, and not be browned. Meat, or indeed any article, should be frequently turned and agitated during frying, to promote the evaporation of the watery particles. To make fried things look well, they should be done over twice with eggs and stale bread crumbs.

If eggs be very dear, a little flour and water may be substituted for them in preparing fish to fry.

In frying use a slice to lift the articles in and out of the pan, and drain them.

To make batter for frying; melt two ounces of butter in a little warm water, and pour it upon half-a-pound of flour; stir it and add water enough to form a batter, thick enough to adhere to whatever is put into it; but it should run freely: add some salt and the beaten whites of two eggs.

A small shallow frying-pan, is very useful to fry articles to be stewed: this method differs from common frying, as it only requires butter enough to keep the article from sticking to the pan and burning.

The fire for frying should be free from smoky coals, sharp, and even. Charcoal makes the best frying fire.

The fat should be carefully drained from all fried articles; indeed, they should be so dry as scarcely to soil a cloth. Fish is best drained by wrapping it in soft whited-brown paper, by which it will so dry as not to soil the napkin upon which it is served.

STEWING.—All articles to be stewed should first be boiled gently, then skimmed and set aside in an even heat: on this account, charcoal makes the best fire for stewing.

All stews, or meat dressed a second time, should be only simmered; as the meat should only be made hot through.

A stewpan is the most advantageous vessel in which stews, hashes, soups, or gravies, can be made; indeed, for all purposes of boiling, a stewpan is preferable to a deep saucepan, as, in the former, the articles are exposed to more even heat than when they are placed one upon another in the saucepan, and are likely to be broken in stirring.

The best stewpans are made of copper or iron; they should be kept covered as much as possible, unless you wish to reduce the gravy.

Be careful not to fry in a stewpan; or, if so, with great care, and sufficient butter to save the tinning from melting.

Most of the directions for making soups and gravies apply also to this branch of cookery.

LARDING.—Have ready larding-pins of different sizes, according to the article to be done, cut slices of bacon into bits of a proper length, quite smooth, and put on a larding-needle to suit it, with which pierce the skin and a very little of the meat, leaving the bacon in, and the two ends of equal length outwards. Lard in rows the size you think fit.

The same effect with regard to flavor, may be produced by raising the skin and laying a slice of fat bacon beneath it.

DOUBING consists in passing bacon through meat, while larding is on the surface only.

BRAISING.—Put the meat you would braise into a stewpan, and cover it with thick slices of fat bacon: then lay round it six or eight onions, a faggot of sweet herbs, some celery, and, if to be brown, some thick slices of carrots, and trimmings of any fresh meat-bones you have, with a pint and a half of water, or the same quantity of stock, according to what the meat is, and add seasoning. Cover the pan close, and set it over a slow stove; it will require two or three hours as its size and quality may direct. Then strain the gravy; keep the meat quite hot: take the fat off by plunging the basin into cold water, which will cause the fat to coagulate; and boil it as quickly as you can till it thickens. If, however you wish the gravy to adhere to the meat, it must be still further thickened; then with a brush kept for the purpose do over the meat, and if that has been larded, put it into the oven for a few minutes. This is called "glazing," and is much in use for made-dishes.

GLAZING is done by brushing melted glaze or jelly over the article, and letting it cool; in some cases it is requisite to cover the articles with two or three coats of glaze, allowing each to cool as it is laid on. The glaze should be of a clear yellow brown, and as thick as good treacle.

If you have not the glaze ready, sift a little sugar over the article to be glazed, and finish in the oven, with a salamander, or red hot shovel.

BONING.—In disengaging the flesh from the bones, work the knife always close to the bone, and take care not to pierce the outer skin. Minute directions are given in other parts of the work for boning fowls, &c.

BLANCHING makes the article plump and white, and consists in putting it into cold water over the fire, allowing it to boil up, and then plunging it into cold water, where the article should remain until cold.

DANGER FROM COPPER SAUCEPANS.—The precise danger from the use of copper saucepans, or stewpans, imperfectly tinned, is far from rightly understood. It appears that the acid contained in stews and other made dishes, as lemon-juice, though it does not dissolve copper by being merely boiled in it a few minutes, nevertheless, if allowed to cool and stand in it for some time, will acquire poisonous matter, as verdigris, in the form of a green band, or crust, inside the vessel. It has likewise been proved that weak solutions of common salt, such as are daily made by adding a little salt to boiling vegetables, meat, or fish, act powerfully on copper vessels, although strong solutions, or brine would not affect them.

It is, however, in vain to hope that cooks will attend to the nice distinctions by which copper stewpans may be rendered safe; the general advice given by prudent physicians is, therefore, against their use at all.

The kettles in which the soups are made should be well tinned, and kept particularly clean, by being washed in hot water and rubbed dry before they are put away. If they are not kept well tinned, the taste as well as the color of the soup will be liable to be affected by the iron; and if the soup-kettle be made of copper, and the tinning not quite perfect, everything cooked in it will be more or less poisonous, as everything which is sweet, salt, or sour, extracts verdigris from copper.

How to Choose Meats.

BEEF.—True well-fed beef may be known by the texture and color; the lean will exhibit an open grain of deep coral red, and the fat will appear of a healthy oily smoothness, rather inclining to white than yellow; the suet firm and white. Yellow fat is a test of inferior quality. Heifer beef is but little inferior to ox beef; the lean is of a closer grain, the red paler, and the fat whiter. Cow beef may be detected by the same signs, save that the older the beast, the texture of the meat will appear closer, and the flesh coarser to the sight, as well as harder to the touch.

The round of beef is, in large families, one of the most profitable parts: it is usually boiled, and, like most of the boiling parts of beef, is generally sold in our markets at less per pound than the roasting joints.

The brisket is also less in price than the roasting parts; it is not so economical a part as the round, having more bone to be weighed with it, and more fat. Where there are children, very fat joints are not desirable, being often disagreeable to them, and sometimes prejudicial, especially if they have a dislike to it. This joint also requires more cooking than many others; that is to say, it requires a double allowance of time to be given for boiling it: it will, when served, be hard and scarcely digestible if no more time be allowed to boil it than that which is sufficient for other joints and meats. When stewed it is excellent; and when cooked fresh, (i. e. unsalted,) an excellent stock for soup may be extracted from it, and yet the meat will serve as well for dinner.

The edgebone, or aitchbone, is not considered to be a very economical joint, the bone being large in proportion to the meat; but the greater part of it, at least, is as good as that of any prime part. It sells for less per pound than roasting joints.

The rump is the part of which our butchers make great profit, by selling it in the form of steaks. In the country, as there is not an equal demand for steaks, the whole of it may be purchased as a joint, and at the price of other prime parts. It may be turned to good account in producing many excellent dishes. If salted, it is simply boiled; if used unsalted, it is usually stewed.

The veiny piece is sold at a low price per pound; but if hung for a day or two, it is very good and very profitable. Where there are a number of servants and children to have an early dinner, this part of beef will be found desirable.

5

From the leg and shin excellent stock for soup may be drawn; and if not reduced too much, the meat taken from the bones may be served as a stew with vegetables; or it may be seasoned, pounded with butter, and potted; or chopped very fine, and seasoned with herbs, and bound together by egg and bread crumbs; it may be fried in balls, or in the form of large eggs, and served with a gravy made with a few spoonsful of the soup.

Of half an ox cheek excellent soup may be made; the meat, when taken from the bones, may be served as a stew.

Roasting parts of beef are the sirloin and the ribs, and these bear in all places the highest price. The most profitable of these two joints at a family table is the ribs. The bones, if removed from the beef before it is roasted, will assist in forming the basis of a soup. When boned, the meat of the ribs is often rolled up, tied with strings, and roasted: and this is the best way of using it, as it enables the carver to distribute equally the upper part of meat with the more skinny and fatter parts at the lower end of the bone.

VEAL.—When you observe the kidney well surrounded with fat, you may be sure the meat is of a good quality. The whitest is not the best veal; but the flesh of the bull-calf is of a brighter color than that of the cow-calf. The fillet of the latter is generally preferred, on account of the udder. There is a vein in the shoulder, very perceptible; and its color indicates the freshness of the meat; if a bright blue or red, it is recently killed; if any green or yellow spots are visible, it is stale. The suet will be flabby, and the kidney will smell.

The leg of veal from which the fillet is taken, the shoulder, the neck, and loin, are all in turn serviceable in a family. When the leg is purchased altogether, without dividing the knuckle from it, the butcher usually considerably remits the price.

MUTTON.—The best is of a fine grain, a bright color, the fat firm and white. It is better for being full grown. The meat of the ewe is not so bright, while the grain is closer. The ram mutton may be known by the redness of the flesh and the sponginess of the fat.

The leg and haunch of mutton, are the most profitable joints, although in price higher than the shoulder or neck. But these last joints are sold at a less price per pound than others.

The loin and saddle (the two loins not separated) are expensive joints, not in price only, but in the great proportion of fat and bone belonging to them. They are considered to be prime parts.

LAMB.—This meat will not keep long after it is killed. The large vein in the neck is blueish in color when the fore-quarter is fresh, green when becoming stale. In the hind quarter, if not recently killed, the fat of the kidney will have a slight smell, and the knuckle will have lost its firmness.

The hind quarter of lamb is more advantageous in use than the fore, but can scarcely be regarded as an economical part. In hot weather, and in a small family, the joints which the quarters form, when divided, are of so convenient a size as to render them much in request.

PORK.—In young pork the lean when pinched will break; the thickness and toughness of the rind shows it to be old. In fresh pork the flesh is firm, smooth, a clear color, and the fat set. When stale it looks clammy and flabby. Measly pork may be detected by the kernels in the fat; it should not be eaten. Dairy-fed pork bears the palm over all others.

BACON should have a thin rind, and the fat should be firm and tinged red, by the curing; the flesh should be of clear red, without intermixture of yellow, and it should firmly adhere to the bone. To judge of the state of a ham, plunge a knife into it to the bone; on drawing it back, if particles of meat adhere to it, or if the smell is disagreeable, the curing has not been effectual, and the ham is not good; it should, in such a state, be immediately cooked. In buying a ham, a short thick one is to be preferred to one long and thin. There are such a variety of qualities that to enumerate all would be too tedious.

VENISON.—When good, the fat is clear, bright, and of considerable thickness. To know when it is necessary to cook it, a knife must be plunged into the haunch; and from the smell the cook must determine on dressing or keeping it.

POULTRY.—In choosing poultry, the age of the bird is the chief point to be attended to.

An old turkey has rough and reddish legs; a young one smooth and black. Fresh killed, the eyes are full and clear, and the feet moist. When it has been kept too long, the parts about the vent begin to wear a greenish discoloured appearance.

COMMON DOMESTIC FOWLS, when young, have the legs and combs smooth; when old, they are rough, and on the breast long hairs are found instead of feathers. Fowls and chickens should be plump on the breast, fat on the back, and white legged.

GEESE.—The bills and feet red when old, yellow when young. Fresh killed, the feet are pliable, stiff when too long kept. Geese are called green when they are only two or three months' old.

DUCKS.—Choose them with supple feet and hard plump breasts. Tame ducks have yellow feet, wild ones red.

PIGEONS are very indifferent food when they are too long kept. Suppleness of the feet show them to be young; the state of the flesh is flaccid when they are getting bad from keeping. Tame pigeons are larger than the wild.

RABBITS when old, have the haunches thick, the ears dry and tough, and the claws blunt and ragged. A young rabbit has claws smooth and sharp, ears that easily tear, and a narrow cleft in the lip.

PARTRIDGES when young, have yellow legs and dark colored bills. Old partridges are very indifferent eating.

WOODCOCKS AND SNIPES, when old, have the feet thick and hard; when these are soft and tender, they are both young and fresh killed. When their bills become moist, and their throats muddy, they have been too long killed.

Fish.

That Fish is an important agent to the comfort of thinking minds may be readily understood by only a slight examination of what fish (particularly salt water fish) does for us—It supplies us with nerve matter. We will instance phosphorus. An idiot has a brain of which about one per cent of phosphorus is present, a healthy active brain about two per cent, a maniac's brain nearly three. We may perhaps here remark without offence that poisonous ingredients such as alcohol, taken immoderately, are apt to destroy the brain power of rejecting (phosphorus for instance) a superfluity of nourishment, and to this cause may be mainly attributed the great danger in what is called "drinking" and traced incipient maniacism.

Fish supplies our system with brain power, and makes good the waste,

"that toiling thought employs."

We advise that Fish be made an article of diet twice a week.

Before dressing fish of any kind, great care should be taken that it is well washed and cleansed, but be cautious not to wash it too much, as the flavor is much diminished by too much water. When boiling fish, put a little salt and a little vinegar into the water to give it firmess. Be careful to let the fish be well done, but not to let it break. When very fresh, cod and whiting are very much improved by keeping a day, and rubbing a little salt down the back bone. Fresh-water fish often have a muddy smell and taste which is got rid of by soaking it. After it has been thoroughly cleansed in strong salt and water, if the fish is not too large, scald it in the same; then dry and dress it.

Put the fish in cold water, and let it boil very gently, or the outside will break before the inside is warm. Put all crimped fish into boiling water, and when it boils up some cold water should be put into it, to check it and keep it simmering. All fish should be taken out of the water the instant it is done, or it will become woolly. To ascertain when it is done, the fish plate may be drawn up, and, if done, the meat will leave the bone. To keep it hot, and to prevent it losing its color, the fish plate should be placed across the fish kettle, and a clean cloth put over the fish.

Small fish may be nicely fried plain, or done with egg and bread crumbs, and then fried. On the dish on which the fish is to be served should be placed a damask napkin, folded, and upon this put the fish, with the roe and liver; then garnish the dish with horse-radish, parsley and lemon.

To broil or fry fish nicely, after it is well washed, it should be put in a cloth, and when dry, wetted with egg and bread crumbs. It will be much improved by being wetted with egg and crumbs a second time. Then have your pan ready with plenty of boilling dripping or lard, put your fish into it and let it fry rather quickly till it is of a nice brown and appears done. If it is done before being nicely browned, it should be taken from the pan, and placed on a sieve before the fire to drain and brown. If wanted very nice, put a sheet of cap paper to receive the fish. Should you fry your fish in oil, it obtains a much finer color than when done in lard or dripping. Never use butter, as it makes the fish a bad color. Garnish your dish with green or fried parsley.

In broiling fish, be careful that your gridiron is clean; place it on the fire, and when hot rub it over with suet, to hinder the fish from sticking. The fish must be floured and seasoned before broiling. It must be broiled over a clear fire only, and great care must be taken that it does not burn or become smoky.

Broiled fish for breakfast should always be skinned, buttered, and peppered.

Fish are boiled, fried, broiled, baked, stewed, in fact cooked in every imaginable fashion; those named are the chief methods. In every kind the greatest attention and cleanliness must be exercised. A broken, disfigured, abrased, or ill-cooked dish of fish presented at table, is quiet sufficient to destroy the taste for it for ever; on the contrary, when neatly done, it heightens the relish which every one possesses more or less, and imparts an appetite where one may be wanting, while the cook is held in grateful remembrance.

Among the bivalves Oysters are said to contain the most of the phosphoric principle, and are held in universal estimation. They are cooked in a greater variety of ways than any other fish—but the leading principle with them is to obtain them fat and in season, and then not to forget that a stew must not be a deluge of water; a fry must not shake off its batter; a roast must not get dried up; a steam must not be done with dirty shells; a fritter must not be all batter, and whether stewed, fried, roasted, steamed or frittered, they must be served up hot.

To Choose Fish.—Cod.—The best fish are thick at the neck, very red gills, firm white flesh, bright, and blood-shot eyes, and small head.

Cat Fish.—When large they will be found very coarse and strong, consequently the small ones are best. Always cook whilst fresh.

Eels.—Silver eels are the best; dark skinned and yellow tinged are not good; the bright silver-hued belly and thickness of back are the guides in their selection.

Flounders.—Thick bodies and the bellies of a creamy white, show them to be good; a flabby flounder, with a pale blue tinge on the belly, should be avoided.

Halibut.—Should be very firm, the fish a clean white when cut into, and with no outward sliminess.

Herrings.—Very red gills, blood-shot eyes, bright scales, and the fish stiff, shows them to be good and fresh.

Mackerel.—Bright eyes, thick bodies, the prismatic colours very predominant on the belly, denote freshness and goodness.

Rock Fish, Black Fish, &c—The remark as to firmness and clear fresh eyes apply to these varieties of the finny tribe. They should be eaten when very fresh, otherwise their flavor becomes destroyed.

SALMON.—The fish stiff, scales very bright, the belly thick, the gills a brilliant colour and the flesh when cut a beautiful red, will prove it to be a fine fresh fish, and upon which alone depends its flavor and excellence, for no method can completely preserve the delicate flavor it has when just taken out of the water.

SALT FISH should be properly soaked in water previous to being dressed, for at least twelve hours, then taken out, scrubbed with a coarse cloth, and laid on a stone or table to drain for six or eight hours, when it should again be put into water, just lukewarm, to remain there ten or twelve hours.

SEA BASS.—When fresh, will exhibit very clearly defined stripes, a clear eye and firm flesh. When too large they are rather coarse. Should be eaten as soon as posible after catching.

SHAD.—When fresh and good, the gills are bright, the scales silvery, and the flesh firm. Shad should be cleaned and salted, at least six hours before cooking.

TROUT.—See that the gills are a bright red, the spots on the sides well colored, with the belly a clear white or slightly tinged with yellow. If the eye is in the slightest degree flabby the fish is not fresh.

TURBOT, and all flat white fish, are rigid and firm when fresh; the under side should be of a rich cream colour. When out of season, or too long kept, this becomes a bluish white, and the flesh soft and flaccid. A clear bright eye in fish is also a mark of being fresh and good.

Of the many other varieties of fish offered in our markets nothing more need be said—by following the above general rules, (which will be found applicable in all cases) fresh fish, and of good quality, can always be chosen.

SHELL FISH.— Lobsters, to be had in perfection should be boiled at home; choose the heaviest. When they are boiled the tail should have a good spring; the cock lobster has a narrow tail in which the two uppermost fins are stiff and hard; the hen has a broad tail and these fins are softer. The male has the best flavour; the flesh is firmer, and the colour when broiled is brighter then the hen.

CRABS.—Like lobsters, should be selected by weight; when prime, the leg-joints are stiff and the scent pleasant.

OYSTERS.—There are so many *named* varieties of the oyster, that it would be rather a difficult matter to classify them. None but fresh ones should be used for any style of cooking, and these are easily known from their general appearance on opening, (as they exhibit a cleaness of liquid and full roundness of flesh) which should be done with care and by an expert. If on inserting a knife between the shells they close firmly, then they are fresh and in good condition, if on the contrary they shut slowly and remain open, they are not fit for use. The smallest and most delicate are considered by most persons best in their raw state whilst the larger or coarser varieties are those generally used for cooking.

RECEIPTS.

Cat Fish, Fried.—Remove the head and tail, and the upper part of the back bone and wash and clean thoroughly; having scored the sides and backs dredge with flour and fry in a pan of boiling lard. They can also be fried in a batter made of eggs and fine bread crumbs, seasoned with salt and pepper.

Cod, to boil—Wash, clean, and rub the inside of the fish with salt. Let it be completely covered with water, in the kettle. A small fish will be done in fifteen minutes after the water boils; a large one will take half an hour; but the tail being so much thinner than the thick of the fish, it will be done too much if it be all boiled at once; therefore, the best way is, to cut that part in slices to fry, and garnish the head and shoulders with, or to serve in a separate dish. Lay the roe on one side, and the liver on the other side of the fish. Serve it with oyster sauce, or plain melted butter.

Cod Chowder.—Lay some slices of good fat pork in the bottom of the pot, cut a fresh cod into thin slices, place a layer on the pork, then a layer of biscuit, then pork, then cod, then a layer of biscuit again, and when all is used, add a quart of water. Let it simmer till the fish is done; before quite done, add pepper, salt, and such seasoning as you like, and a thickening of flour, with a coffee cup of sweet cream or rich milk. Add oysters to the above if you fancy them.

Clam Chowder is made the same way, only cut off the hard leathery parts of the clams.

Cod, to Fry.—Cut in thick slices; flour, or egg, and cover these with bread-crumbs, or biscuit powder. Fry in plenty of hot dripping or lard. Slices of cod may also be stewed in gravy, like eels.

Cod's Head and Shoulders.—Wash it clean, then quickly dash some boiling water over it, which will cause the slime to ooze out; this should be carefully removed with a knife, but take care not to break the skin; wipe the head clean, and lay it on a strainer, in a turbot-kettle of boiling water; put in the salt and a teacupful of vinegar. Take care that it is quite covered. Let it simmer from thirty to forty minutes. It should drain before it is dished, and the dish be rather a deep one. Glaze it with beaten yolks of eggs, then strew over it fine grated bread-crumbs, lemon-peel, pepper and salt, stick into it some bits of butter, and set it before the fire; as it browns baste it with butter, constantly strewing more bread-crumbs and chopped parsley over it. A rich sauce for the above is made as follows: have made, in preparation, a quart of strong beef or veal stock; or, if to be maigre, a rich, well seasoned, fish stock; thicken with flour mixed into butter, and then strain it; add it to 30 oysters, picked and bearded, the hard meat of a boiled lobster cut up, and the soft part pounded, 2 glasses of white wine (sherry is best,) and the juice of one lemon. Boil it, altogether, for 5 minutes, skim it, and pour part of it into the dish where the fish is; the rest serve in a sauce tureen. This dish may be garnished with fried smelts, flounders, or oysters. When the French cook cod's-head in this way it has the addition of being stuffed with either meat or fish forcemeat and some balls of the same, fried, as a garnish. Cold cod may be dressed as cold turbot. Slices of cod may be boiled, as well as fried; but they should be as short a time as possible in the water; it should, therefore, boil soon after the slices are put into it. About ten minutes ought to do them. Shrimp sauce may be poured over these, or anchovy sauce. If you wish it to be rather rich, make a sauce of veal stock, a boned anchovy and pickled oysters, all chopped fine, pepper, salt, a glass of red wine, and a thickening of butter and flour. Boil up and skim, and pour over the slices of cod.

Cod Sounds, Boiled.—Soak the sounds in warm water for half an hour, then scrape and clean well. Boil in milk and water, and when tender, serve in a napkin, with egg sauce.

Cod Sounds Ragout.—Scald, clean, and rub the sounds well with salt; then stew in some good highly seasoned gravy, and when tender add a little cream and floured butter to thicken; give a boil, and season with grated lemon-peel, nutmeg, and a little allspice.

Eels, Broiled.—Skin and clean them, cut into pieces about three inches long, and broil slowly over a good fire: then serve with melted butter.

Eels, to Collar.—Skin, gut, remove the back-bone, and cut off the heads of as many eels as you want; then dip into a mixture of salt, common pepper, cayenne, grated nutmeg, pounded cloves, lemon-peel grated, and some finely-rubbed sage. Roll up in fillets, tie with string as usual, boil in salt water, with an equal portion of vinegar, until tender, and then remove; add some whole pepper to the pickle, which should be placed in a deep dish, and when cold, plunge the eel fillets into it.

Eel Pie.—Clean a pound or more of eels, cut them in lengths of two and three inches, season with pepper and salt, and put them in a dish with some lumps of butter; and a wine-glassful of water; cover with a light paste, and bake. Some add a couple of bay-leaves and a fagot of herbs, with a few cloves and an onion, and veal stock thickened with flour, instead of water. Cream added after the pie is done, instead of butter before, also improves it vastly.

Eels, to Pot.—Skin and clean the eels, split them, and remove the back-bone, then cut into pieces two or three inches long, and season with pepper, salt, dried sage rubbed fine, and powdered allspise and nutmeg. Place the pieces in a baking-dish in layers, pour in clarfied butter until full; cover with paper, and bake in a moderaetly quick oven for an hour and a half. When cold remove them, press into pots, and cover with clarified butter.

Fish Cakes.—Remove all the bones carefully from any given quantity of either fresh or salt codfish of a previous days cooking, mix it well with mashed potatoes and butter, (having an excess of the potatoes,) to which now add well beaten eggs, so as to make the whole into a thick paste, and season with black or cayenne pepper as may be desired. Make up into balls or cakes, sprinkle with flour and fry in lard.

Flounders, Fried.—Clean and dry the fish well, egg over dip, in bread crumbs, and fry a light brown. Garnish with fried parsley, and serve with plain melted butter.

Haddock, to boil.—Boil entire, if not very large; and throw a little salt, vinegar, and horseradish, into the water, which improves the look of the fish, and prevents the skin breaking. Serve hot, with oyster sauce.

Hake Cutlets.—Cut a moderate sized hake into cutlets, lengthwise, about the size of ordinary veal cutlets, dry well with a cloth, egg well, dip in bread crumbs, and fry light brown; then serve hot on a napkin, with fried parsley garnish.

Halibut, Fried.—The best pieces for frying, are obtained from the middle of the fish, which wash and dry very carefully; extract all the bone and cut into slices about an inch in thickness. Take beaten yolk of eggs well seasoned and prepare in a pan and in another grated bread crumbs. Now season the fish with salt, pepper and butter and dip twice alternately in the egg and bread crumbs, and fry in boiling lard over a quick fire.

Herrings, to Fry.—Scale, wash, and dry them in a cloth, but do not cut off their heads. Dredge them with flour, and fry them with clean dripping or lard over a brisk fire, and when done, serve hot, garnished with fried parsley round the dish, and parsley and butter for sauce.

Mackerel, to Broil.—Clean, split down the belly, spread open, cut off the heads, and pepper well inside: then flour them lightly to prevent their sticking to the bars of the gridiron, and put over a clear fire, until done a light brown, then serve spread open with the inside uppermost, with a lump of butter the size of a walnut rubbed over each or with plain melted butter.

Mackerel, Fried.—Take the swollen sized mackerel for the purpose, perfectly fresh, and wash and dry them thoroughly; then make some cuts and scores in the back and cover them well with beaten egg and bread crumbs. Let the lard be boiling before putting them in to fry, and serve them hot.

Perch as Water Souchy.—Take a dozen fish, place in a stew pan, with about two quarts of water, some parsley roots and leaves chopped, but not fine. Boil until nearly the whole of the flesh of the fish will run through a coarse sieve with the gravy to them, season with pepper and salt, and stew until done; then turn gravy and all into a soup tureen. Some add onions, but in our opinion it spoils the flavor of the souchy.

Pike, to Bake.—Scale and clean the fish, cut off its fins, and stuff the belly with pudding meat of best quality; then place the tail in the mouth, as recommended for stewing, and put it upon its belly in a baking-dish. Flour the fish well all over, cover with a few lumps of butter, and place in an oven, or a Dutch-oven before the fire, taking care to baste it occasionaly with some of the fat. When done, remove the pike, place on a clean dish, add a squeeze of lemon, a little soy and melted butter together, mix, and pour into the dish; garnish with sliced lemon, and serve as hot as possible.

Pike to Stew.—Take stale bread crumbs, finely-chopped sweet herbs and parsely, a little lemon peel, three ounces of butter, mixed up with the yolks of two eggs, and seasoned with nutmeg, cayenne, common pepper, and salt, and form into a pudding to stuff the fish with. A few pickled or fresh oysters chopped fine and mixed with it improves the flavor consideratbly. Clean and wash the fish, stuff with pudding, fix the tail in the mouth, and stew gently in the same manner as the turbot and garnish with sliced lemon.

Rock Fish, Sea Bass and Black Fish.—These are all best boiled plain, after having drawn, scaled and carefully washed them, then dredge a cloth with flour, place the fish in it, and place in the fish kettle with plenty of water, to which add salt in sufficient quantity. The head and tail should be left on. They require about thirty minutes, steady boiling; when done remove the cloth, drain well the fish, and serve either with egg sauce, or hard boiled eggs sliced, and cold butter to the taste.

Rock Fish, Stewed.—Cut the fish in slices about an inch thick and sprinkle with salt; put in a stewpan with some fresh butter, and about half a dozen large onions thinly sliced. The fish should be placed in layers seasoning each with pepper, and nutmeg, chopped parsely and small lumps of butter rolled in flour. Cook one hour over a slow fire, and serve hot with egg sauce.

Salmon, to Broil.—Cut the fish in slices an inch thick, season with cayenne and common pepper, a little nutmeg and salt, roll well in buttered white paper, and broil over a slow fire; serve in the paper, with plain melted butter, anchovy, lobster, or shrimp sauce.

Salmon Collared.—Split enough of the fish to make a handsome roll, wash, and wipe it well; rub the inside and outside well with powdered white pepper, mace, salt, and Jamaica pepper, carefully mixed; roll it tight, and bind it up; put as much water, and one-third of vinegar, as will cover it, add salt, long pepper, allspice, and two bay leaves; cover it close, and simmer till done enough. Drain and boil the liquor quickly, and pour it over the fish when cold; serve with parsley.

Salmon dressed, to pot.—Take the remains of a dressed salmon, remove the bones, mash it upon a board, season with a little allspice, pepper, and salt; then add some thick melted butter, sufficient to form into a paste, but do not make it too moist, then press into a pot, and pour clarified butter over the top. If at hand, the coral and spawn of a lobster, or a few shrimps or prawns, improve it both in flavor and appearance.

Salmon to Pickle Cold.—Boil some of the liquor in which the fish was dressed with an equal part of vinegar, and add some whole peper-corns: when it bubbles, remove from the fire, and pour over any cold salmon you have at hand. If the salmon is not well done, boil it up in the pickle until well dressed.

Salmon, to Pickle Undressed.—Scale the fish, rub well with a cloth, and scrape away all the blood about the back bone, but do not wash it; cut off the head, and divide the fish into pieces about six inches long, then boil the pieces in pickle made of equal parts of vinegar and water, with a few cloves, and two or three blades of mace, until done; skim carefully all the time the fish is boiling and when done remove the fish, and pour the liquor into a jar or a tub, so that both may become cold; when cold, put the fish into the liquor, with one-third more vinegar, and some whole pepper.

Salmon-Trout Pie.—*A Plain Way.*—Clean and nicely trim, then cut into handsome fillets, as many trout as may be required; season each fillet with pepper, salt, mace, and cayenne, which should be well rubbed into the inside, and each fillet afterwards rolled up and well packed into the pie-dish. Put bits of butter above and among the fillets, and add six or eight oysters. Take a pint of fish-stock, or the same quantity made of the head and trimmings, thicken and strain this over the fish; then cover in the dish with a good paste, and bake as usual, but remember that it will not require so long a time to bake as a meat pic.

Sea Bass Fried.—Remove the head and tail of the fish and fry in plenty of lard. By adding about a pint of either stewed and stuffed or pickled tomatoes, and dredging with a little flour, they will be greatly improved.

Skate, to Boil.—The fish having been previously skinned, the flesh cut into slips about an inch wide, and then immerse in salt and water for four or five hours, the pieces should be rolled, tied with a piece of string, and boiled for about twenty minutes. The thinner parts not requiring so long should not be put in until a short time after the water boils. Anchovy, and butter sauce, or crab sauce, should be served with it.

Skate, to Fry.—Prepare the fish as directed to boil egg well; dip in bread crumbs, and fry carefully in plenty of dripping. Garnish with fried parsley, and serve with crab sauce, anchovy and butter sauce, soy or ketchup.

Sunfish, and Perch to Fry.—Clean, cut all the fins close off, open by the belly, dry well, dust with flour, and fry a light brown, in plenty of lard or olive oil. Serve with melted butter, anchovy, soy, or ketchup.

Trout, Boiled.—Clean, scale well, and boil whole in cold water, allowing it to boil gradually; vinegar and horseradish put in the water improve the flavor. When done, carefully drain off the water so as not to break the skin, and serve with lobster, shrimp, or anchovy butter sauce.

Trout Stewed.—Take white wine and cold water, in equal quantities, as much as may be required to cover the fish well, and stew until done, serve them hot with a gravy composed of flour, butter, beaten eggs and seasoning to taste.

Turbot Baked.—Prepare as above, then season with cayenne, mace and nutmeg powdered, a few sprigs of herbs, butter and grated bread crumbs, and place in a deep baking dish and bake. Serve hot.

Turbot, to Boil.—Choose a sufficiently large kettle, pour in sufficient water to cover the fish, add a handful of salt, a table-spoonful of shred horseradish, and two table-spoonfuls of vinegar. Boil until the water has acquired some flavor, and then allow it to become cool. Score the fish just through the skin on the dark side, so as to prevent it cracking on the other, and then place it in the kettle with the dark side downwards, and check the boiling as soon as ebullition takes place; observe also that the scum is removed frequently, and that no blacks fall into the kettle. When done, remove, sprinkle the surface with the dried spawn of a hen lobster, or if it cannot be procured, a little scraped horseradish. Serve with lobster, shrimp, or crab sauce. A moderate sized turbot requires about half an hour to cook it well, a large one from three quarters of an hour to an hour, a thick slice from twenty to twenty-five minutes.

Shell Fish.

Crabs, Dressed.—Choose a good heavy crab, boil for about half an hour in salt and water, remove the pot, let the crab get cold; take off the great shell without breaking it, extract the fish from the body and claws, and mince it well. Put some floured butter in a stew-pan with six or eight small mushrooms, parsley, and green asparagus tops, shred fine, fry a little, and put in the minced fish with half a wine-glass of white wine, and pepper, salt, and sweet herbs to season; stew gently for fifteen minutes, thicken with flour, and flavor with lemon juice. Fill the shell with this mixture, having previously removed the herbs, set in a baking-pan, or dish, strew stale bread crumbs over the top, set in an oven to brown, and then serve hot. Garnish with lemon, and parsley.

Crab, Minced.—Remove the meat, mince small and place in a saucepan with a wine-glassful of white wine, pepper and salt, nutmeg, cayenne pepper, and two table-spoonfuls of vinegar. Let it stew for ten minutes; melt a piece of butter the size of a hen's egg, with an anchovy and the yolks of two eggs; beat up and mix well, stir in the crab, and add sufficient stale bread crumbs to thicken. Garnish with thin toast cut with a pastry leaf-cutter, or with the claws, and parsley. Lobster may be dressed in the same manner.

Lobster Balls.—Take the meat of a lobster with the coral and spawn, pound in a mortar, add bread crumbs, about a quarter the proportion of the lobster, and season with cayenne, white pepper, mace, and salt. Mix sufficient melted butter with the whole to form into a mass, make into balls the size of small apples, egg well, dip in bread crumbs, and fry a pale brown.

Lobster Cutlets.—Choose a large lobster and two small ones, reserve a piece of the coral, pick and pound the remainder with a little fresh butter, a little salt, red and white pepper, a blade or two of mace, a little nutmeg, and a dessert-spoonful of anchovy sauce: when well pounded, add the yolks of two eggs and the white of one; lay the mixture on a paste-board, roll it out with a little flour until an inch thick, cut into small squares, do them over with egg, dip in bread crumbs, and fry a light brown in lard. Mix the coral remaining with a little melted butter and anchovy sauce, pour it into the middle of the dish with the cutlets arranged round, cut the horns of the lobster into pieces an inch and a half long, place them between each cutlet and serve hot. A very pretty way to dress them is to form into the shape of lamb cutlets, placing a piece of the horn in centre of the extremity to resemble the bone.

Lobster, to Pot Cold.—Choose a hen lobster. Remove the spawn, coral, flesh, and pickings about the head, and mix with the meat from the claws; pound well in a mortar, seasoning with white pepper, cayenne, and pounded mace; then add some thick melted butter, until it forms a good thick paste. Remove the meat from the tail, pound and season the same, then put half of it in the bottom of the pot, and cover with the other paste. Pour clarified butter over the top of each pot, and keep in a cool place.

Lobster Salad.—Take three yolks of hard eggs, two yolks of raw eggs, two tea-spoonsful of mustard, a little salt and cayenne pepper, four table-spoonsful of salad oil, one and a half table-spoonful of tarragon vinegar, and one of essence of anchovies; mix well, and add three table-spoonsful of cream. Cut two large lobsters up small, and mix with finely cut salad, cucumber, hot pickles, and beet-root. Pour the mixture given above over the salad, put in a dish not a bowl, and garnish with hard boiled eggs cut in thin slices.

Lobster Sauce.—Break the shell of the lobster, extract the meat from the claws and body, cut small; boil the shells in half a pint of water, with a little ground allspice and scraped horseradish, until all the strength is extracted; strain the liquor into a stew-pan; add the lobster, half a pound of cream or thick melted butter, a teaspoonful or two of anchovy sauce, and a squeeze of lemon. If you have a hen lobster, remove the coral and spawn, and pound it up fine in a mortar; stir well in the stew-pan, and let simmer gently for about five minutes, but do not let it boil; season with cayenne and salt while stewing.

Oyster Sausages.—Chop and pound some veal well in a mortar, then chop up an equal proportion of oysters, mix well and add some bread crumbs and a little beef suet shred fine; moisten with some of the liquor of the oysters, season with pepper salt and a little mace, bind together with well beaten egg form into sausages or flat cakes, and fry a pale brown in good dripping.

Oysters Scolloped.—Butter the bottoms of your scollop shells, then sprinkle with bread crumbs, and lay a sufficient number of bearded oysters to cover the bread, season with pepper and salt, and place some pieces of butter over them; place another layer of bread crumbs, oysters, and butter until the shells are full then cover the whole with bread crumbs add a few pieces of butter on the top, and place in a Dutch-oven before the fire; when done, brown with a salamander, or a red-hot shovel held over the top, and serve in the scollop shells.

Soups.

WHAT constitutes Soup and what are its constituents are two very different questions—many persons think that a medley of market supplies thrown carelessly into a pot of boiling water after an indefinite period or hurried cooking makes *Soup* but such is not the case; it requires due proportion of each item, due attention to the manner of mingling, and due time to each of the ingredients, and indeed if the soup-er-in-ten-dant is not half a scientist it will be but a sorry recompense for getting good materials. The French are the best soup makers in the world, and this aptitude is so natural, that even the common soldiers divide themselves into soup squads, and thus extract from their rations, probably double the nutriment of their neighbors the English—who traditionally go in for every thing as solid as possible.

The constituents of soup, then, are not enough to constitute soup, without very careful management. This will be easily understood when it is taken into consideration that the extraction of gelatine from meat, which is the basis of good soup, may be or nearly so lost to the soup by fierce boiling, and then, what avails the rest? The vegetable additions too may be spoiled by equal inattention. To make good soup, it matters not what the ingredients are, if there is a proper knowledge of their conditions and nature—a skilled cook can make soup out of material that would otherwise be wasted, while the best materials without skill would yield nothing worth the name.

There is no form of nutriment so palatable and healthful as properly prepared soup, while it may be said that few articles of the dinner table are more distasteful than what generally passes under its injured name. Whether we regard the season of the year, or not as suggestive of different soups, one thing is certain that what cannot be got cannot be made into soup; the market must decide, and whether meat or vegetable, or a mixture of both, the same rule must be followed—boil steadily, adjust sorts and quantities judiciously, and never over-season—all that is wanted is what epicures call *piquancy*—something to call out the flavors of the meat and vegetable compound. Too little attention is paid to color in soup, it should be clear and rich, and if there is no natural browning or kitchen stock on hand, the addition of a little sugar browned will supply this need. It is a matter however of some consequence to take into account whether it is winter or summer: in the winter, soup is better made before it is wanted, and the vegetable addition and seasoning added afterwards, for, by this means, the gelatine is much richer after being cooled, and the coarse fat can be easily removed.

In summer only the leaner and best meat should be used and only such vegetables as are in the highest perfection; but there is one thing that in both and all seasons should be especially noted, and that is, both before and after use, carefully clean and dry the soup-pot, and friends who love to feed their brethren well should remember that upon the first dish, soup, depends mainly the relish for the rest. Many inferior dishes may follow without remark if good soup leads; but if this fail, the appetite will criticise every succeeding delicacy, and a disappointed fancy often condemn a whole dinner. So much depends on the subject of these remarks and which the following receipts will illustrate.

RECEIPTS.

Barley Soup—. Two pounds of shin of beef, quarter of a pound of pearl barley, a bunch of parsley, four onions, four potatoes, two sweet potatoes, salt, pepper a blade or two of mace, and four quarts of water. A small piece of a boiled knuckle of ham will improve it. Put all the ingredients together, and simmer gently for three hours.

Beef, Family Soup.—Get what is called a good beef soup bone, boil two hours, leaving about two quarts of broth, break two eggs into it, about the size of a pigeon's egg, and fried, and add them to the soup just before sending to table.

Calf's Head.—Scald, and wash the head clean with salt and water, then place in a stewpan with sufficient water to cover it: add a faggot of sweet herbs, an onion stuck with cloves, six blades of mace, and a table-spoonful and a half of pearl barley. Stew till tender, and add a head of stewed celery. Season with pepper, pour the soup into the tureen, place the head in the centre, and serve. This is an excellent soup when carefully prepared.

Carrot Soup.—Take half a dozen full grown carrots, scrape them clean and then rasp off the outer rind, or soft red part only, add a sliced ripe tomato. Prepare any kind of fresh meat broth, and take two quarts of it whilst hot, season it with two onions fried in butter, a small quantity of mace, and a little salt—nothing else; add the raspings, put the whole in a stewpan covered close, and let it simmer by the side of the fire for two or three hours, by which time the raspings will have become soft enough to be pulped through a fine sieve; after which boil the soup until it is as smooth as jelly.

Clam Soup.—The secret of this soup is merely in the opening of the clams; they must be opened into two dishes, the bodies in one the "tongues" in another—Scald the tongues and skin them, then cut them small and put with the bodies. Cook slowly, with the addition of a little water, some white potatoes, parsley, peper, and a trifle of salt.

Green Pea Soup.—(*Plain*).—Take a quart of large fresh green peas, boil them in water with salt until thoroughly tender—then pass the pulp through a sieve; take a quart of fresh milk and beat up in it the yolk of two eggs and the white of one; add the pulp to this and boil for a quarter of an hour; just before taking off the fire sweeten a little with white sugar, and add a little grated nutmeg and lemon peel.

Lobster Soup.—Take three or four young lobsters boiled, and remove the fish and cut it into small pieces; take out the coral, not the berries, pound it so as to separate it and sift it through a coarse strainer; take two quarts of good veal stock quite a jelly and cold; add to it the berries bruised, a tablespoonful of anchovy sauce, two ounces of melted butter, rubbed into two tablespoonsful of flour; add it to the stock with a blade of mace, let it boil ten minutes, then strain it; add to it the meat of the lobsters and the whole of the coral, stir it all up so as to make thoroughly warm but do not let it boil. Make forced meat balls (minced) out of the head of lobster, with the soft part, the tips of the tails and other scraps, some bread crumbs, a teaspoonful of flour, a little grated nutmeg, mixed up, with the yolk of one egg, made into balls.

Mixed Vegetable Soup.—Take half a pint of small barley, and having washed well, put it into four quarts of cold water, with a lump of fat from any kind of roasted meat, a teaspoonful of salt, and half a one of pepper. Let this boil gently for two hours, the four quarts will then be reduced to two. Cut up two large well scraped carrots, four large onions, two heads of celery, and three or four turnips, into thin slices or small pieces, and put them in when the soup is boiling. Let it boil gently for an hour and a half. Mix in a basin, a piled teaspoonful of flour with a little cold water until it is like cream. Mix a little flour clear of lumps and add it; stir the soup up well, let it simmer a moment and it is done.

Mock Turtle Soup.—Take a Calf's or full grown lamb's head, thoroughly clean it, breaking the bones and taking out the brains, separating the tongue and detaching the scalp; add the giblets of two tender full-grown chickens, and having washed them carefully in cold water, put them all into a pot and boil gently in a gallon of water, adding a little salt; skim, and when cooked enough peel the tongue and boil down until all the meat has boiled from the bones. Take then a large stewpan and line the bottom with good fat ham, mix such vegetables as you please with the meat, with pepper and a little mace and a few cloves, and place on the ham, and then gently pour on the soup. Simmer the whole slowly for one hour, adding more seasoning if necessary, and serve whilst hot.

Mutton Broth.—Take the blood out of two pounds of scrag of mutton, by putting it in a stewpan and covering with cold water; when the water becomes milk-warm pour it off; then put in it four or five pints of water, with a teaspoonful of salt, a tablespoonful of best grits, and an onion; set it over a slow fire, and when all the scum has been removed, put in two or three turnips. Let it simmer very slowly for two hours, then strain through a clean sieve.

Oyster Soup.—Take a quart of milk and a quart of stock; boil them for ten minutes, with a blade of mace, and a tablespoonful of essence of anchovy; then set it to cool. Take three dozen oysters, put them with their liquor and a little water over the fire, and barely let them boil; then drain them, taking care of the liquor and throw away their beards. Take four tablespoonsful of flour, mix in a paste, with two ounces of melted butter before the fire, add a little cold water, then a little of the soup; then put it over the fire until it is thick, strain it into the soup, and throw in the oysters. The whole of the soup will now be nearly cold; let it boil up rapidly at once, and carefully scum it, and serve it as hot as possible.

Pea Soup.—Cut up two and a half pounds of pickled pork, or some pork cuttings, or the same quantity of scrag of mutton, or leg of beef, (but always with a little pork flavoring) and put away one of these kinds of meat into a pot with a gallon of water, three pints of split or dried peas previously soaked in water over night, two carrots, four onions, and a head of celery, all chopped small; season with pepper and salt if necessary; boil very gently for three hours, taking care to skim it occasionally, and stirring it up from the bottom now and then. Serve while hot.

Soup Stock.—Take four pounds of shin of beef, or four pounds of knuckle of veal, or two pounds of each; any bones, trimmings of poultry, or fresh meat, quarter of a pound of lean bacon or ham, two ounces of butter, two large onions, each stuck with three cloves, one turnip, three carrots, one head of cellery, three ounces of white sugar, two ounces of salt, half a teaspoonful of whole pepper, one large blade of mace, one bunch of savory herb, and four quarts and a pint of cold water. Cut up the meat and bacon or ham into pieces of about three inches square; rub the butter on the bottom of the stewpan; put in half a pint of water the meat, and all the other ingredients. Cover the stewpan, and place it on a sharp fire, occasionally stirring its contents. When the bottom of the pan becomes covered with a pale jelly-like substance, add the four quarts of cold water, and simmer very gently for five hours. Do not let it boil quickly, and carefully remove every particle of scum whilst it is doing, and strain it through a fine hair sieve. This stock, or one similar to it in most respects, is the basis of most of the soups made, and will be found excellent for ordinary purposes.

Sago Soup.—Take two quarts of good clear, brown, gravy soup, and add to it sufficient sago to thicken it to the consistency of pea soup. Season it with any favorite ketchup, and add a little lemon juice.

Veal White Soup.—Take four calf's feet, and a knuckle of veal and boil them in five quarts of water, with three onions sliced, a bunch of sweet herbs, four heads of white celery cut small, a tablespoonful of whole pepper, and a small teaspoonful of salt, adding five or six large blades of mace. Let it boil very slowly until the meat is in rags and has dropped from the bone, and the gristle quite dissolved. Skim it well while boiling. When done, strain it through a sieve into a tureen, or a deep white-ware pan. When cold, skim off all the fat, and put the jelly (for such it ought to be) into a clean soup-pot with two ounces of vermicelli, and set it over the fire. When the vermicelli is dissolved, stir in gradually a pint of thick cream, while the soup is quite hot; but do not let it come to a boil after the cream is in lest it should curdle. Cut up one or two rolls into small pieces, put in the bottom of a tureen, pour in the soup and send it to table.

Vermicelli.—Put on a quart of soup stock and when it boils add two ounces of vermicelli; simmer gently for half an hour, stirring frequently.

Meats.

Bacon, Boiled and Vegetables.—Take a ten gallon pot and put therein a piece of bacon; let it boil up gently, and take care to keep it well skimmed; then add some cleaned, washed and split cabbage; a few parsnips and carrots also split, and when it has boiled an hour and a half, put in a dozen, more or less as may be required, peeled potatoes, and when these latter are done the whole will be ready to serve. The liquid in which this has been cooked makes an excellent soup by adding a little seasoning and some spices or crusts of bread.

Bacon Pudding.—Take a pound of moderately fat bacon and boil for half an hour, and then cut it up into thin slices; peel an onion and half a dozen apples and cut them also into thin slices; work two pounds of flour into a stiff dough, and having rolled it out thin lay the slices of bacon upon it, and the slices of onion and apples upon the bacon; roll up the dough so as to secure its contents, securing it well, put into a pudding cloth and boil full two hours in a good sized pot and an abundance of water.

Beef a-la-mode.—Cut out the bone from the beef, and convert it with the trimmings into gravy; stuff the orifice with rich forcemeat. Half roast it, and before putting in the stewpan lard the top with dried and pickled mushrooms, adding mushroom powder in the orifice; then put in two quarts of gravy from the bones, a large onion stuck with cloves and two carrots cut in slices. When the beef has stewed until it is quite tender, strain and thicken the sauce, add to it a glass of wine, mushroom or oysters and small pieces of fried paste. The mushroom or oysters may be omitted if desired.

Beef, Baked, and Potatoes.—The cheapest pieces of beef, suitable for baking or roasting, consist of the thick part of the ribs, cut from towards the shoulder, the mouse buttock and the gravy pieces, and also what is commonly called the chuck of beef, which consists of the throat boned, and tied up with a string in the form of a small round.

Whichever you may happen to buy, it should be well sprinkled over with pepper, salt and, flour, and placed upon a small iron trivet in a baking dish, containing peeled potatoes and about half a pint of water. If you bake the meat in your own oven remember that it must be turned over on the trivet every twenty minutes, and that you must be careful to baste it all over now and then with the fat which runs from it into the dish, using a spoon for that purpose.

Beef Collops.—Cut thin slices of beef from the rump, or any other tender part, and divide them into pieces two or three inches long; beat them with the blade of a knife and flour them. Fry the collops in butter two minutes; then lay them into a small stewpan, and cover them with a pint of gravy; add a bit of butter rubbed in flour.

Beef, Corned, with Cabbage.—Select for boiling small white cabbages with firm heads; cut them in quarters, and examine carefully that there is no vermin lodged in them; lay them for an hour in salted water to draw out any that may have escaped observation. Wash your corned beef well and put on the fire in cold water, and let boil sufficiently, remove it, skim the fat from the pot and put in the cabbage while the liquor is boiling. When done, replace the meat in the pot to warm unless it is desired cold.

Beef, Corned Hash.—Take corned beef boiled very tender and chop it up fine when entirely cold. The potatoes intended for the hash should be boiled in the meat liquor, and peeled and chopped fine whilst warm. To every teacupful of chopped meat allow four of chopped potatoes, stirring them gradually the one into the other, until the whole is mixed. Put the pan on the fire with a lump of butter about the size of an egg, add a little pepper and salt if necessary. When the butter has melted put the hash in the pan; add four tablespoonsful of water and stir the whole well together. After it has become pretty hot, stir it from the bottom, keep it covered and place it where it will merely stew. If a dry brown hash is desired, put no water, and prepare over a quick fire. It is always best to mix the beef and potatoes over night.

Beef, Dutch.—Corn lean beef with a mixture of molasses and moist sugar for three days, then salt it well with common salt and saltpetre rubbed well in, and turn it well every day for a fortnight. Then roll up tight in a coarse cloth and place for some hours under heavy pressure, after which hang up in wood smoke, turning it every day. After boiling if well pressed, it will grate up or cut in shavings equal to the finest Dutch beef. One pound of salt is sufficient for twelve pounds of beef.

Beef, Fricasse of Roast Cold.—Cut underdone beef into very thin slices, chop some parsely very fine, put it with an onion cut up into a stew pan, a little butter and a spoonful of flour; let it fry; then add some strong broth, season with salt and pepper, and simmer very gently a quarter of an hour; then mix into it the yolks of two eggs, and a spoonful of vinegar. Stir it quickly over the fire a minute or two, then put in the beef, make it hot, but do not let it boil, and serve while hot.

Beef Hung.—Rub a piece of beef with one eighth of its weight of salt, to which a little salt-petre has been added, then put in a tub or other suitable vessel, place a board over it and pile heavy weight upon it: let it remain so for fourteen or twenty days then take out and hang up for a month to dry. It eats well boiled tender with greens, carrots, &c., or by cutting a lean bit and boiling until extremely tender it can be grated and whilst hot put under a press. When cold it can be folded in a sheet of paper and will keep in a dry place for two or three months, and can be served on bread and butter.

Beef, Minced.—Take the lean of some cold roast beef, chop it very fine, adding a small minced onion; and season it with pepper and salt. Put it into a stewpan, with some of the gravy that has been left from the day before, and let it stew for a quarter of an hour. Then put it (two thirds full) into a deep dish; fill the deep dish with mashed potatoes, heaped high in the centre, smoothed on the surface, and browned with a salamander or red hot shovel.

Beefsteak Pie—Take rump steaks that have been well hung, cut in small scollops: beat them gently with a rolling pin; season with pepper, salt, and a little shalot minced very fine, put in a layer of sliced potatoes, place the slice in layers with a good piece of fat and a sliced mutton kidney; fill the dish; put some crust on the edge, and about an inch below it and a cup of water or broth in the dish. Cover with rather a thick crust and bake in a moderate oven.

Beef, Plain.—Persons desiring economy may learn from the following how to practice it without losing their character for good cookery. Take a piece of beef, and divide it—that is to say cut about half of it into steaks and the rest reserve for boiling. Into a saucepan two thirds full of water place all that is not wanted for steaks, and a dozen or two of whole onions—stew slowly till the onions are done—then fry the steaks, and serve them with the onions, making plenty of gravy—what may remain uneaten of the steaks and gravy put into the boiling meat, and continue it slowly boiling. Let this stand over night to cool—then skim off any fat that may have risen—take out the meat and cut it all up into small pieces. Season with pepper, and salt, and add from six to a dozen sweet potatoes peeled and cut into dice sizes. By this management two meals may be made out of what ordinarily is cooked for one.

Beef Roast, with Yorkshire Pudding.—Five tablespoonsful of flour mixed with one of salt, one pint of milk, and three well beaten eggs. Butter a square pan, and put the butter in it; set it in the oven until it rises, and is slightly crusted on top; then place it under the beef roasting before the fire or the oven, and baste it as well as the meat.

Beef, Rump of.—This is one of the most juicy of all the joints of the beef, but is more frequently stewed than roasted. As it is two large to serve whole, generally, cut as much from the chump end to roast as will make a good dish. Manage it as though a sirloin. When boned and rolled into the form of a fillet of veal, it requires more time.

Beef, (shin or leg of) or knuckle of Veal.—A shin or leg of beef, or a knuckle of veal, of about six pounds in weight will make an excellent soup and is thus easily prepared. Cut half a pound of bacon into slices, about half an inch thick; lay it at the bottom of a soup kettle, or deep stewpan, and on this place the beef or veal, having first chopped the bone in two or three places; garnish it with two carrots, two turnips, a head of celery, two large onions, with two or three cloves stuck in one of them, and a good bundle of lemon thyme, winter savory and parsley. Just cover the meat with cold water, and set it over a quick fire until it boils; having skimmed it well, remove your soup kettle to the side of the fire, and let it stew very gently about four hours: then take out the meats, strain the soup and set it in a cool place till wanted, when the fat must be taken off from the surface of the liquor, which is to be decanted into a clean pan, keeping back the settlings. If thick soup is desired, take a tablespoonful of the fat off the soup into a stewpan and mix it with four tablespoonsful of flour, pour a ladleful of soup to it, and mix it with the rest by degrees, and boil it up until it is smooth. Cut the meat, gristle and bacon, into small eating sized bits, and put them into the soup to get warm; and then serve up.

Beef, Spiced.—Take a round of beef, put in a quarter of a pound of saltpetre finely pounded, let it stand a day, then season it with a pound of bay salt, an ounce of black pepper, and the same of allspice, both well pounded. Let it lie in pickle a month turning it every day. When required for use, chop some shred suet very finely, and cover the beef with it, and bake it in a moderately heated oven from five to six hours. Whilst baking it may be placed either upon a meat tin, or in an earthen dish as nearly of its size as possible. In both cases there should be a cupful of gravy, or water under the meat to prevent it from burning.

Beef Steak, Spanish.—Take the tender loin of beef, have onions cut fine and put into a frying pan, with some boiling butter. When quite soft, draw them to the back part of the pan, and having seasoned well the beef with pepper and salt, put it in the pan, and rather boil than fry it. When done, put the onions over it, and just as much boiling water as will make gravy. Let it stew a few minutes, and serve while well hot.

Beef Tongue, Dried.—Soak the tongue well over night, then put in a pot of cold water over a slow fire for an hour or two, before it comes to a boil. Let it simmer gently from three to four hours, according to its size; ascertain when it is done by probing with a skewer. Take the skin off and serve either hot or cold.

Beef Tongue, Fresh.—Take a fresh tongue, stick it well with cloves, and boil gently for three hours; then brush it over with the yolk of an egg, dredge it well with bread crumbs, and roast it, basting it well with butter, when dished, serve it with a little brown gravy, flavored with a glass of wine if agreeable, and lay slices of currant jelly around it. A pickled tongue may be dressed in the same way.

Beef, Welsh.—Rub two ounces of saltpetre into a round of beef, let it remain an hour, then season it with pepper, salt, and a fourth portion of allspice; allow the beef to stand in the brine for fifteen days, turning it frequently. Work it well with pickle; put it into an earthen vessel, with a quantity of beef suet over and under it, cover it with a coarse paste, and bake it, allowing it to remain in the oven for six or eight hours. Pour off the gravy, and let the beef stand until cold. It will keep for two months in winter.

Browning for Gravies.—Melt four ounces of sugar in a frying-pan, with a little water; add one ounce of butter, and continue the heat until the whole is turned quite brown without burning; then pour in a pint of port wine, stirring well, all the time, and remove the pan from the fire. When the roasted sugar is dissolved, pour it into a bottle and add half an ounce each of black pepper and bruised pimento, six shalots cut small, a little mace and finely grated lemon-peel and a quarter of a pint of catsup. Digest for a week occasionally shaking, then strain through a muslin and keep for use.

Bubble and Squeak.—Cut slices from a cold round of beef; let them be fried quickly until brown, and put them into a dish to keep hot. Clean the pan from the fat; put into it greens and carrots previously boiled and chopped small; add a little, butter, pepper and salt. Make them very hot and put them round the beef with a little gravy. Cold pork boiled is better for bubble and squeak than beef, which is always hard. In either case, the slices should be very thin and lightly fried.

Ham Omelet.—Take two eggs, four ounces of butter, half a saltspoonful of pepper and two tablespoonsful of minced ham. Mince the ham very finely, without any fat, and fry it for two minutes in a little butter; then make the batter for the omelet, stir in the ham, and proceed as in the case of a plain omelet. Good lean bacon, or tongue, answers equally well for this dish; but they must also be slightly cooked previously to mixing them with the batter. Serve very hot and quickly, without gravy.

Ham Pie.—Make a crust the same as for soda biscuit, line a dish, and put in a layer of potatoes sliced thin, with pepper, salt, and butter, then a layer of ham, or corned leg of pork, cooked and cold; add considerable water, bake one hour, and an excellent pie will be the result.

Ham Relish.—Cut some slices of boiled ham, season them as highly as may be desirable with Cayenne pepper, and broil them until nicely browned, basting with a little butter; spread mustard over them, squeeze on a little lemon juice and serve.

Ham Toast.—Grate a sufficient quantity of cold lean ham, and having beaten together the yolks of two or three eggs, as may be necessary, with a little cream, work the grated ham into it until tolerably thick; put the whole into a saucepan over the fire and let it simmer about ten minutes. Pare the crust off some slices of toasted bread, butter them nicely, then spread them thickly over with the ham, and serve whilst hot.

Lamb (Boiled Leg of.)—To make it white, boil in a cloth—cut the loin into stakes, dip them in egg, the yolks and whites beaten up strew them over with crumbs of bread, fry them a nice brown and place them round the dish. Garnish with dried and fried parsley. Spinach should be served with it.

Lamb, Boiled Neck or Breast of.—These being small and delicate joints, are only suited for a very small family. The blood must be carefully cleaned away by washing in warm water. Either of these joints when being boiled, must be put into cold water, well skimmed, and very gently boiled, until done. Half an hour after they begin to boil, will be sufficient for either of them.

Lamb Chops.—Cut chops half an inch thick from a loin of lamb, retaining the kidney in its place; dip them into a thick batter of eggs and bread crumbs, fry and serve with fried parsley. If the chops are made from a breast of lamb, remove the red bone at the edge of the breast, and parboil it in water broth with a sliced carrot and two or three onions before it is divided into chops, which is done by cutting between every second or third bone, and preparing them like the others.

Lamb, Roast Loin, Neck and Breast of.—These joints should be floured and salted about twenty minutes before they are done. The loin will require roasting an hour and a half; neck an hour; and a breast, three quarters of an hour.

Lamb, Roast Leg of.—The hind quarter has an average weight of seven pounds; roast two hours; the leg itself about four pounds; roast one hour and a half; and the fore quarter, about the same time. Ribs are thin, and require more care to do them gently at first, and brisker as finishing. The fire should be brisk, and the joints frequently basted whilst roasting, sprinkled with a little salt, and dredged all over with flour about half an hour before done.

Lamb, Stewed Breast of.—Cut it into pieces, season with pepper and salt, and stew in weak gravy; when tender thicken the sauce. Cucumbers sliced and stewed in gravy form an excellent garnish and should be poured over them on being served.

Lamb's Sweetbread.—Blanch them and put into cold water. Put them in a stewpan with a ladleful of broth, some pepper and salt, small bunch of button onions, and a blade of mace; stir in a bit of butter and flour, and stew half an hour. Have ready the yolks of two or three eggs well beaten in cream, with a little minced parsley and a few grates of nutmeg. Put in some boiled asparagus tops to the other things, and be careful it does not boil after the cream has been added, but kept hot and stirred all the time until it is done.

Lamb, Vegetables and Garnish for.—Joints of roast lamb should be garnished with minced parsley, and served up with either green peas, spring spinach, asparagus and new potatoes, cauliflowers, or French beans and potatoes; and for sauce take three heaped up tablespoonsful of finely chopped mint, and mix it with two of pounded and sifted sugar, and six of the best vinegar, mixing well until the sugar is dissolved.

Meat Cooked (Maccaroni) Pudding.—Take cooked chicken and ham, cold, in equal parts, mince them small and mix well; then take half the quantity by weight of maccaroni boiled in broth, two eggs well beaten, one ounce of butter, and seasoning to please; mix all well together put in a basin or mould and boil for two hours.

Meat Pie with Potato Crust.—An economical Dish.—Take cold cooked beef, mutton, veal, or pork, cut into pieces, and season well with salt, pepper, onion, &c.; take boiled potatoes, mash them with milk, form a crust, with which line a buttered dish, and put in the meat with a teacupful of water, lay the crust thickly over the meat, and bake in a slow oven one hour and a half.

Mutton, Boiled Leg of.—Soak a leg of mutton for a couple of hours in cold water; then put only water enough to cover it, and let it boil gently for three hours, or according to its weight, add some salt and an onion or two. It should be removed from the fire at least fifteen minutes before serving, during which time the pot should remain covered close.

Mutton Chops.—Take them from the loin, and from one half to three quarters of an inch thick. They should not be put on the gridiron until everything else is ready to be served; have a clear cinder fire to broil them; if the fat falling from them should cause a blaze, remove the gridiron for a moment, and strew a handful of salt upon the fire. They should be kept continually turned; the greater part of the chine bones should be chopped off; cut off a good deal of the fat, but do not pepper or flour the chops, and serve them one at a time, immediately they are done.

Mutton, Fillet of.—Cut a fillet or round from a leg of mutton; remove all the fat from the outside and take out the bone. Beat it well on all sides with a rolling pin, and rub it slightly all over with a very little pepper and salt. Have ready a stuffing made of finely minced onions, bread crumbs, and butter, seasoned with a little salt, pepper and nutmeg, well mixed. Fill the place of the bone with some of this stuffing. Make deep incisions or cuts all over the surface of the meat, and fill them closely with the same stuffing. Bind a tape round the meat to keep it in shape. Put it in a stewpan with just water enough to cover it and let it stew slowly during four, five, or six hours, according to size. Serve with its own gravy or tomato sauce.

Mutton, imitation Venison.—Bone a loin of mutton, and lay it on the fat side in a stewpan, with an onion stuck over with cloves, until the meat is slightly brown. Then pour over it one pint of broth, a gill of port wine, half a gill of catsup, and let all stew gently together for about three hours. Serve it with a rich brown sauce.

Mutton, Loin of, Roasted.—Take off the skin and some of the fat; joint it and skewer it from the flap into the fillet; then put the spit through the chump and the skewer at the end will secure the joint in its place. Roast for an hour and a half.

Mutton, Loin of, Stewed.—Bone a loin of well hung mutton; take off the skin and remove the fat from the inside; put it into a stew-pan, with broth enough to cover it, and let it stew gently until it becomes of a good brown color; add a glass of good port wine, a large spoonful of mushroom ketchup, and some vegetables, cut in shapes, or stewed beans.

Mutton, Minced.—Cut some lean meat from a roast leg of mutton, chop it fine, season with pepper and salt, chopped parsley, and a little onion; mix all together with a quarter of a pound of grated bread; moisten with a tablespoonful of vinegar and a cup of good gravy; when put into the dish lay an ounce of butter in small bits on the top, grate bread over it, and add a little more butter; brown it before the fire and serve whilst hot.

Mutton Pie.—Take mutton tolerably fat and cut into slices, seasoning to please the taste, mixing the fat well with the lean, put into a stewpan without water, and when done let it remain until cold: make some gravy from the bones, and add to it the strained gravy from the mutton. Chop a shalot and one or two onions and add them. Use puff paste and make the pie in a dish or in small pattypans, and bake.

Mutton and Rice.—Half boil a shoulder of mutton, then put into a stewpan with two quarts of the water in which it has been boiling, with a quarter of a pound of well picked and washed rice, add a little beaten mace and cinnamon, stew until the rice is done, then take up the mutton, and add to the rice half a pint of cream and two ounces of butter rolled in flour; then pour over the mutton in a dish and serve.

Mutton, Roast Shoulder of.—Have a good clean fire, flour the joint well before spitting, and baste it constantly with its own dripping; be careful not to burn the fat by placing too near the fire. A moderate sized joint will require an hour and a half to roast. It may be served to table with stewed onions.

Pork, Fresh Pot Pie.—Boil a spare rib of pork until quite tender, after removing the fat and cracking the bones; remove the scum as it rises, and when nearly done season with salt and pepper; about half an hour before time of serving, thicken the gravy with a little flour, have ready another pot or pan into which remove all the bones and most of the gravy, leaving only sufficient to cover the pot half an inch above the rim that rests on the stove; put in the crust, cover tight and boil steadily twenty to thirty minutes.

Pork Chops.—Cut the chops about half an inch thick; trim them neatly; put a frying-pan on the fire, with a bit of butter; as soon as it is hot, put in the chops, turning them often until brown all over; fifteen minutes is sufficient to have them well done. Season them with a little nicely minced onion, powdered sage, and pepper and salt.

Pork Olives.—Cut slices from a fillet or leg of cold fresh pork. Make force meat in the usual manner, only substituting for sweet herbs some sage leaves chopped fine. When the slices are covered with the forcemeat, and rolled up and tied round, stew them slowly either in cold gravy left of the pork or in fresh lard. Drain them well before they go to table. Serve them up on a layer of mashed turnips or potatoes, or if in season, mashed sweet potatoes.

Pork, (Pig's Head) with Cabbage.—Pig's head is cheap and when well cooked it is delicious; the tip of the snout chopped off, and put in brine a week is good for boiling, so also the cheeks, though some prefer these latter baked with beans; but the whole head is best with cabbage. Select for boiling small white cabbage with firm head; cut them in quarters, and examine carefully that there are no vermin secreted in there; put them in strongly salted water for an hour before cooking in order to draw out any that may have escaped detection. Put the pig's head or such part as may be required to boil at least an hour before the cabbage, and skim the pot carefully. When done the cabbage should be well drained before serving.

Pork Roast.—Young Pig.—Crumble the soft part of a loaf of bread, add half a pound of butter a good deal of salt, pepper and sage; stuff the pig and sew it up; roast two hours and a half; baste frequently with salt and water. For gravy, boil the liver, feet, &c, quite tender with salt and pepper; when done, chop up and mix three ounces of butter with a couple of tablespoonsful of flour, stir it well into the gravy, let boil a moment, and when the pig is carved add the brains. Serve it and also apple sauce.

Sausage Cakes.—Chop a pound of good pork fine, add to it half a teaspoonful of pepper, half a spoonful of cloves, half a spoonful of coriander seed, and four tablespoonsful of cold water. Mix all well together form them into small cakes, and fry in a hot pan.

Sausage Dumplings.—Take one pound of flour and two ounces of chopped suet, into a thick paste, with only water enough to mix it.

and having divided it into twelve equal parts, roll each out separately just large enough to retain a beef or pork sausage which place in it; wetting the edge of the paste so as to fasten the dumpling securely; and, as fast as prepared put them into a pot or saucepan with an abundance of water boiling quickly. When the whole are completed reduce to a very gentle boil for over an hour, and then serve whilst hot.

Sausage Fried.—They should always be quite fresh made. Put a bit of butter or dripping into a clean frying pan; as soon as it is melted and before it gets hot, put in the sausages, and shake the pan for a minute or two, and keep turning them, but being careful not to prick them in so doing; fry them over a slow fire until they are nicely brown on all sides; when they are done lay them on a hair sieve for a couple of minutes before the fire to strain the fat from them. The secret of frying sausages is to let them heat gradually; they then will not burst unless they are stale. The common practice to prevent their bursting is to prick them with a fork but this lets the gravy out.

Veal Breast of, Stewed.—Cut a breast, or a portion in pieces; fry them with a little butter, an onion, and a cabbage-lettuce shred small, when browned add a little flour, shake it well together; then add a small quantity of broth or water; let it stew gently. When the veal is three parts done, take a quart of peas, put them in water and handle them with a little butter, so that they adhere together; take away nearly all the gravy from the veal, and put in the peas. When both are done add pepper and salt and a little pounded sugar; thicken the peas with flour and butter, dish up the veal, and pour the peas over. There should be very little sauce with the peas.

Veal, Fillet of Corned.—Take a large fillet of veal and make deep incisions or cuts all over it with a sharp knife, and insert a slip of the fat into each cut, pressing it down well to keep it in. Mix a tablespoonful of powdered saltpetre with half a pound of fine salt, and rub the meat all over with it. Make a brine of salt and water strong enough to swim an egg on its surface, adding a lump of saltpetre about the size of a walnut. Put the meat into the brine, and of which there must be more than enough to cover it, and let it remain ten days, turning it every day. Then take it out wash off the brine, and boil the veal until thoroughly done and tender throughout. It is best eaten cold and sliced thin.

Veal Cutlets and Spinach.—Take cutlets, egg and bread crumbs, salt and pepper to taste, and a little clarified butter. Brush the cutlets over with egg, sprinkle them with bread crumbs, and season with pepper and salt. Dip them into clarified butter, sprinkle over a few more bread crumbs, and fry them over a sharp fire turning them when required. Lay them before the fire to drain, and arrange them on a dish with spinach in the centre, which should be previously well boiled, drained, chopped and seasoned. Peas or asparagus, or beans may be substituted for spinach.

Veal, Knuckle of and Rice.—Put the knuckle of veal into a boiling pot, with a pound of bacon, two pounds of rice, six onions, three carrots cut in pieces, some peppercorns, and salt in moderation on account of the bacon; add three or four quarts of water, and set the whole to stew very gently over a moderate fire for about three hours. This will provide a good substantial dinner for at least ten persons.

Veal Minced.—Take three or four pounds of the lean only of the fillet or loin of veal, and ham, also minced. Add three or four small onions chopped fine, a teaspoonful of sweet marjoram leaves picked from the stalks, the yellow rind of a small lemon grated, and a teaspoonful of mixed mace and nutmeg powdered. Mix all well together, and dredge it with a little flour. Put into a stewpan, with sufficient gravy of cold roast veal to moisten it and a large tablespoonful or more of fresh butter. Stir it well and let it stew until thoroughly done. If the veal has been previously cooked, a quarter of an hour will be sufficient.

Veal, Shoulder of French Dressing.—Cut the veal into nice square pieces or mouthsful, and parboil them. Put the bone and trimmings into another pot and stew them slowly a long time, in a very little water, to make the gravy. Then put the meat into the dish in which it is to go to table, and season it with a very little salt and Cayenne pepper, the yellow rind of a large lemon grated, and some powdered mace, and nutmeg. Add some bits of fresh butter rolled in flour, or some cold drippings of roast veal. Strain the gravy and pour it in. Set it in a hot oven and bake it brown. Any piece of veal may be cooked in this way.

Veal, Roast Breast of.—Cover it with care, and if the sweetbread is retained, skewer it to the back, but take off the caul when the meat is nearly done; it will take two and a half to three hours roasting. It may be also baked in the same way.

Veal Sausages.—Chop fat bacon and lean veal in equal parts, with a handful of sage, a little salt, pepper, and, if at hand, an anchovy. It must be well chopped and beaten together, then made into sausages, or rolled into small cakes, and fried.

Poultry and Game.

Capons or Fowls, Roast.—Capons, and fowls, and chickens are roasted or baked and served as turkeys, with the addition of egg sauce, requiring of course less time and are seldom stuffed. From half an hour to an hour and a quarter will suffice, according to age and size.

Chicken or Fowl Broiled.—Split them down the back; season well with pepper and put on the gridiron with the inner part next to the fire, which must be very clear. Hold the gridiron at a considerable distance from the fire, and allow the chicken or fowl to remain until it is nearly half done; then turn it taking care it does not burn. Broil it to a fine brown, and serve with stewed mushrooms or their sauce. A duck may be broiled in the same way.

Chicken Fricassee.—Half-boil a chicken in a little water, let it cool, then cut it up, and simmer in a gravy made, of some of the water in which it was boiled, and the neck, head, feet, liver, and gizzard stewed well together. Add an onion, a faggot of herbs, pepper and salt, and thicken with butter rolled in flour added to the strained liquor, with a little nutmeg, then give it a boil, and add a pint of cream, stir over the fire, but do not let it boil. Put the hot chicken into a dish; pour the sauce over it; add some fried forcemeat balls; and garnish with slices of lemon.

Chicken Pudding Baked.—Cut up two young chickens, and season them with pepper, salt, a little mace and nutmeg. Put them into a saucepan with two large spoonsful of butter, and water enough to cover them. Stew them gently; and when about half cooked, set them away to cool. Pour off the gravy, and reserve it to be served up separately. Make a batter as if for a pudding, of a pound of flour stirred gradually into a quart of milk, six eggs well beaten and added by degrees to the mixture, and a very little salt. Put a layer of chickens in the bottom of the pie-dish, and pour over it some of the batter; then another layer of chickens, then more batter, and so on having a layer of batter on top. Bake until it is brown. Break an egg into the gravy, give it a boil, and send to table with the pudding.

Chickens stewed whole.—Prepare a pair of fine fat chickens with the liver under one wing and the gizzard under the other, and fill the insides with large oysters secured from falling out by fastening them round the bodies with tape. Put them into a tin butter-kettle with a close cover, set the kettle into a larger pot or saucepan of boiling water, taking care that the water does not quite reach the top of the kettle, and place it over the fire. Keep it boiling steadily until the chickens are done, which will be in about one hour after the pot has begun to boil. As the water boils away replenish it with boiling water, which should be kept ready in a teakettle. When done remove them from the gravy about them, and leave them clearly covered in the kettle; put the gravy in a saucepan and add to it two tablespoonsful of butter rolled in flour ; two of chopped oysters ; the yolks of three hard-boiled eggs, fine minced, some nutmeg, mace and a little cream. Boil five minutes, and send the chickens to the table with it.

Ducks, to Roast.—After plucking and singeing carefully, let them be well washed and dried. Make a seasoning of onion, sage, pepper, and salt. Fasten it tight at the neck and rump. Paper the breast-bone, baste well, and when the breast is rising take off the paper, and serve before the breast falls, with plenty of good gravy. Be sure to have apple-sauce ready.

Ducks, Canvas-back, Roast.—Truss the ducks, and put into each a thick piece of bread that has been soaked in port wine. Place them before a quick fire and roast them from three quarters to an hour. Before they go to table squeeze over each the juice of a lemon or orange; and serve them up very hot with their own gravy around them. Eat with currant jelly. Make also a gravy by stewing slowly in a saucepan the giblets to the ducks in butter rolled in flour, and as little water as possible. Serve this gravy up like wine.

Fowls, Cold, to Dress.—Take the remains of a cold fowl, remove the skin, then the bones, leaving the flesh in as large pieces as possible; dredge with flour, and fry a light brown in butter: toss it up in a good gravy well seasoned, thicken with butter rolled in flour, flavour with lemon, and serve hot.

Fowls Curried Malabar Fashion.—Cut a fowl into small joints, and wash it well in cold water. Mince an onion or two, put three ounces of butter, in a stew-pan, fry the onion a nice brown, then add the meat, a tablespoonful of flour, the same of curry powder, and simmer for ten minutes, then add a pint of veal broth or water, and stew for half an hour, with a stick of cinnamon. Scrape some cocoa-nut into a basin with a gill and a half of warm water, press it well with the back of a spoon, strain through a sieve, and add with two or three bay-leaves before serving. Shake the pan once or twice, squeeze half a lemon in, add a tablespoonful of vinegar, and serve hot, with the rice separate, having previously removed the bay-leaves.

Goose Roast.—Prepare a goose by picking, singeing and cleaning it well, and making the stuffing with four common sized onions, about an ounce of green sage finely chopped, a large cup of stale bread crumbs, one of mashed potatoes, pepper, salt, a small lump of butter, and an egg or two; mix them well together and stuff the goose. As the stuffing will swell it is important not to fill the goose too much. Pass the spit through it and tie at both ends, to prevent its swinging round, and the stuffing from coming out. Roast with a lively fire. At first baste with salt and water but afterwards with its own dripping. Two hours will roast it. It may be baked in the same manner.

In all cases have the goose well and thoroughly cooked, otherwise the meat is strong and not easily digested.

Partridge Pie.—Pick, singe, and clean four partridges, cut off the leg, at the knee, season with pepper, salt, thyme, chopped parsley, and two mushrooms of moderate size chopped fine. Put the partridges at the *bottom* of the dish, and lay over them some veal steak and ham, cut into pieces about two inches square; add half a pint of good veal broth, cover with a good puff paste in the usual way, brush over with egg, and bake for an hour. The general way of laying the meat at the bottom of the dish is wrong, because by the method given above, the partridges receive the flavor of the meat, which is in a measure prevented by adopting the old method. In some pies—pigeons for instance—some of the meat should be placed at the bottom as well as the top.

Pheasant, larded and roasted, Sportman's fashion.—
When the pheasant gives off a peculiar odor, and the skin of the breast changes color a little, it should be plucked carefully, but not sooner. When plucked, lard it with some good fresh bacon very carefully, and then stuff with the following:—Take two woodcocks, and divide the flesh into one portion, and the tail and liver into another; mince and mix the meat with some good beef marrow, a little scraped bacon, salt, pepper, and lemon-thyme, or other herbs; add truffles sufficient to fill up the rest of the inside of the bird, then stuff it in and secure well, so that none of it may escape, which may be effectually done by placing a crust of bread over the opening, and sewing it up. Make a paste of the livers of the woodcocks, some truffles, grated bacon, an anchovy boned, and some fresh butter; cover the bird with this, put down to roast, and when done serve upon a slice of toasted bread, surrounded with slices of orange, and

some of the gravy round the bird, [This receipt was obtained from an old epicurean sportsman, who vouched for its being a first-rate way of cooking the bird, and further recommended that a table-spoonful of champange or burgundy, should be poured over the bird, in addition to a good libation of the same wine during the time it is being partaken of.]

Pheasants, and Partridges.—They are rarely stuffed, it is more customary to send them to table accompanied by forcemeat in the dish, and in many cases with the simple gravy only; the real epicure in game prefers the flavour of the bird uncontaminated by any accessories, save those which just assist to remove the dryness common to most game. Pheasants are sometimes larded; but as the flavour is entirely distinguished by the taste of the bacon, incorporated with the flesh of the fowl, unless it is done for appearance than palate we would not advise it. In dressing a pheasant, it should be drawn and cleaned as other game, and trussed, and should be roasted before a clear, not a fierce fire; it will take forty minutes, but it must not be sent to table underdone.

They may be, and are oftener, plain roasted than not, but very frequently larded, and if two are served in a dish have one larded; but when stuffed, by some, larding is most approved. Mince very fine some raw veal with a small quantity of fat bacon, with a few bread crumbs, pepper and salt; with this stuff your birds, baste frequently, and flour and salt them before you take them up. To any game of this kind you may introduce either chestnut stuffing or truffles; only to be cut in slices or put in whole.

Pigeons, Broiled.—Cut the pigeon down the back flatten and truss it as a fowl for broiling. Egg it on both sides; season with pepper and salt, dip it in chopped sweet herbs and bread crumbs; warm a little butter sprinkle it over, and then dip the pigeon again in the crumbs. Broil it a light brown. Serve with any agreeable sauce.

Pigeons Compote.—Truss six pigeons as if for boiling; grate the crumb of a small loaf: scrape a pound of fat bacon; chop parsley, thyme, an onion or two shalots, and some lemon peel, fine; grate some nutmeg, season with pepper and salt, and mix up with two eggs. Put this forcemeat into the craws of the pigeons, lard the breasts, and fry them brown. Place in a stewpan with some beef-stock, stew three quarters of an hour, thicken with a piece of butter rolled in flour, and dish up with force-meat balls around the dish; strain the gravy over the pigeons and serve hot.

Rabbits.—There are several ways of cooking this little animal—and when properly dressed is a nourishing luxury that ought to be in more general use:—

To Boil Whole.—When cleaned, skewer into a compact form and fill the inside with onions, eschalots, or leeks, taking care that the liver properly freed from the gall is not left out. Put into cold water and only just as much as will cover it, and boil slowly till done. Then take the onions and cut them in pieces and put into some of the liquor the rabbit was boiled in, and boil up, thickening with a little flour, and adding some pepper and salt. Remove the skewer, place on a dish, pour over the sauce and having chopped the liver very fine, sprinkle it over or around the rabbit. Serve as hot as possible.

Rabbits Baked.—Take slices of streaky pork or bacon cut very thin and skewer over the back of the rabbit. Having stuffed with mashed potatoes, and seasoned with fine dry sage, pepper and salt.

Rabbit Curry.—Cut up a rabbit as for a fricassee; fry it a light brown, and stew in gravy. Add a table-spoonful of curry powder, and, if necessary, cayenne pepper and salt. When stewed sufficiently, thicken with butter rolled in flour, and add lemon juice, shalots or garlic; serve with rice, and garnish with lemon.

Rabbit, Fricassee of.—Wash and cut a young rabbit into joints, and put them in a stewpan, with a quarter of a pound of streaky bacon cut small, an onion stuck with cloves, a faggot of herbs, a blade of mace, and some salt; cover the whole with water, and let it simmer twenty minutes, keeping it well skimmed; pass the liquor through a sieve. Into another stewpan put two ounces of butter, a tablespoonful of flour, and a little of the liquor; set on the fire, stir well until it boils; add the rabbit and bacon, with a dozen and a half of small onions; let the whole simmer until the onions are done; skim well; then pour in a wine-glassful of white wine, mixed with the yolks of two eggs, and a little grated nutmeg; leave it to thicken, remove the rabbit, pile it on sippets, sauce over, garnish with sliced lemon, and serve hot.

Rabbit Pie.—Cut up a rabbit and season it; bake it with eggs and sausage meat, as usual; or in a raised crust, and when cold cover with savory jelly.

Rabbit, to Stew.—Divide the rabbit into quarters, lard them with large slices of bacon, and fry them; then put into a stewpan; with a quart of good broth, a glass of white wine, a bunch of sweet herbs, a little pepper and salt, and a piece of butter rolled in flour. When done, dish up, and pour the gravy sauce on them. Garnishing with sliced lemon.

2.—Having stewed some onions until only skins are left; strain through a cullender. In this liquor place one or more rabbits cut into convenient pieces—season with pepper and salt—and when nearly done say within fifteen minutes add two or three sweet potatoes cut up into dice sized pieces.

"Repley Rabbit Pie," the celebrated.—This is a popular dish in all the villages round the new Forest in England, and is prepared in the following manner:—Take a deep pie dish and line with thin slices of bacon. Prepare a mixture of dry sage in powder, pepper and salt. Cut the rabbit in pieces, peel a few white potatoes, and cut to the size of half an egg. Chop up some onions; when all is prepared lay them in the dish, alternately, and sprinkle the seasoning and onions as you proceed. Bake this slowly and thoroughly, and when done slightly loosen the contents from the dish and place on the table and if any one who partakes does not ask, like Oliver Twist, for "more," the fault must lie with the cook.

Small Birds, Baked.—These should be picked clean, trimmed close, and stuffed with a paste made of any rich gravy, oatmeal and a little butter, flavored with powdered summer savory pepper and salt. Skewer in rows, and bake slowly, serve on toast and pour over a little hot rich gravy.

Teal, to Roast.—Dress the same as wild ducks but it is well, unless ordered otherwise, to dress one well and the other rather less, as some epicures prefer wild-fowl underdone, as it is said to be finer flavored. Epicures eat wild-fowl without sauce, but a good brown gravy, flavored with shalot, cayenne, salt, and port or claret, is usually served hot over the birds.

Turkey Boiled.—Make a stuffing consisting of bread crumbs very fine, or pounded crackers, raw salt pork chopped very fine, a shredded onion, some sage or any other desired herb, seasoning with pepper; work all together with the yolks of one or two eggs. Put on the turkey in boiling water, just enough to cover it well; let boil slowly and remove the scum as it rises. Boil from one hour and a half to two hours according to size. Serve with oyster sauce. The turkey may be boiled by putting into a stewpan over boiling water, and instead of stuffing as above, oysters may be used.

Turkey Devilled.—Mix a little salt, black pepper and cayenne, and sprinkle the mixture over the gizzard rump, and drumstick of a dressed turkey; broil them and serve very hot with this sauce; mix with some of the gravy out of the dish, and a little mustard, some butter and flour, a spoonful of lemon juice, and the same of soy; boil up the whole.

Turkey, Dutch way.—Boil, season with salt, pepper, and cloves; add a quarter of a pound of rice or vermicelli to every quart of broth, serve hot, garnishing with toasted bread cut with a pastry-cutter.

Turkey Patties.—Mince part of the breast fine, season with salt, nutmeg, grated lemon, white pepper, and a little butter warmed. Fill the patties, and bake as usual.

Turkey Roast.—Make a stuffing of pork sausages, an egg or two beaten up, some bread crumbs and a shredded onion. Fill the body and under the breast with the stuffing, and put to roast before a sharp, clear fire, at a moderate distance for some twenty minutes, but closer afterwards. Baste with butter and when nearly done dust it over lightly with flour and baste again with melted butter. Serve it with its own gravy from the dish, with the liver, gizzard, &c., cooked and added to it, with bread sauce. A large turkey will require three hours roasting, a smaller one in proportion. A turkey may be prepared and baked in the same manner.

Venison, to Hash.—Carve your venison into thin slices, and put them into a stewpan with two small glasses of port wine; add a spoonful of browning, one of ketchup, an onion stuck with cloves, and half an anchovy chopped small, and let it boil, then put in your venison, making it thoroughly hot through. Lay sippets of toast, in various shapes in a soup dish, pour the hash upon it, serve with currant jelly.

Venison, to Roast.—All venison for roasting should have a paste made of lard over it; after having prepared the meat with buttered paper, then lay your stiff paste upon the top of that, either dangle it or put it in a cradle spit; a few minutes before you require to take it up take off the paste and paper, baste it with some butter, salt it and flour it; when done give it a few more turns round, and send up very hot, your dish to be very hot also; and the dry pieces and the shank you will boil down with brown stock for the gravy; send currant jelly in a boat, and French beans in a vegetable dish.

There are no Sportsmen whether of the Gun or Rod who do not enjoy "the fruits of their labor" served up to them, in sportsmanlike style—that is "under the shady greenwood tree" and as few know except the very experienced, how simple is

> Enjoyment, when the toil is o'er
> And prizes counted by the score;
> To gather round a crackling fire
> The young and old, the son and sire,
> And from the spoils of sport to feed
> Together, on the grassy mead.

We will give our sporting friends a few directions calculated to enhance and prolong the manly results of such out door enjoyment. Some pepper and salt, a sheet of clean paper, a few matches and a pocket knife are all that is needed, except of course a few crackers. These each person should carry for himself in his own gamebag or pockets.

Suppose birds are to be cooked, the following is the plan—hollow a basin shaped hole and press it close—then build a fire over it till the ground all around it is hot, then clean out the hole and place your birds, feathers and all, snugly together therein on their backs and pile over them the hot embers wood ashes and all.

Now make up another good fire, and you may disperse for an hour and come back to dinner. Carefully remove the fire and as carefully lift the birds—each one takes his bird and strips off the skin, which comes off leaving the bare breast, juicy and clean—this he transfers to his plate (i. e. his sheet of paper) and eats the out side only, the breast, thighs, &c—and if he does not enjoy his "bread and cracker," it is because

> His disposition doth complain
> For want of common sense and brain.

Fish and small animals are as easily cooked out of doors, but each one will require a little study of its own "ways and means."

Puddings, Pastry, Cakes, &c.

This Department of Cooking requires more than ordinary caution and should be attended to with the strictest care. If the cook through negligence should fail to have washed and dried the pudding cloth well, the outside will taste disagreeable and thus spoil the flavor of the whole pudding. Most puddings are better boiled in an earthen bowl or tin boiler, than in cloth alone. These however must be tied in a cloth, not only for convenience in removing them from the pot, but in order to prevent the admission of water Where a bag alone is used it should be cut narrower at the bottom than at the top, the corners rounded, and the stiching very firm and close, and when in use the seams turned outside. A few inches from the top of the bag a tape should be sewed on to tie it with. Always dip your bag in boiling water, squeeze it dry, and flour it well before using; pour in the pudding, draw the bag together as closely as possible, tie it securely, allowing sufficient room for the pudding to swell. Immerse it thoroughly, in the pot in boiling water and every five or ten minutes during the first half hour, turn it over to prevent the fruits settling on one side; keep a tea-kettle of boiling water ready to replenish the pot as it boils away, as it must be kept covered with boiling water when a cloth bag is used. When you take it up, put into a strainer or colander, and pour a little cold water over it to prevent its sticking to the cloth; untie the bag, and put it over the dish it is to be served in, turn it over and remove the strainer and bag.

When eggs are used in puddings, they should be strained before adding the eggs, butter the pans or basins and flour the cloth. Where hot milk and eggs are used together be careful not to add the milk whilst too hot otherwise the eggs will be partially cooked and the lightness and appearance of the pudding spoiled. Excellent puddings can be made without eggs, but they must only have milk enough to mix them, and must boil three or four hours.

The most digestible pudding is that made with bread, or biscuit, or boiled flour grated. Paste puddings or dumplings are extremely indigestible; batter pudding is not easily digested and suet puddings are to be considered not only mischievous but even dangerous to invalids. Pancakes are to many objectionable on account of the frying imparting a greasiness. Boiled Indian Meal puddings are not very indigestible and are far preferable to wheat flour. It is always well to mix puddings, an hour or two before cooking them, except when self-raising flour is used, when they should be put into the boiling water as soon as mixed.

A bread pudding should be tied loose; if batter, it must be tied tight over, and a batter-pudding should be strained through a coarse sieve when all is mixed. In others, the eggs only. If you boil the pudding in a basin or pan, take care, that it is always well buttered.

PANCAKES are very generally liked, though not the most wholesome things in the world. The batter requires long beating; but the art in making pancakes consists in frying them. The lard, butter, or dripping must be sweet, fresh, and hot, as for fish. Beat two eggs, and stir them, with a little salt, into three tablespoonsful of flour [or allow an egg to each spoonful of flour,] add, by degrees, a pint of new milk; and beat it to a smooth batter. Make a small round frying-pan quite hot, put a piece of butter, or lard, into it, and, when it has melted, pour it out and wipe the pan; put a piece more in, and when it has melted and begins to froth, pour a ladle or teacupful of the batter in, toss the pan round, run a knife round the edges, and turn the pancake when the top is of a light brown; brown the other side; roll it up, and serve very hot. Before it is rolled up, some people spread currant jelly lightly over, or orange or apple marmalade. Cream, and more eggs may be used to make the pancakes richer. A little brandy, or peach water is an improvement. Serve with white wine sauce. Lemon should be on the table as some people like to flavor pancakes with the juice.

Receipts.

Apple Bread.—Take good sweet apples pared and cored, and stew to a pulp, then while yet warm add double their weight of flour, the usual quantity of yeast for making common bread is to be added; put in a proper vessel and allow to rise eight to twelve hours, then bake in long loaves. If the apples are good and fresh no water will be necessary for the mixing.

Apple Dumplings.—Choose six or eight good sized baking apples pare them, roll out some good paste, divide it into as many pieces as you have apples; roll and cut two rounds from each, put an apple on one piece and put the other over; join the edges neatly, tie them in cloths, and boil them.

Apple Pie.—Russetings, ribstone pippins, and such other apples as have a little acid, are the best for baking. Pare, core, and slice the apples, throwing them into cold water to prevent their turning black, sprinkle sugar between, as you put them into the pie dish, also a little pounded cinnamon and cloves. Some slices of quince are a great improvement, or quince marmalade, or candied orange peel. Put a strip of paste round the edge of the dish, and cover with a rich light paste.

Apple or Peach Pudding Plain.—Take stale bread and soak thoroughly in water; squeeze out the surplus water and work into a kind of paste, and having buttered a dish lay the bread paste on the bottom and sides of the dish, and put a thin layer of butter over the whole surface. Prepare some apples or peaches by paring, slicing and then add a lump of butter, some fine loaf sugar and some grated orange or lemon peel; make a cover of some of the bread paste, buttering the under side and place over all. Now cover it with a plate reversed, put a weight upon to keep the fruit down and bake in a slow oven two hours. Take off the weight and plate and bake another hour.

Apple Tart.—Pare, core, and cut the best sort of baking apples in small pieces, and lay them in a dish previously lined with a puff-crust; strew over them pounded sugar, cinnamon, mace, nutmeg, cloves, and lemon peel chopped small, then a layer of apples, then spice and so on till the dish is full, pour over the whole a glass and a half of white wine. Cover it with puff-crust, and bake it. When done, take off the crust and mix in with the apples two ounces of fresh butter, and then pour in two eggs well beaten; lay the crust on again, and serve either hot or cold. You may add pounded almonds and a little lemon juice.

Apple Toast Pudding.—Cut toasted white bread into squares the size of the palm of the hand and cross-wise in slices. Butter the toast and place alternately edgeways in a buttered baking dish sprinkle over the whole some white sugar and half cover with hot water. Bake quickly and serve without sauce.

Arrowroot Blancmange.—Take four good tablespoonsful of arrowroot; have four breakfast cups of milk well spiced, add a little ratifia and some isinglass to it, and when quite boiling pour it over the arrowroot stiring quickly all the time; put into a mould and when cold turn it out and serve with preserves and cream.

Arrowroot Breakfast Cakes.—Mix together two cups of arrowroot, half a cup of flour, and a tablespoonful of salt butter, an egg and as much milk or water as will bring it to the consistency of paste; roll it out and cut with a breakfast cup, and put the cakes upon a baking iron; a few minutes will bake them; split and butter them and send them to table hot.

Arrowroot for Sick Persons.—Mix a spoonful or two of arrowroot in double the quantity of cold water, then pour on boiling water slowly until it changes color, and it becomes transparent, then put on the fire and boil gently three minutes; sweeten to the taste, adding a little cinnamon or grated nutmeg to make it more palatable, and wine or brandy if necesary.

Arrowroot Pudding.—Take four tablespoons of sifted arrowroot, and put into a basin breaking four eggs into it; rub them together until smooth, then pour over three quarters of a pint of boiling milk, mixing it well whilst pouring on the milk. If it comes to the consistency of a thick custard it is properly done; butter a mould pour your pudding into it, tie it in a towel and put it into a pot of boiling water—let boil one hour. Should the milk not make it thick enough pour the mixture into a pan and hold it over the fire until it thickens, and then proceed as above. The same mixture can be made with the addition of a little spice, butter and sugar, and baked in an oven.

Baked Gooseberry Pudding.—Scale the fruit, and when quite tender, rub it through a sieve, and sweeten to taste with brown sugar. Melt a quarter of a pound of butter in some cream, beat the yolks of six and the whites of three eggs, grate a little lemon peel, and mix the whole well together, adding a little brandy if you wish it highly flavored. Bake in a dish lined with puff paste.

Batter Pudding.—Mix well together the whites and yolks of three eggs well beaten, three salt spoonsful of flour which must be worked in gradually and in small quantities. Work in one pint of milk with a little salt and boil in a mould or basin tied up in a cloth. It will require one hour's boiling. The mould or basin should be well filled.

Biscuits, Devilled.—Butter pilot's biscuits, or any similar kind, on both sides, and pepper them well; then make a slice of good cheese into a paste, and lay it on one side of each biscuit; spice with cayenne pepper and grill them.

Biscuits, Sponge.—Add the whites and yolks of twelve eggs, previously well beaten, to one and a half pounds of finely powdered sugar, and whisk it until it rises in bubbles, then add one pound of flour and the rind of two lemons grated. Form them into shapes, sift a little sugar over them, and bake them in buttered tin moulds, in a quick oven for one hour.

Barley Pudding.—Take a pound of pearl barley well washed, three quarts of new milk, one quart of cream, and a half a pound of double refined sugar, a grated nutmeg, and some salt; mix them well together, then put them into a deep pan, and bake it; then take it out of the oven, and put into it six eggs well beaten, six ounces of beef marrow, and a quarter of a pound of grated bread; mix all well together; then put it into another pan, bake it again, and it will be excellent.

Blancmange.—Milk, one quart; isinglass or calves feet jelly, one ounce; sweet almonds, one dozen; bitter almonds half a dozen; loaf sugar, half a pound; cream, four tablespoonsful; grate the almonds and then boil the whole together until of a proper thickness; when cold, add one or two tablespoonsful of rose-water, before letting it cool; when nearly cold pour into the moulds previously rubbed with a little salad oil.

Blancmange, Rice.—Ground rice, two ounces; milk, one pint; lump sugar, three ounces; a little lemon peel and cinnamon. Dissolve the rice in the milk by boiling, reduce it to a proper consistence, then add the spice and sugar, boil for one minute, strain, and when nearly cold, mould as before. The powdered rice must be rubbed up with a little cold water before adding it to the milk, to prevent lumps.

Blancmange, West India.—Make a jelly with arrowroot, and to every pint when nearly cold add a glass of sherry, a spoonful each of brandy and orange flower water, and two bunches of lump sugar. Mould as before.

Bread Pudding.—Cut two or three French rolls, in slices, and soak them in a pint of cream or good milk; beat up the yolks of six eggs with them, and add sugar, orange-flower water, three pounded macaroons, and a glass of white wine; tie it up in a basin of buttered cloth, let the water boil when you put in the pudding, and boil it for half an hour. Serve with wine sauce.

Brown Bread Pudding.—Mix well together half a pound of dried bread crumbs, and the same weight of beef suet; one pound and a half of currants; half a pint of fresh bread crumbs; a large spoonful of sugar; the yolks of six and the whites of three eggs, and having seasoned it with nutmeg and cinnamon, boil it for two hours. It may be served with or without sauce.

Buns.—One pound of flour, six ounces of butter, two teaspoonsful of baking powder, a quarter of a pound of sugar, one egg, nearly a quarter of a pint of milk, a few drops of essence of lemon. Bake immediately. This receipt will make twenty-four buns.

Buns, English.—Flour, two and a half pounds; sifted white sugar, half a pound, a little mace, cassia, and coriander seed powdered fine; then make a paste with half a pound of butter, dissolved in half a pint of hot milk, work in three tablespoonsful of yeast and a little salt; set it before the fire for an hour to rise, then make it into buns and again set them before the fire on a tin for half an hour; lastly brush them over with warm milk, and bake them to a nice brown in a moderate oven.

Buns, Family.—Flour, two pounds; well washed currants, half a pound; butter, a quarter of a pound; sugar, six ounces; a little salt, powdered caraway and ginger; make a paste with four spoonsful of yeast and warm milk a sufficient quantity, and finish as for English buns.

Buns, Madeira.—Butter, eight ounces; eggs, two; flour, one pound; powdered sugar, six ounces; half a nutmeg grated; powdered ginger and carraway seeds, each one teaspoonful; work well together, then add sherry wine, one glassful, and as much milk as required. Bake in tins in a quick oven.

Buns, Tea.—Warm and dried flour, three pounds; powdered sugar, one pound; butter, two and a half pounds, melted and beat up with four ounces of rose water; form into a light paste, with three quarters of a pint of yeast, and place it for an hour to rise, then add a little candied lemon and orange peel, and one pound of currants, and make the whole into buns; set them before the fire for forty minutes, then wash them over with milk, and put a little grated peel and a few caraway comfits on the top of each.

Cakes, Almond.—Sweet blanched almonds, flour and powdered sugar, each one quarter of a pound, seven eggs and the outside peel of four lemons shredded very small. Pound the almonds until they are very smooth, adding gradually the sugar and the lemon peel, add the eggs, and beat the whole until it becomes as white as sponge paste; next add the flour, work well, put into well buttered moulds, and bake in a slack oven with eight or ten thicknesses of white paper under them and one over.

Cakes Banbury.—Work one pound of butter into the same weight of dough, made for white bread, as in making puff paste, then roll it out very thin, and cut into oval pieces, or as the cakes are wanted. Mix some good brown brandy, then put a little upon each piece of paste; close them up, and place them on a tin with the closed side downwards, and bake them. Flour some powdered sugar with candied peel, grated or essence of lemon, and sift a little over the cakes as soon as they come out of the oven.

Cake, Bath.—Mix well together, half a pound of butter, one pound of flour, five eggs, and a cupful of yeast. Set the whole before the fire to rise, which done, add four ounces of finely powdered sugar and one ounce of caraways. Roll the paste out into little cakes. Bake them on tins.

Cakes, Cheese.—Curdle some new milk previously warmed with rennet, drain the curd in a linen bag, then beat it as fine as butter, and add one fourth its weight, each of sugar and butter; six eggs, some grated nutmeg, and a little orange flower or rose water. Work the whole well together, make into cakes of the desired size and bake in a moderate oven.

Cake, Ginger.—Make a paste with one pound of sugar, four ounces of powdered ginger, two pounds of flour, one pint of milk or water, half a pound of butter, and three ounces of candied orange peel, grated; form them into cakes and pick them with a fork before baking.

Cakes, Plain.—Flour, four pounds; currants, two pounds; butter half a pound; caraway seed, a quarter of an ounce; candied lemon peel grated, one ounce; four eggs; wet it up with milk, and half a pint of yeast. Let it rise well before baking.

Cake Pound.—Take equal parts of sugar, flour, currants and sultana raisins, and half that quantity each of butter, brandy, and candied peel, with such spices as may be desirable in the proportion as for Runnel's plum cake, and bake in a hot oven.

Cakes, Icing for.—Beat the white of two eggs, to a full froth, with a little rose or orange flower water; then add gradually as much finely powdered sugar, as will make it thick enough, beating it well all the time. In using it, dust the cake over with flour, then gently rub it off; lay on the icing with a flat knife, stick in the ornaments while wet, and place it in the oven a few minutes to harden, but not long enough to discolor.

Cake, Plain Plum.—Mix half a pound of butter in three pounds of dry flour, and eight ounces of finely powdered white sugar; add stoned raisins and currants, each three quarters of a pound, well washed and dried; some pimento finely powdered. Make a dough of three spoonsful of yeast and a pint of milk, well warmed, with the above, mixing in the fruit last. Make into a cake, and bake on a floured tin half an hour.

Cake, Plain Seed.—Mix one quarter of a peck of flour with half a pound of sugar, a quarter of a pound of allspice, and a little ginger; melt half a pound of butter with half a pint of milk; when just warm, put it to quarter of a pint of yeast, and work up to a good dough. Let it stand before the fire a few minutes, before it goes to the oven, add seeds or currants, and bake an hour and a half.

Cakes Rich—Equal weights of flour, butter, sultana raisins, eggs, currants, and brown sugar, mixed up with milk, and seasoned with candied peel, caraways, nutmeg, and a little ginger, then batter all in fine powder. Bake in a quick oven.

Cake, Rundell's Plum.—Beat one pound of fresh butter with a strong wooden fork until it resembles cream; add one pound of sifted white sugar, and mix them very completely; have ready the whites of ten eggs beaten, and pour them into the butter and sugar; then add the yolks of eighteen eggs, also well beaten and beat them all up for ten minutes. Take one pound of flour, two ounces of pounded and sifted spices, namely, cloves, cinnamon, mace, nutmeg, and allspice, and mix them by degrees with the other ingredients; then, beat the cake ten minutes longer, and, when the oven is ready, add one pound of currants four ounces of sliced almonds, half a pound of raisins, stoned and chopped, and a large glass of brandy (if agreeable). Bake the cake in a hot oven. When sufficiently baked, let the oven cool, and, afterwards put the cake back in the warm oven, and allow it to remain several hours to dry.

Cake, Mrs. Rundell's Sponge.—Prepare eight eggs, three quarters of a pound of lump sugar, half a pound of flour, quarter of a pint, of water, and the juice of a lemon and mix as follows:—Overnight pare a good sized lemon thin and put the peel into the water; when about to make the cake, put the sugar into a saucepan, pour the water and lemon peel into it, and let it stand by the fire to get hot. Break the eggs into a deep earthen vessel that has been made quite hot; whisk the eggs for a few minutes with a whisk that has been well soaked in water; make the sugar and water boil up and and pour it boiling hot over the eggs; continue to whisk them briskly for about a quarter of an hour or until they become quite thick and white, which is a proof of their lightness. Have the flour well dried and quite warm from the fire, then stir lightly in, put the cake into tins lined with white paper and bake them immediately in a moderately hot oven.

Cakes, Lemon or Orange.—Flour and sugar, of each one pound; eggs, one dozen; grated peel or juice of four lemons or oranges; whisk the eggs to a high froth, then gradually add the rest. Bake in small oval tins, well buttered, and place six thicknesses of paper beneath each tin. Thinly ice them.

Cakes Soda.—Flour, one pound; bicarbonate of soda, one quarter of an ounce; sugar and butter, each half a pound; currants, three quarters of a pound; make a paste with milk, and add candied orange, lemon or citron peel, or the fresh peels grated, according to fancy.

Cake Scotch.—Butter and sugar, each half a pound; nine eggs; beat up the eggs, then mix well together, and add a little cinnamon, grated nutmeg, and cloves; carraway seeds, a quarter of an ounce; candied citron, one pound; candied orange peel, three quarters of a pound; and blanched almonds half a pound, pounded fine; mix well then add flour three pounds, and brandy one fourth of a pint. Work the whole well and bake.

Cakes, Tipsy.—Steep small sponge cakes in brandy; then cover them with grated almonds and candied peel; or almonds cut into spikes and stuck in them; pile them in a dish, surround them with a custard, and cover them with preserves, drained as dry as possible.

Cream Cake.—The whites of three eggs, a drop of essence of lemon, and as much powdered sugar as will thicken; whisk the white to a dry froth, then add the sugar, a teaspoonful at a time, until it is as thick as very thick batter. Wet a sheet of white paper, place on a tin, and drop the egg and sugar on it in lumps about as big as a walnut; set them in a cool oven and so soon as the sugar is hardened, take them out; remove from the paper with a broad bladed knife, place the white of two together and place on a sieve in a cool oven to dry.

*** It is of the last importance before proceeding to the making of CAKES or FANCY bread that the various articles required for the purpose should be prepared some short time before needed. As soon as they are ready they should be placed upon a stove or near a fire so as to become gently heated, without which it is impossible to obtain good results. The flour should be well dried and thoroughly warmed, the fruit or other article washed, powdered, grated or cut up fine, as may be required, and dusted over with a little flour and also set before the fire : the sugar rubbed to a fine powder; the eggs well beaten and strained, the butter melted by being placed in a basin set in hot water and afterwards well beaten up with a little milk, lemon cut very thin and beaten in a mortar to a paste or powder with lump sugar, the caraways, ginger and other similar flavoring ingredients prepared as a fine powder, and the milk and water well warmed. All these things should be put into a pan in their proper order and well beaten up, as the lightness of the cakes depend a good deal upon this. A little yeast is a great improvement in various kinds of cakes. Good stale bread well soaked in hot milk or water then beaten to a paste and passed through a fine sieve forms an excellent article to mix up the ingredients with and produces a light and very nutritious cake.

Ginger Bread Nuts.—One pound of flour, rubbed in a quarter of a pound of butter, three quarters of a pound of white powdered sugar, one ounce of grated ginger, and the peel of a lemon. Let the articles be well worked in together, and bake in a slow oven.

Good Rusks.—Take a piece of bread dough, large enough to fill a quart bowl, one teacup of melted butter, one egg, one teaspoonful of saleratus ; knead quite hard, roll out thin, lap it together, roll to the thickness of thin biscuit, cut out with a biscuit mould and set to rise in a warm place, (unless self-raising flour is used when bake as soon as mixed) twenty to thirty minutes will be sufficient. Bake them and dry thoroughly, and they are an excellent rusk to eat with coffee.

Ground Rice Pudding.—Grind half a pound of rice into a fine powder and work smoothly into a small quantity of fresh milk, boil a quart of milk and beat into it smoothly the rice as prepared. Let it cool and then add the whites and yolks of six or eight eggs well beaten up, a few bruised almonds, some nutmeg, cinnamon, and grated orange peel. It may be baked in a buttered dish for three quarters of an hour in a quick oven or boiled in a bowl tied up in a cloth, for the same time.

Flaked Crust for Tart.—Mix a pound of flour with a little salt and add sufficient water to make it into a paste of medium consistency, neither very thick nor very thin. Let it stand for two hours; roll out the paste, place in the centre a piece of butter nearly equal in weight to the quantity of flour used, double the paste over the butter, and roll it out to the thickness of about a quarter of an inch, fold it into three, and having strewn a little flour between the folds roll it out again; repeat this operation four or five times and the crust is completed.

Fruit Cake.—Mix one pound of butter and one of sugar to a cream, then beat in twelve eggs, yolks and whites separately; work in two pounds of stoned raisins, two pounds of currants, one pound of fine chopped citron, and as much spice as is liked in flavoring, one glass of brandy and one of wine. When all these ingredients are well mixed then work in last one pound of finely sifted flour; beat the whole well up and bake four hours in a slow oven.

Light Currant Dumplings.—For each dumpling take three tablespoonsful of flour, two of finely chopped suet, three of currants, a pinch of salt, and as much milk as will make a thick batter of the ingredients. Tie in well floured cloths and boil an hour.

Macaroni Pudding.—Take an ounce or two of the pipe sort of macaroni, and simmer it in a pint of milk, and a bit of lemmon-peel and cinnamon, till tender; put it into a dish, with milk, three eggs, but only one white, some sugar, nutmeg, a spoonful of almond-water, and half a glass of raisin wine; lay a nice paste round the edge of the dish, and put it in the oven to bake. If you choose you may put in a layer of orange-marmalade, or raspberry-jam; in this case you must not put in the almond-water, or ratafia, you would otherwise add too much flavor to it.

New Year's Rich Fruit Pudding.—Seedless raisins, one and a half pounds; currants, one pound; figs, chopped coarse, one pound; stoned prunes and dates half a pound each; citron, four ounces; lemon peel, one ounce; cinnamon, half an ounce; mace, a teaspoonful; mix all the above together well. Beat up one dozen eggs, whites and yolks separately, then mix, and add to and work well in to the following—best self-raising flour two pounds; suet well picked and chopped fine, one pound; white crushed sugar, one and a half pounds; now work in the mixed fruits rapidly, and put the whole into a pudding cloth, allowing ample room to swell and put into a large boiler of water, and allow one hour for each pound in weight. Turn it every fifteen minutes of the first two hours; on taking from the boiler dip it in cold water two or three times before removing from the cloth. Serve with sauce to please the taste.

Pancakes.—Make good batter, in the usual way with eggs, milk and flour; pour this into a pan, so that it lays very thin; let your lard, or whatever else you fry them in, be quite hot. When one side is done, toss it up lightly to turn it. Serve with lemon and sugar.

Peach Leaves.—Boil peach leaves in milk and add it to the other ingredients in making puddings, and a better flavor is obtained than with any spice. Experience will teach the necessary number.

Plain Rice Pudding.—Take four large spoonsful of well washed rice, and boil it in a pint of milk until it thickens, add then a small lump of butter and give one boil to dissolve and spread the butter; let cool then mix in the yolks of six and the whites of three eggs well beaten, sugar, nutmeg and grated lemon to please the taste. Butter cups, three parts fill them, and bake half an hour in a slow oven.

Plain Plum Pudding.—Take of sifted flour, suet, butter, loaf sugar, raisins, (stoned,) and currants, one pound each; ten eggs, beat up separately, the whites to a froth, and then mix with the yolks, cinnamon, cloves and nutmeg to please the taste, and one ounce of candied lemon peel. The suet must be chopped up fine and then mixed in well with the flour, rub the sugar and butter together and add them, then the eggs, cinnamon, &c., and lastly raisins and currants by alternate handsfull having first sprinkled them with a little flour. Now add about four ounces of yeast (unless self-raising flour is used) and set the whole in a warm place for about twelve hours—then put into a clean pudding bag or cloth, and boil one hour for every pound it weighs.

Plum Cake (Rich).—Rub together one pound each of fresh butter and white sugar, now work in one pound each of candied citron and of orange peel finely cut up and chopped, one quarter of an ounce of allspice, a quarter of an ounce of cinnamon, two ounces of sweet almonds ten eggs, and a glass of brown brandy; work the whole well and then add and thoroughly mix one pound of best sifted flour. Bake in a hot oven with a sufficiency of paper under it to keep from burning. It will require three hours baking.

Polka Pudding.—Mix four tablespoonsful of arrowroot in a pint of cold milk; beat four eggs well, add them with three ounces of fresh butter cut in small bits; a few drops of essence of lemon or ratafia a dessert-spoonful of rose water, and a teacupful of sugar; boil a quart of milk in a saucepan and when boiling stir in the other ingredients, without taking the pan off the fire; let it boil until thick, then pour into a mould to cool.

Pineapple Custard.—Strain three wine glassesful of pineapple juice through a fine sieve; beat nine eggs yolks and whites, strain them also and add them to the pineapple juice, with a quarter of a pound of powdered loaf sugar, a glass of white wine, and half a wine glass of water, with a little grated lemon peel. Mix all together, and put all the ingredients into a saucepan on the fire, stirring it until it becomes thick, and of a proper consistence.

Raspberry Biscuit.—Select fine clean raspberries and boil to a pulp; take the fruit off the fire and add an equal weight of powdered white sugar. Stir well until all the sugar is dissolved, when pour the paste on tins to dry. As soon as the top surface is dry cut the paste into cakes, of different sizes and shapes, and dry them in a slow oven until they are crisp; put in tin boxes, and keep in a dry place for use.

Rice Custard.—Sweeten a pint of milk with loaf sugar boil it with a stick of cinnamon, then use sifted ground rice till quite thick. Take it off the fire; add the whites of three eggs well beaten; stir it again for two or three minutes, then put into cups that have lain in cold water; do not wipe them, when cold turn them out, and put them into the dish in which they are to be served; pour round them a custard made of the yolks of the eggs, and a little more than a half a pint of milk, put on the top a little red currant jelly, or raspberry jam. A pretty supper dish.

Ramakins.—Scrape a quarter of a pound of Goshen cheese, add a quarter of a pound of butter, then beat all in a mortar with the yolks of four eggs and the inside of a small French roll boiled in cream or milk till soft. Mix the paste with the whites of the eggs previously beaten, bake in a Dutch oven till of a fine brown color; they should be eaten quite hot. Some like the addition of a glass of white wine.

Rhubarb Fool.—Scald a quart or more of rhubarb, nicely peeled, and cut into pieces an inch long, pulp through a sieve, sweeten, and let it stand to cool. Put a pint of cream, or new milk, into a stew-pan with a stick of cinnamon, a small piece of lemon-peel, a few cloves, coriander seeds, and sugar to taste; boil ten minutes. Beat up the yolks of four eggs, and a little flour, **stir into the cream,** set over the fire till it boils, stirring all the time; remove, and let it stand till cold. Mix the fruit and cream together, and add a little grated nutmeg.

Russe, Charlotte.—Mix with the yolks of four eggs, a quarter of a pound of powdered sugar, and add to this half a pint of new milk; put it over the fire till it begins to thicken like custard, but do not let it boil; then add half pint of very thick calves foot jelly strain it through a napkin; put it in a pan placed on ice. A pint of very thick cream, flavored or not as you like, and whip it until it looks like float—pour the cream into another dish, and pour the custard in the pan on the ice. Stir it on the ice with a paddle, until it becomes thick like jelly; then add the cream very lightly. The mixture should look like light sponge cake before it is baked. A round tin pan must prepared with sponge cake, called ladies' fingers, placed around the bottom very evenly and closely; pour the Charlotte into it, and place it on the ice until wanted. When wanted put a round dish or plate on it, and turn it out, the bottom will then be at the top, and no cake at the bottom.

Sago Pudding.—Boil two ounces of sago with some cinnamon and a bit of lemon-peel, till it is soft and thick; mix the crumbs of a small roll finely grated, with a glass of red wine, four ounces of chopped marrow, the yolks of four eggs well beaten, sugar according to taste; when the sago is cold, add this mixture to it; stir the whole well together, and put it in a dish lined with a light puff paste; and set it in a moderate oven to bake; when done, stick it all over with citron cut in pieces, and almonds blanched and cut in slips.

Or, Boil two ounces of sago until tender, in a pint of milk; when cold, add five eggs, two biscuits, a little brandy, and sweeten according to taste; put this into a basin and boil. Serve with melted butter mixed with wine and sugar.

Or, Wash half a pound of sago in several waters (warm); then put it into a saucepan with a pint of good milk, and a little cinnamon; let it boil till thick, stirring frequently; pour it into a pan, and beat up with it half a pound of fresh butter; add to it the yolks of eight, and whites of four eggs beaten, separately, half a glass of white wine, sugar according to taste, and a little flour; mix all together well and boil. Serve with sweet sauce.

Sippet Pudding.—Cut a small loaf into extremely thin slices, and put a layer of them at the bottom of a dish, then a layer of marrow, or beef-suet, a layer of currants, then a layer of bread again, &c., and so continue until the dish is filled; mix four eggs, well beaten, with a quart of cream, a nutmeg, a quarter of a pound of sugar, and pour over; set it in the oven, it will take half an hour baking.

Spanish Fritters.—Cut the crumb of a French roll into square lengths half an inch thick; mix nutmeg, powdered cinnamon, sugar, and an egg together. Soak the roll in the mixture, and fry a nice brown. Serve with wine sauce.

Strawberry Cake.—Take two quarts of flour, and rub in about two ounces of butter, a little salt, two teaspoonsful of cream of tartar, and in a little milk; dissolve one teaspoonful of soda, add this to the flour and as much more milk as will make it a dough. Bake in a flat dish, and when done, and while hot split in two; spread both sides with butter: sprinkle on a little sugar, spread on fresh ripe strawberries, then more sugar, on one half, and place the other over it. A little sweet cream poured over the whole, enhances this delicacy. This must be eaten hot.

The Philadelphia Raspberry and the Lawton Blackberry, can be used in the same way but are inferior to the Strawberry.

Suet Pudding.—Chop finely and pick carefully half a pound of beef suet, and work well into one pound of flour, beat up the white, and yolk, of six eggs separately, then mix the whole together and add as much fresh milk as may be required to thicken properly. Flavor with a little powdered allspice, cinnamon and salt; tie closely in a cloth leaving it room to swell and boil two hours.

Sweetheart Pudding.—Grate the crumb of stale bread, and having buttered a dish lay in a thick layer of the crumbs; pare core and cut-up ten or twelve apples and put a layer of them with sugar on the crumbs, then alternate layers of crumbs and apples until the dish is full, putting a small lump of butter on top, and bake it in a moderately hot oven.

Sweet Potatoe Pudding.—Boil the potatoes and mash them very smooth. To two cups full of potatoes add two cups of sugar, one of butter, one glass of brandy or wine, five eggs, one nutmeg and the grated rind of a lemon. Bake with an under crust.

Tea Biscuit.—One quart of flour, a pinch of salt, and two teaspoonsful of cream of tartar; mix these together thoroughly whilst in a dry state; then dissolve a small spoonful of soda and a small piece of butter in a pint of milk and work the whole well together. Bake in a quick oven.

Tea Cake, (FRENCH).—Rub two ounces of fresh butter with one pound of flour, then add four tablespoonsful of warm milk, one of yeast and a beat up egg. Mix well and let rise near the fire, when risen make into cakes, place before the fire a short time then bake with a quick oven fifteen minutes.

Victoria, Queen, Pudding.—Three sponge biscuits soaked in wine laid in the bottom of a glass dish; then a pudding made as follows. A pint of milk, with the peel of a lemon stewed half an hour, then thicken with two spoonsful of ground rice and lump sugar; when a little cold, add the yolks of four eggs; butter a dish that will just hold it, then bake it sufficiently to turn out on the sponges, then cover it with jam, and over that a thick custard.

Note.—When essences or oils are added to puddings, &c., always drop them on to a lump of sugar; if you attempt to put any oil in without so doing, it will not mix with the other ingredients, but float on the surface.

Preserves, Jams, Jellies, and Marmalades.

FRUITS and VEGETABLES may according to age and condition be preserved. Two methods are employed, the one to secure an acid or sour result, the other saccharine or sweet result. The former plan yields what are familiarly known as Pickles, the latter Jams, Jellies, &c. The two processes demand a few separate remarks.

In making pickles, a great many nonsenscial ideas have crept into formulas and complications of spice and mysteries in preparation, have tended to introduce some of the most mischievous ingredients, as Dr. Hassall's great work on Adulterations abundantly proves. But the wise pickle maker will not be misled by receipts, because they are given in expensive cook books; he will learn what does and what does not make the pickles—and leave out all else.

The best pickles are the simplest in there manufacture—the best looking and the purest flavored—as well as most wholesome.

For instance let any one slice a bright well colored and hard red cabbage, and sprinkle about two handsful of dry salt over it, turning over occasionally till it is all salt-wilted; all it then needs is enough good salt vinegar to cover it and it is a brilliant pickle, as far superior to the *cooked* preparations called "pickled cabbage," as can be imagined. If the taste is so perverted as to need spice and pepper, they may be added, but they are out of place. This simple rule is more or less applicable to all so called Pickles.

One word, however, on vinegar. Few understand that vinegar is simply water-diluted acetic acid, and the different names given to vinegar, such as white wine, malt, cider, &c., merely indicates from what substance the acetic acid is extracted, and why different vinegars have flavors. Vinegar that has no flavor but the acid is to be preferred, and if the weather be cold enough to freeze water slightly, vinegar may be exposed in flat dishes, and the surface ice removed to give it strength—for it is pure and strong vinegar that makes good pickles, by a sour preservation. The other, or sweet process of making preserves, is equally simple, needing sugar only to effect all the delicious changes that Fruits undergo in the form of Preserves, which includes the whole fruit crystallized, the broken fruit of Jam, or the juice only as in Jellies. Here a word of counsel is needed; the whitest sugar is not the best preserver, but strong tasting should not be used, as it spoils the delicacy of the fruit flavor.

Porcelain dishes should be preferred to copper or brass, that is to say, iron ones with porcelain lining, and the fruit should be most carefully watched while cooking, skimmed and stirred frequently. Preserves cannot be hurried—must not be economised—and may not be neglected while over the fire. They must have their own time, their proper amount of sugar, and their own watchful attendance. Common tumblers covered with paper on which white of egg has been spread, makes the best vessels to keep them in, and a dry cool closet to store them. Self sealing cans may be used by those preferring them.

Apples Stuffed.—Take large apples, cut off the crown thick :—scoop the cores fill with mixed butter and sugar; replace the crowns, and bake with a little water in the dish.—

Apple Fool.—Peel and core a number of apples and put them into a jar with sufficient sugar to make them palatable, and add a very small quantity of cider. Place the jar in a pot of water over the fire and continue the heat until the apples become quite soft, then pass through a strainer, add milk and cream and sweeten with sugar to the taste.

Brandy Peaches.—Take four pounds of peaches and two pounds of powdered loaf sugar. Put the fruit over the fire in cold water; simmer, but not boil, until the skins will rub off easily. Stone them if so preferred. Put the sugar and fruit in alternate layers in the jars until filled, and then pour in sufficient white brandy to cover the whole. Cork tightly and put by for use.

Jams.—All jams are made by boiling either pulped or bruised fruit over the fire along with certain proportions of loaf sugar, experience alone dictating the proper quantities, until the mixture jellies, which can be ascertained by pouring a little on a cold plate. When arrived at that condition the semi-fluid mass should be passed through a coarse hair sieve while hot, to remove the stones and skins of the fruit, and then poured into pots or glasses.

Blue Plum.— Take eight dozen fully ripe blue plums, stoned and pared or three and a half pounds of the pulp and three pounds of loaf sugar. Treat as above.

Cherry.—Stoned cherries, four pounds; white sugar, two and a half pounds; red currants, fully ripe, two pounds. Treat as above.

Blackberry.—Clearly picked and ripe blackberries, fifteen pounds; loaf sugar, twelve pounds; black currants, two pounds. Treat as above.

Gooseberry.—Picked and stalked gooseberries, any color, twenty pounds, white sugar, twelve pounds. Treat as above.

Plum.—To seven pounds of common blue plums add four pounds of sugar, one quart of vinegar, one tablespoonful of ground cloves and one of mace. Boil four hours over a slow fire stirring occasionally. Treat as above.

Raspberry.—Picked raspberries and white sugar, each twelve pounds; white or red currant juice one pint. Treat as above.

Rhubarb—Boil gently together for three hours an equal weight of white sugar and rhubarb stalks, with the juice and grated rind of a lemon to each pound of the fruit. When a strong flavor of the rhubarb is liked, omit the lemon-peel.

Strawberry Jam is made similar to the Raspberry.

Jellies.—All jellies are prepared by first boiling the fruit and pressing out the juice direct from the fruit which in most cases is better and boiling down with proportions of sugar, carefully removing the scum as it simmers. The sugar should not be added until the juice begins to thicken. The whole process must be conducted with a gentle heat.

Apple Jelly.—Strained apple juice, four quarts; loaf sugar, five pounds. Boil to a jelly.

Cherry.—Cherries, six pounds; water, one pint and a half; bruise, boil and strain, then add, sugar three pounds; boil down until the liquid jellies.

Currant.—Currant juice, six quarts; loaf sugar three pounds. Boil as before. Black Currants in the same quantity will require five pounds of sugar. Blackberries, Gooseberries, Raspberries and Strawberries are prepared in the same way and with the same proportions.

Lemon.—Isinglass, four ounces; water two quarts; boil and add sugar two pounds; clarify and when nearly cold, add the juice of one dozen lemons and the grated yellow rinds of three oranges and three lemons; mix well, strain off the peel and put into pots or glasses.

2.—The grated rind and juice of four lemons, one box of Cox's gelatine, a few whole cloves, pieces of cinnamon stick, and one pint of cold water. Let it stand an hour, then add three pints of boiling water, and one and three quarter pound of sugar. Strain into mould.

Orange.—Orange juice, two quarts; infuse in it the grated rinds of one dozen of the oranges for five or six hours; then strain and add loaf sugar, three pounds; isinglass eight ounces dissolved in twelve pints of water. Mix, boil down, put into glasses before it cools.

Marmalade, Green Gage.—Take off the skins, stone, weigh, and *boil quickly*, without sugar for one hour keeping them well stirred; then to every four pounds add three of finely powdered white sugar, and boil for six or eight minutes; let cool and scum carefully before putting in the jars. If the flesh of the fruit will not separate easily from the stones, boil the whole, pass through a sieve and deduct the weight of the stones before adding the sugar. Any good plums may be served in the same way.

Mixed.—Take equal parts of peaches, plums, pears, apples, &c., and boil them down to a pulp; pass through a sieve and equal weight of loaf sugar; heat again sufficiently to dissolve and mix well in the sugar and put in pots before it is cool.

Orange.—Take equal weight of Seville oranges and loaf sugar; grate half the orange rinds, choosing the roughest parts and pour boiling water over them; cut the oranges into slices across and strain through a sieve; boil the ungrated parts of the skins until tender, then wipe them on the inside with a clean cloth, cut them into very thin slices, and let them boil in the sugar, which should be previously clarified, until they are transparent, put in the orange juice and the water strained from the gratings and boil down together until it becomes a jelly which can be easily known by cooling a little on a plate or saucer.

2.—Boil the peelings of one dozen good well flavored oranges in sufficient syrup to cover them, until reduced to a pulp, then pass through a sieve; add the juice in which they were boiled, the juice of the fruit and as much loaf sugar as is necessary to bring them to the required consistence.

Peaches, Economical way of Preserving whole.—To fifteen pounds of cling-stone peaches, take seven and a half pounds of loaf sugar; put two or three quarts of water in a preserving kettle, with one teaspoonful of pearlash to destroy the skin of the fruit. When the water is hot throw in a few of the peaches and let them remain a few minutes; take them out and wipe off the skins with a coarse towel, and then throw them into cold water. Take half the sugar, with as little water as possible to dissolve it; then put in a layer of peaches and let them boil twenty to thirty minutes; take them out on a flat dish to cool. After two or three layers have been boiled in this way the syrup will increase, then by degrees add the rest of the sugar. When all the peaches are done, boil the syrup until it becomes a little thick; then add while in the kettle, half a pint of alcohol, which will cool and thicken it sufficiently, to put on the peaches which should be ready in the jars. Do not cover them until the next day. They will not have the least taste of the alcohol and are a very fine preserve.

Quince.—Equal parts of quince flesh or pulp and sugar, and half a pint of white wine. Gently evaporate until prepared.

Scotch.—Sweet orange juice, two quarts; yellow peel of the fruit grated from eight oranges; honey, three pounds; loaf sugar, two pounds. Boil to the required thickness.

Ice Cream.—The following is excellent:—heat one quart of milk nearly scalding in a pan over boiling water, then pour in three eggs well beaten, one tablespoon even full of flour mixed with a little cold milk, a half saltspoonful of salt, and one half pound of sugar. Stir constantly until it thickens, then strain it. When cold add half a pint of cream and flavor to taste.

Preserving Peaches.—Take half a pound of sugar to each pound of pared, stoned, and quartered peaches. The sugar must be put into a preserving kettle with half a pint of water to every pound of sugar, heated to boiling point and carefully skimmed. Into this syrup the peaches are placed and boiled for ten minutes. Put them in cans, and seal up whilst hot. The peaches can be treated in the same way whole by simply paring them.

Pickles, Sauces, &c.

Anchovy Sauce.—Two dozen anchovies chopped; butter one and half pounds; water, twelve ounces; vinegar, six ounces; flour, six tablespoonsful; stir the whole over the fire until it thickens, then rub through a coarse hair sieve; when cool bottle close for use.

Chow Chow.—Half a peck of green tomatoes chopped not very fine, six green peppers, and sprinkle over them a teacupful of salt. Let them drain well, and then add a teacup of grated horse-radish, a tablespoonful each of ground mustard, allspice, cloves, and ground pepper. Cover with good vinegar.

Family Dish of Raw Tomatoes.—For a family of half a dozen persons take six eggs, boil four of them hard, dissolve the yolks with vinegar, add about three teaspoonsful of mustard, and mash as smooth as possible; then add the two remaining eggs, raw; yolk and white well beaten up; stir well and add salad oil to make altogether sauce enough to cover the tomatoes; add plenty of salt and cayenne pepper, and then beat the whole thoroughly until it froths. Scald the tomatoes, skin and cut them a full fourth of an inch thick and pour the sauce over them, and the dish cannot be surpassed.

Fish Sauce.—Twenty four anchovies; ten shalots; scraped horse-radish; three tablespoonsful; mace and cloves, each one quarter of an ounce, two shired lemons; anchovy liquor, eight ounces; water, one pint; Hock or Rhenish wine, one bottle; walnut ketchup, half a pint; boil to two and a half pounds, strain and bottle.

Meat Sauce.—Sharp apples, pared cored, and tomatoes, salt, brown sugar and stewed raisins, each eight ounces; red chillies, and powdered ginger, each four ounces; garlic and shalots, each two ounces; pound well and add vinegar three quarts and lemon juice one quart. Digest with frequent agitation for a month, pour the liquor clear from the sediment and bottle. The sediment of this forms the well known Chetney Sauce, which must be put into jars or pots, and corked close. It is used like mustard.

Piccalilli.—One bushel of tomatoes, three pints of onions, one quart sharp pepper, one pint grated horse-radish, one teacup ground mustard; salt, cloves, cinnamon and alspice to the taste. Press out the juice of the tomatoes and boil in vinegar until tender. It is cheap, good, and wholesome.

Pickled Cucumbers.—Take thoroughly clean full cucumbers—not ripe ones—and steep them for eight days in a strong solution of salt and water; pour it off, boil it a few minutes and then pour on the cucumbers again; let stand twenty-four hours then drain and dry them on a sieve. Put them into wide mouthed bottles or jars, and fill them up with strong pickling vinegar, boiling hot, bung down immediately and tie over with bladder. As soon as thoroughly cold dip the corks into melted bottle wax. If desired, spice in any quantity and of any description can be added either by boiling in a cloth with the vinegar, or by putting in the jars with the cucumbers before the vinegar is added. This general receipt will be found excellent also for the pickling of beans, tomatoes, onions, gherkins, mushrooms, green gooseberries, walnuts, melons, cauliflowers, lemons, peaches, &c. Only observing that the more delicate the article the less time it will require in the brine.

Oyster Sauce.—Open the oysters carefully, so as to preserve their liquor; beard and remove the tough parts, which stew in the liquor, adding sufficient water or veal-broth to make the proper quantity of sauce, and allow for evaporation of about one-half; when done, strain it off, and put it in a saucepan with the oysters, a tea-spoonful of anchovy sauce, and a good-sized piece of butter rolled in flour; keep turning it round to prevent the butter from curdling.

Pickled Oysters.—Take one hundred oysters with their liquor; put them into a kettle with a teaspoonful of salt; let them boil gently for half an hour, shaking the kettle frequently to prevent burning. Take the oysters out of the liquor and throw them into a vessel of cold water for a quarter of an hour to make them crisp and solid. Strain the liquor in which they were boiled, add a pint of sharp vinegar and half an ounce of mace; let the liquor boil five minutes; drain the oysters from the cold water and pour the liquor over them, and when half cold cover close.

Pickled Cucumbers and Onions.—Boil in three pints of vinegar, a quarter of a pound of flour of mustard, mixed as for table use; let it stand till cold. Slice a dozen large cucumbers, and a half a dozen large onions; put them into jars with two ounces of ginger, half an ounce of white pepper, and a small quantity of mace and cloves, and pour the vinegar, when cold, over them. Tie down close.

Pickled Red Cabbage.—Get a firm dark-colored middling sized cabbage, and, having cut out the stalk, divide the cabbage, and cut it into slices of the breadth of narrow straws; sprinkle salt over, and let lie for two days; then drain the slices very dry, and fill the jar, or jars, three parts full, and pour a hot pickle over them, of strong vinegar, which has been heated, with due proportion of black pepper, ginger, and allspice. Cover the jars to keep the steam in, and when the pickle is cold, put in the bungs, and tie bladders over.

Pickled Beet Root.—There are several species of beet root, which are used for different purposes. The white Sicilian beet, from yielding most saccharine matter, is, according to Burnett, chiefly cultivated in France for the manufacture of sugar and spirit. Another kind of beet is grown extensively by farmers, called "mangel wurzel," which translated means "famine's root," but which should more properly have a name indicative of plenty, for many of the roots weigh twenty, thirty, and even sixty pounds each. But we have to speak of the red beet, the beta vulgaris rubra of the botanists; and the only thing we could desire respecting this plant is, that it might in reality be what the botanists term it, vulgaris, or common; for a more nutritious esculent could scarcely be found when properly cooked, that is, boiled from one and a-half to two and a-half hours, according to its size. To pickle beet roots, boil them till three parts done, then, when cold, peel them and cut them into thin slices; put the cut slices into a jar, and pour on them hot spiced vinegar, sufficient to cover the whole. After they have stood a month ask us to come and take bread and cheese with you; put the pickled beet on the table, and there will be a supper "fit for a king."

Superior Sauce Piquante.—Brown vinegar, three quarts; tomatoes' juice boiled and strained, one quart, salt two ounces, mace, allspice, ginger and nutmeg each one quarter of an ounce; cloves and shalots each half a dozen; cayenne pepper. Simmer the whole gently over the fire a few minutes, let stand for two weeks and then bottle.

To Preserve Cucumbers, Gerkins, or Melons.—Take large cucumbers, green, and free from seed, put them into a jar of strong salt and water, with vine leaves on the top; set them by the fireside until they are yellow; then wash them, and set them over a slow fire in alum and water, covered with vine leaves, let them boil until tender, take them off, and let them stand in the liquor until cold; then quarter them, and take out the seed and pulp: put them in cold spring water, changing it twice a day for three days. Have ready a syrup made thus:—to one pound of loaf sugar, have half an ounce of bruised ginger, with as much water as will wet it; when it is quite free from scum, put in when boiling the rind and juice of a lemon; when quite cold, pour the syrup on the preserves. If the syrup is too thin, after standing two or three days, boil it again, and add a little more sugar. A spoonful of rum gives it the West India flavour. One ounce of powdered alum is sufficient for a dozen melons or cucumbers, or a proportionate quantity of gerkins. The vine leaves may be omitted, if not obtainable.

Vinegar, Spiced.—For every pint it is intended to make, take one ounce of black-pepper, half an ounce of salt, half an ounce of ginger, a quarter of an ounce of allspice, and if desired to be hot, add also a quarter of a drachm of Cayenne, or a few capsicums. Bruise the whole of these materials in a mortar, and put them into a jar, or wide-mouthed green glass bottle, tied over with a bladder. Place this in a saucepan of water, and keep it hot for three or four days, shaking it now and then. If the maker has an enamel saucepan, this operation can be facilitated by simmering the ingredients together. Spiced vinegar is used hot for walnuts and cold for cabbage.

Tomatoes Bottled or Canned.—Procure the tomatoes as late in the season as possible and peel them whilst ripe and fresh. Season with salt and pepper as if for immediate use. Put them in cans or bottles, cork them up leaving a hole in the centre of the corks, and then put them in cold water and set them over a fire and boil them twenty minutes; take them up, cork and seal them tight and keep for use in a cool place.

Tomato Catsup.—Heat the tomatoes until they become quite soft, and then pass them through a fine sieve. To six quarts of the juice add three quarts of first quality cider vinegar. Boil slowly and when it begins to thicken, add alspice, cloves, pepper, cinnamon, and mace, each half an ounce, and of salt three tablespoonsful. Boil until reduced to the proper thickness.

To Pickle Onions.—Put the onions into cold salt water, let them stand all night; boil the spice in white vinegar, let it remain till it is cold; drain the onions well and pour the vinegar over; they will be fit for use in a few days.

2.—Peel the onions till they look white; boil some strong salt water, and pour it over them; let them stand in this twenty-four hours, keep the vessel closely covered to retain the steam; after that time wipe the onions quite dry, and when they are cold, pour boiling vinegar, white ginger and white pepper over them. Take care the vinegar always covers the onions.

Tomato Soy.—One peck of tomatoes peeled, sliced, and sprinkled with a little salt; let them stand twenty-four hours, then pour off all the juice; add to the tomatoes one quarter of a pound of mustard seed, one ounce each of ground pepper, cloves, and allspice, and twelve large onions; cover the whole with good vinegar and boil twenty minutes.

To Pickle Mangoes.—Take small musk-melons, cut out one piece large enough to remove all the seeds from the inside. Prepare a filling of scraped horse-raddish, whole mustard seed, sliced onions, whole cloves, and allspice. Put this mixture into the mangoes and then put in the piece you have cut out, sewing it with coarse thread in its original shape. Pickle the same as other pickles.

Walnut Ketchup.—Thoroughly well bruise one hundred and twenty young walnuts; put to them three quarters of a pound of salt, and a quart of good wine vinegar; stir them every day for a fortnight; then strain and squeeze the liquor from them through a cloth, and set it aside; put to the husks half a pint of vinegar, and let it stand all night: then strain and squeeze them as before, adding the liquor which is obtained from them to what was put aside the preceding day, and add to it one ounce and a quarter of whole black pepper, forty cloves, half an ounce of nutmegs bruised, or sliced, half an ounce of ginger, and five drachms of mace, and boil it for half an hour; then strain it off from the spices, and bottle it for use.

To Make Mustard.—Take some of the best flour of mustard and mix it, by degrees, to a proper thickness with boiling water, rubbing it extremely smooth; add a little salt, and loosely cover, and only put as much into the mustard-pot as will be used in a few days; the mustard-pot should be daily wiped round the edges.

Artichokes.—Boil the artichokes till you can pull the leaves off; take out the choke and cut away the stalk, but be careful that the knife does not touch the top; throw them into salt and water, when they have lain an hour, take them out and drain them, then put them into glasses or jars, and put a little mace or sliced nutmeg between; fill them with vinegar or spring water; and cover your jars close.

Asparagus.—Cut and wash the green heads of the largest asparagus; let them stand two or three hours in cold water; scald them very carefully in salt and water, then lay them on a cloth to cool: make a pickle according to the quantity of your asparagus, of white wine vinegar and bay salt, and boil it. To a gallon of pickle put two nutmegs, a quarter of an ounce of mace, the same of whole white pepper, and pour the pickle hot over them; cover the jar with a thick cloth, and let it stand a week, then boil the pickle; when it has stood another week, boil it a third time; when cold, cover the jar close.

French Beans.—Lay them in salt and water for nine days, then add a little vinegar and boil them in the liquor; when they become green, drain them, wipe them dry, and put the beans into a jar; boil some vinegar, mace, pepper, cloves, and mustard-seed, all bruised, and while hot, pour it on the beans; cover them close when cold.

Celery.—Separate the stalks from the head, clean them thoroughly and put them into salt and water strong enough to bear an egg, let them remain in this a week or ten days, or until wanted to pickle, then take them out, wash them well in clear water, drain dry, place in a jar and pour boiling vinegar over, to which any approved spices may have been added.

Gherkins.—Choose your gherkins very green and straight, brush and place a layer in a pan, sprinkle them with fine salt, then another layer of gherkins, which sprinkle with salt also, and continue this operation until you have used nearly a bushel of gherkins; leave them in the salt for twenty-four hours, which will draw all the water from them; at the end of that time, drain, and place them in a jar, with a handful of allspice, the same of tarragon, a little balm, ten shalots, six cloves of garlic, two or three long peppers, twenty cloves, a lemon cut in quarters, and two small handfuls of salt. Boil two gallons of the best vinegar, a second time, and pour it on again the following day; boil the vinegar for the third time, pour it over the gherkins, and when quite cold, cover the jar with a wet parchment.

CHAPTER IV.

Milk—Tea—Coffee—Tapioca—Sago, &c.

MANY infants subsist entirely upon the milk of the cow; that nutritious fluid also forms a large portion of the diet of most young children, and in some shape or other enters into the daily food of almost every adult; it therefore becomes a matter of primary importance to determine whether milk, as supplied for the consumption of the public, is in a genuine state or not.

If the testimony of ordinary observers, and even of many scientific witnesses is to be credited, there are but few articles of food more liable to adulteration (and this of the grossest description) than milk.

The relative proportions of the different constituents of cows milk, especially the fatty matter, are subject to very great variation. The age of the cow, the time after calving, food, temperature, and the time and frequency of milking, all occasion considerable difference in the quality of milk.

A very large proportion of the milk used in some of our large cities was, until very recently, much deteriorated by the improper feeding of the cows, and the manner in which they were bound and confined. We regret to say that this practice still prevails to some extent in New York and other places.

In a vitiated atmosphere, reeking with everything pernicious to the health of the animal, the poor creatures are kept close shut up, night and day, till their milk failing, they are consigned to the butcher.

Thanks, however, to our railroads, the greater portion of our supplies are now obtained from country dairies, and hence it is to be hoped that ere long, the practice of having and confining cattle in our cities will cease.

The specific gravity of milk is usually determined by means of an instrument termed a lactometer. This is a graduated glass tube, weighted so as to float upright when immersed in any fluid, sinking deep in liquids of low specific gravity, and but little in those of high density; the scale serves to show the exact density in degrees, contrasted with distilled water. In estimating then the quantity of milk, this instrument should be used for determining the density of either skim milk or, what is better still, the serum of milk, for numerous observations have shown that the density of these, when pure and genuine, the first ranging between 1027° and 1031°, and the second between 1025° and 1028°.

But there is a second means by which it may be ascertained whether any milk be rich or not in butter; namely, by the microscope.

Butter is suspended in milk, in the form of innumerable droplets of various sizes; in rich milk, these are particularly abundant, so that when a drop of milk is viewed under an object-glass of high magnifying power the field is crowded with myriads of these globules.

In an impoverished milk, the globules will be smaller in size and fewer, and the field of vision will present a different appearance.

When curd of Milk is examined under the microscope, the butter is still seen as droplets of fat, and the cheese as a granular substance of a yellowish color.

It has been stated at the outset, that if the testimony of ordinary observers is to be credited, that milk of all articles of consumption, is most adulterated.

The most common method of adulteration practiced is that with water, although other means are often resorted to. When adulterated with water, it is found that the serum of milk, that is, the fluid left after the precipitation of the cheese, by the addition of acetic acid, possesses a density which is almost constant, the limits being 1025° to 1028°; it is further ascertained that the specific gravity of this serum, varies in proportion to the quantity of water added to the milk; now the addition of water would of course lessen the specific gravity in proportion to the quantity added,—we have thus a fixed point from which to determine the adulteration of milk with water.

The specific gravity of skim-milk, although less uniform than that of the serum, is yet much more so than pure milk; on this account, the next and most accurate method of determining the admixture of water with milk, is to take the density of skim-milk *after* the per centage of cream has been ascertained by the lactometer.

The medicinal properties of milk have, until recently, been in a great measure overlooked. Yet in the early symptoms of consumption, it may be doubted if there is a better or more efficacious remedial agent than buttermilk, combined with a small portion of quick lime, poured on a quantity of wild lettuce, by which means a strong infusion is obtained in about twenty-four hours. We have seen persons restored to perfect health, in a few months, by the constant use of this infusion taken as an ordinary drink. A simple diet and gentle exercise were, in all cases, the only accessories.

The subject of a "Milk Diet," and its curative effects in diseases of the heart, dyspepsia, dropsy, and affections of the breast, is at present commanding a good deal of the attention of the medical profession, and no doubt some valuable and important results will be obtained for the benefit of suffering humanity, the more its powers and sanitary virtues become known and appreciated.

It used to be said that when the teapot was a permanent "tenant of the hob," the owner was able to "talk some," and the idea is not yet lost sight of, though other beverages have disputed sovereignty with "the cup that 'cheers but not inebriates;" we still find it customary to call sociable chats by the name of tea parties—indeed, "come to tea," is almost the same as "come to talk" would be, and it is thought nothing strange, if when we are invited to tea, we don't find any, but have its substitutional infusions—perhaps Coffee, Chocolate, Cocoa or Rye. Tea however is an important item of diet—it lessens the wear and tear of the system—and the experience of many is, they would more readily do without their loaf than their tea. The reason of this is, that tea assists digestion, that is to say, helps to disolve the food in the stomach, and thus obtains from a given amount a larger proportion of nourishment. This is the rule in the use of tea. With plenty of food, tea is beneficial, because it is a powerful digestive agent, but where tea is taken without corresponding food to digest, it wastes the tissues of the body and lowers all the vital powers.

Coffee has not so many friends among the medical profession as tea, for it is always forbidden in treatment, and by many discouraged entirely—but the effect of coffee on some constitutions is unmistakeably good; as an accompaniment of a good segar it is not likely to be discarded. It is supposed to act, however, adversely upon the reproductive organs, and may, in many ways be injurious—and the unfashionable make-believe Coffee called Rye, after all may be more wholesome.

Chocolate, cocoa and such like are however in all their forms to be commended for they contain nutriment as well as aid in digestion.

If however we might give our advice on the use of these articles, it would be to use them all, at different times, and confine yourself to none—taking care however that in their preparation as much care and common sense is used as in their purchase and selection.

SAGO, is a species of fecula or starch, obtained from the pith of the sago palm-tree, and is highly nutricious and much used in sickness.

GELATIN, as an article of diet, is highly nutricious when combined with other food abounding in proteine matter, but alone, it appears that, notwithstanding the opinion of ages to the contrary, it is incapable of supporting life. The commendation of it as an alimentary substance has been too general and lavish, and has led to its employment as an article of diet for the sick, in cases in which it is manifestly improper. "Gelatin may be considered as the least perfect kind of albuminous (?) matter existing in animal bodies; intermediate, as it were between the saccharine principles of plants, and thoroughly developed albumen. Indeed, gelatin in animals, may be said to be the counterpart of the saccharine principle of plants, it being distinguished from all other animal substances by its ready conversion into a sort of sugar, by a process similar to that by which starch may be so converted." The similarity of composition between the first and third of the above substances, will be readily recognized by the reader, but this similarity does not convey like properties; gelatin, in reality, more nearly resembles sugar than albumen. It has none of the properties of a compound of proteine. It neither yields proteine, when acted on by potassa, nor does it produce a purple color with hydrochloric acid. It therefore does not contain proteine. Animals fed exclusively on gelatin die of starvation. For as gelatin contains no proteine, it cannot yield albumen, fibrine, or caseine, substances necessary to the composition and support of animal bodies. Blood cannot be produced from gelatin alone; for it does not contain its most essential ingredient. But when mixed with other food, especially compounds of proteine, or substances abounding in albumen, caseine, or fibrine, gelatin may be useful as an aliment, and serve directly to nourish the gelatinous tissues.

To dress Vegetables.

VEGETABLES should be fresh gathered, and washed clean; when not recently gathered, they should be put into cold spring-water some time before they are dressed. When fresh gathered, they will not require so much boiling, by a third of the time, as when they have been gathered the usual time those in our market have. Shake the vegetables carefully to get out the insects; and take off the outside leaves. To restore frost-bitten vegetables, lay them in cold water an hour before boiling, and put a piece of saltpetre in the saucepan when set on the fire. Soft water is best for boiling vegetables; but if only hard water can be obtained, a very small bit of soda, or carbonate of ammonia, will soften it, and improve the appearance of the vegetables. Pearlash should never be used, as it imparts an unpleasant flavor, as will also soda, if not cautiously used. All vegetables (except carrots) should be boiled by themselves, and in plenty of water. Salt should be used with green vegetables. And the water should be skimmed before they are put in. Fast boiling, in an uncovered saucepan, will preserve their color. When they sink they are done, and should be taken out and drained, else they will lose their color, crispness, and flavor. Green vegetables, generally will require from twenty minutes to half an hour, fast boiling; but their age, freshness, and the season in which they are grown, require some variation of time. They should, almost invariably, be put into boiling water. Vegetables are very nutritious and wholesome, when thoroughly boiled; but are very indigestible when not sufficiently dressed. The principal points in cooking them are, to boil them so soft as to be easy of digestion, and sufficiently to get rid of any rankness, without losing their grateful flavor.

METHODS OF COOKING.—*Asparagus.*—Let the stalks be lightly, but well scraped, and as they are done, be thrown into cold water; when all are finished, fasten into bundles of equal size ; put them into boiling water, throw in a handful of salt, boil until the end of the stalk becomes tender which will be about half an hour ; cut a round of bread, and toast it a clear brown, moisten it with the water in which the asparagus was boiled, and arrange the stalks with the white ends outwards. A good melted butter must accompany it to table. Asparagus should be dressed as soon after it has been cut as practicable.

Angelica.—When the stalks are tender, cut them in lengths of three or four inches, and boil them well in a very little water, keeping them covered; then take them up and peel them, and boil again until a nice green, when take the stalks up on a cloth to dry, lay them in an earthan pan, adding to every pound of stalks a pound of sifted sugar, let it lie several days, and then boil the angelica until very green, when take it up on your sieve to drain, and sift well over it some fine pounded sugar ; lay it in the sun, or in your hot closet, to dry, if for candying.

Artichokes.—Cut away the outside leaves, and make the stalks as even as possible, then put them into boiling water with some salt; if they are very young, they will be tender in half an hour, if rather old, they will require an hour before they are thoroughly tender ; drain and trim the points of the leaves, and serve with melted butter. They are better for being kept two or three days.

French Beans.—When very young, the ends and stalks only should be removed, and as they are done, thrown into cold spring water ; when they are to be dressed, put them in boiling water which has been salted with a small quantity of common salt, in a quarter of an hour they will be done, the criterion for which is when they become tender ; the saucepan should be left uncovered, there should not be too much water, and they should be kept boiling rapidly. When they are at their full growth, the ends and strings should be taken off, and the bean divided lenthways and across, or, according to the present fashion, slit diagonally or aslant. A small piece of soda a little larger than a good-sized pea, if put into the boiling water with the beans, or with any vegetables, will preserve that beautiful green which is so desirable for them to possess when placed upon the table.

Cabbages.—A full grown or summer cabbage should be well and thoroughly washed; before cooking, cut them into four pieces, boil rapidly, with the saucepan uncovered, half an hour; a young cabbage will take only twenty minutes, but it must be boiled very rapidly; a handful of salt should be thrown in the water before the cabbage is put in.

Cauliflowers.—Trim them neatly, let them soak at least an hour in cold water, put them into boiling water, in which a handful of salt has been thrown, let it boil, occasionally skimming the water. If the cauliflower is small, it will only take fifteen minutes; if large, twenty minutes may be allowed; do not let them remain after they are done, but take them up, and serve immediately. If the cauliflowers are to be preserved white, they ought to be boiled in milk and water, or a little flour should be put into the water in which they are boiled, and melted butter should be sent to table with them.

Green Peas.—A delicious vegetable; a grateful accessory to many dishes of a more substantial nature. Green peas should be sent to table *green.*—No dish looks less tempting than peas if they wear an autumnal aspect. Peas should also be young, and as short a time as possible should be suffered to elapse between the periods of shelling and boiling. If it is a matter of consequence to send them to table in perfection, these rules must be strictly observed. They should be as near of a size as a discriminating eye can arrange them; they should then be put in a cullender, and some cold water suffered to run through them in order to wash them; then, having the water in which they are to be boiled slightly salted, and boiling rapidly, pour in the peas; keep the saucepan uncovered, and keep them boiling swiftly until tender; they will take about twenty minutes, barely so long, unless older than they should be; drain completely, pour them into the tureen in which they are to be served, and in the centre put a slice of butter, and when it has melted, stir round the peas gently, adding pepper and salt; serve as quick and as hot as possible.

Potatoes.—In Ireland potatoes are boiled to perfection; the humblest peasant places his potatoes on his table better cooked than could half the cooks in our city, trying their best. Potatoes should always be boiled in their "jackets;" peeling a potato before boiling is offering a premium for water to run through it, and making them waxy and unpalatable; they should be thoroughly washed and put into cold water. In Ireland they always nick a piece of the skin off before they place them in the pot; the water is gradually heated, but never allowed to boil; cold water should be added as soon as the water commences boiling, and it should thus be checked until the potato is thoroughly done; the skins will not then be broken or cracked until the potato is thoroughly done; pour the water off completely, and let the skins be thoroughly dry before peeling.

Spinach.—The leaves of the spinach should be picked from the stems; it should then be well washed in clean cold water, until the whole of the dirt and grit is removed; three or four waters should be employed, it will not otherwise be got thoroughly clean; let it drain in a sieve, or shake it in a cloth, to remove the clinging water. Place it in a saucepan with boiling water, there should be very little, it will be done in ten minutes; squeeze out the water, chop the spinach finely, seasoning well with pepper and salt; pour three or four large spoonsful of gravy over it, place it before the fire until much of the moisture has evaporated, and then serve.

Turnips, Whole.—Pare several large turnips, and scoop out with an iron cutter for the purpose; throw them in water as you cut them; when done, blanch them, then strain them off; if for white sauce, add bechemel to them; if for brown, brown sauce; season as before.

WE cannot conclude this Department of our book better than by giving the following valuable

Domestic Hints.

EAT slowly and you will not over-eat.

Keeping the feet warm will prevent head-aches.

Late at breakfast—hurried for dinner—cross for tea.

Between husband and wife little attentions beget much love.

Always lay your table neatly, whether you have company or not.

Put your balls or reels of cotton into little bags, leaving the ends out.

Whatever you choose to give away, always be sure to *keep your temper.*

Dirty windows speak to the passer-by of the negligence of the inmates.

In cold weather, a leg of mutton improves by being hung three, four, or five weeks.

When meat is hanging change its position frequently, to equally distribute the juices.

There is much more injury done by admitting visitors to invalids than is generally supposed.

Matches, out of the reach of children, should be kept in every bed-room. They are cheap enough.

When you dry salt for the table, do not place it in salt-cells until it is cold, otherwise it will harden into a lump.

Never put away plate, knives, and forks, &c., uncleaned, or sad inconvenience will arise when the articles are wanted.

Feather beds should be opened every third year, the ticking well dusted, soaped and waxed, the feathers dressed and returned.

Persons of defective sight, when threading a needle, should hold it over something white, by which the sight will be assisted.

In mending sheets and shirts, put the pieces sufficiently large, or in the first washing the thin parts give way, and the work is undone.

Reading by candle light, place the candle behind you, that the rays may pass over your shoulder on the book. This will relieve the eyes.

A wire fire guard, for each fire-place in a house, costs little, and greatly diminishes the the risk to life and property. Fix them before going to bed.

In winter, get the work forward by day-light to prevent running about at night with candles. Thus you escape grease spots, and risks of fire.

Be at much pains to keep your children's feet dry and warm. Don't bury their bodies in heavy flannels and wools, and leave their knees and legs naked.

Apples and pears, cut into quarters, and stripped of the rind, baked with a little water and sugar, and eaten with boiled rice, are capital food for children.

After washing overlook linen, and stich on buttons, hooks and eyes, &c.; for; this purpose keep a "housewife's friend," full of miscellaneous threads, cottons, buttons, hooks, &c.

CHAPTER VI.

Swimming—Home Bathing—Turkish Baths.

BEFORE meals rather than after, and especially before breakfast and before supper, are proper seasons for bathing. The heats of the day are to be avoided, but, in very hot weather a bath is useful to cool the blood, and secure refreshing leep. If in the middle of the day, a shaded place should be chosen, or the head protected from the sun by being kept wet, or by wearing a straw hat, as is practised by the fashionable French ladies at their watering places.

The sea is the best place for swimming. Owing to the greater specific gravity of salt water than fresh, the body is more buoyant in it, as are other substances. A ship coming out of salt water into fresh sinks perceptibly in the water. The difference is nearly equal to the weight of the salt held in solution.

The bottom should be of hard sand, gravel, or smooth stones. Sharp stones and shells cut the feet—weeds may entangle them. The swimmer must avoid floating grass and quicksand. The new beginner must be careful that the water does not run beyond his depth, and that the current cannot carry him into a deeper place also that there be no holes in the bottom. As persons are ever liable to accidents, cramps, &c., it is always best that boys or girls should be accompanied by those who are older than themselves, and who will be able to save them in any emergency.

Probably one of the best ways of learning to swim is to go with a competent teacher, in a boat in deep water, thus supporting the body more buoyantly than that which is shallower, and preventing the constant tendency of beginners to touch bottom, which here is of course impossible.

The teacher should fasten a rope carefully around the waist, or better still, to a belt, which can neither tighten nor slip down. The rope may be fastened to a short pole. Supported in this manner, the pupil may take his proper position in the water, and practise the necessary motions, and the support of the rope may be gradually lessened, until the pupil finds himself entirely supported by the water.

Corks and bladders are often used as supports for learners; but it is much better to begin without them. As, however, they may be a protection in some cases against accidents, and enable the learner to practise the proper motions for rapid swimming more carefully, they are not to be entirely condemned.

Swimming with the plank has two advantages. The young bather has always the means of saving himself from the effects of a sudden cramp, and he can practise with facility the necessary motions with the legs and feet, aided by the momentum of the plank. A piece of light wood three or four feet long, two feet wide, and about two inches thick, will answer very well for this purpose. The chin may be rested upon the end, and the arms used, but this must be done carefully, or the support may go beyond the young swimmer's reach.

A better method, still, as many think, is for the teacher to wade into the water with his pupil, and then support him in a horizontal position by placing his hand under the pupil's chest, while he directs his motions.

Those persons who plunge into the water when they are heated by exercise, and remain in it until they are benumbed with cold, or exhaust themselves by very violent exertion, are the more subject to attacks of cramp. The moment the swimmer is seized by cramp in the legs, he must not suffer himself to feel alarmed;

but strike out the limb affected with all his might, keeping the heel downward, and drawing the toes as far upward as he can, although at the time these movements give him great pain; he may also turn on his back, and jerk the limb into the air, though not so high as to throw himself out of his balance. Should these attempts prove unsuccessful, he must try to reach the shore with his hands; or, at all events, keep himself afloat until assistance can be procured. If he cannot float on his back, he may swim upright, keeping his head above the surface, by striking the water downward with his hands near his hips; and he can thus make steady progress without using his legs. If only one leg be attacked, the swimmer may strike forward with the other; and to acquire confidence in cases of cramp, it is advisable to practise swimming with one hand and leg; with the hands only, or even with one leg.

We now come to the most important directions. As the pupil must gradually acquire confidence in this new element, he should not be urged to plunge in against his inclination. After wetting his head, he may wade in until the water is up to his breast, then turning towards the shore, inflate his lungs and incline forward, until the water covers his chin. The head should be thrown backward, and the back hollowed, and the chest as much as possible expanded. In swimming, the feet should be about two feet below the surface.

The hands should be placed just in front of the breast, pointing forward, the fingers kept close together, and the thumb to the fingers, so as to form a slightly hollow paddle. Now strike the hands forward as far as possible, but not bringing them to the surface; then make a sweep backward to the hips, the hands being turned downward and outward; then bring them back under the body, and with as little resistance as may be, to their former position, and continue as before.

The hands have three motions—First, from their position at the breast, they are pushed straight forward; second, the sweep round to the hips, like an oar, the closed and hollowed hands being the paddle portion, and their position in the water and descent serving both to propel and sustain the body; and third, they are brought back under the body to the first position.

Having learned these motions by practising them slowly, the pupil should proceed to learn the still more important motions of the legs. These are likewise three in number, one of preparation, and two of propulsion. First, the legs are drawn up as far as possible, by bending the knees, and keeping the feet widely separated; second, they are pushed with force backward and outward, so that they spread as far as possible; and, third, the legs are brought together, thus acting powerfully upon the wedge of water they enclose.

In leaping into the water, feet first, which is done from rocks, bridges, and even from the yards and lofty masts of vessels, the feet must be kept close together, and the arms either held close to the side or over the head. The hands are also in a proper position for striking out. In diving head foremost, the hands must be put together, so as to divide the water before the head.

It is wonderful how easy the swimmer directs his course under water. If he wishes to go down or come up, or swim to the right or left, he has but to bend his head and body in that direction, and after a little use he will do this almost unconsciously, as if his movements were the result of volition alone.

In descending in the water, bend the head so as to bring the chin near the breast, and curve the back in the same direction; in ascending, hold back the head and hollow the back. In swimming over the surface, look up to the sky.

In the swimming schools of Prussia, the pupils are taught in deep water, sustained by a belt, and a rope attached to a pole, which the teacher holds as a lever over a railling. The motions of the arms, then of the legs, and then both together, are practised by word of command, like military exercises. The support is given as required. After a few lessons the pole is dispensed with—then the rope; but the pupil is still kept, until proficient, within reach of the pole.

Treading is a favorite position in the water, and useful as a means of resting in swimming long distances. The position is perpendicular; the hands are placed upon the hips, or kept close to the side, to assist in balancing the body, being moved like fins at the wrist only. The feet are pushed down alternately, so as to support the head above water; and the body may be raised in this way to a considerable extent. While in this position, if the head be thrown back so as to bring the nose and mouth uppermost, and the chest somewhat inflated, the swimmer may sink till his head is nearly covered, and remain for any length of time in this position without motion, taking care to breathe very slowly.

In swimming on either side, the motions of the legs have no alteration, but are performed as usual. To swim on the left side, lower that side, which is done with the slightest effort, and requires no instructions. Then strike forward with the left hand, and sideways with the right, keeping the back of the latter to the front, with the thumb side downward, so as to act as an oar. In turning on the other side, strike out with the right hand, and use the left for an oar. To swim on each side alternately, stretch out the lower arm the instant that a strike is made by the feet, and strike with the other arm on a level with the head at the instant that the feet are urging the swimmer forward; and while the upper hand is carried forward, and the feet are contracted, the lower hand must be drawn toward the body. This method is full of variety, and capable of great rapidity, but it is also very fatiguing.

Thrusting is a beautiful variety of exercise, and much used by accomplished swimmers. The legs and feet are worked as in ordinary swimming, but the hands and arms very differently. One arm —say the right—should be lifted wholly out of the water, thrust forward to its utmost reaching, and then dropped upon the water with the hand hollowed, and then brought back by a powerful movement, pulling the water toward the opposite arm-pit. At the same time the body must be sustained and steadied by the left hand, working in a small circle, and as the right arm comes back from its far reach to the arm-pit, the left is carrying in an easy sweep from the breast to the hip. The left arm is thrust forward alternately with the right, and by these varied movements, great rapidity is combined with much ease.

Swimming on the back, is the easiest of all modes of swimming, because in this way a larger portion of the body is supported by the water. It is very useful to ease the swimmer from the greater exertion of more rapid methods, and especially when a long continuance in deep water is unavoidable. The swimmer can turn easily to this position, or, if learning, he has but to incline slowly backward, keeping his head on a line with his body, and letting his ears sink below the surface. Then placing his hands upon his hips, he can push himself along with his feet and legs with perfect ease, and considerable rapidity.

The hands may be used to assist in propelling in this mode by bringing them up edgewise toward the arm-pits, and then pushing them down, the fingers fronting inwards, and the thumb part down. This is called "winging."

The hand may be used at discretion, the application of force in one direction of course giving motion in the other; and the best methods are soon learned when once the pupil has acquired confidence in his bouyant power.

Home Bathing.

"THERE are certain rules connected with our ablutions that ought to be known and carefully observed. Many persons bathe after a full meal, in ignorance of the fact that a period of at least three hours ought to intervene. It is wise also to consider not only the conditions of our stomach, when we are about to take a bath, but the degree to be exerted by the bath—for it is a proven fact, that the more empty the stomach the greater is the ability of the system to bear powerful bathing and the more loaded the stomach is with undigested food, the less desirable is any bathing indulgence. Persons when heated by exertions ought not to apply cold water to their bodies, but it is quite a beneficial luxury, to use the cold bath when even profusely perspiring from the use of a hot bath; but it must not be forgotten that all sudden changes are riskful, of the respiration be disturbed, or a fatiguing exhaustion experienced, Under all circumstances when a cold bath is taken the body should be comfortably warm. The means are, when means are required, fresh and dry wrapping, or fire, according to circumstances at command. When feeble or debilitated persons commence a course of bathing, it should be borne in mind that tepid or warm water should be used, and attention paid to its temperature, so that at each succeeding use of the bath, the temperature may be lowered until the body can bear ordinarily cold water without inconvenience.

The application of water to the skin differs in its effects according to the manner of its use. It may be general or partial, hot or cold, and continue for a longer or shorter period.

The Home bath should always have at hand two bathing sheets, each capable of enveloping the whole body—for there are two processes requiring a wet sheet; and a dry one should always be ready to wrap in after any bathing, in which to remain a few minutes before dressing.

A sheet dripping wet may be wrapped round the body, the person standing up in a tub or bath and then rubbed by an attendant with the hands over the sheet, the bather assisting, so as speedily and actually to finish it—or by placing flannel cloths dipped in hot water, and wrung out nearly dry in any thin cloth, so that the part may be steamed, and a sedative effect produced.

He is then to be transferred to a dry sheet and the like outside rubbing repeated.

The other wet sheet process is termed packing, from the fact that other wrappings are added to the sheet. In preparing for this operation two or three bed covers or comfortables, are required; one spread or mattress, then a pair of woollen blankets, then a wet sheet, (pillows having been placed on the mattress to raise the head and shoulders) and then the person is placed on his back and the sheet closed over him tightly; then the clothes and the comfortables—taking care to wrap the feet well and leave the head free. He then remains from fifty to sixty minutes—on removal he may enter a cold bath or not, but rubbing with a crash towel is important, varying in activity according to the person's condition.

If during this process, headache is felt apply a folded wet towel to the forehead, if the feet continue or become cold, apply a bottle or jar of hot water to the wrappings up.

There is also a wet sheet process which is only partial, that is to say only the trunk is enveloped, from the armpits to the hips, but otherwise the treatment is the same as the preceeding.

The wet girdle is applied by the use of a few yards of crash toweling; one half wet, the other dry and wrapped round the abdomen. This should be frequently, or as often as it gets dry, re-applied until alleviation from troublesome symptoms is obtained. It may be worse at night.

The sweating process is accomplished easily by a wet bandage round the throat, and all the rest of the body enclosed in blankets or other warm flannels.

The half bath is any vessel convenient to a sitttng posture with the legs extended—and the water should reach half way up the abdomen; an attendant should then rub the upper while the bather rubs the lower parts of the body.

In the use of the hip bath, a blanket should be clasped at

the throat and hang down outside the bath tub, which may at the same time be used to assist the fraction of the abdomen and sides.

The FOOT BATH is simply a small vessel for the feet filled with the water, in which the feet are kept in motion as if walking for ten or fifteen minutes and then put into cold water for the shortest possible time and then well dried with crash toweling.

The best FOOT BATH however for those who can bear it is obtained by a stream of water, such as a running hydrant would produce, and walking up and down in it with the bare feet—then rubbing them dry with crash towelling and putting on clean dry socks or stockings.

The SHOWER BATH known to every one is not recommended in consequence of the shock to the head, but there may be cases in which if the head be first wetted or protected by covering, in which this plan may be beneficial.

The STREAM DOUCHE is an impartial remedy for many local difficulties, and can be easily obtained by a common hose pipe attached to the hydrant, and the height and strength regulated by the faucet.

The PAIL or BUCKET DOUCHE is an easy one (when used to it) an agreeable steam bath. This is done by standing in a tub, the head having been first dipped in a basin of water and pouring over the shoulders the contents of a water bucket—quickly followed by good rough drying and rubbing.

The TOWEL BATH is simply the use of a dripping towel or sponge, applied all over the body, and followed by unfolding in a large dry sheet.

INJECTION BATHS are used warm or tepid, or cool or cold—a warm injection is used abundantly to quiet pain and produce free evacuations—a cold injection to check excessive evacuations and to strengthen the bowels.

FOMENTATION BATHS are used to relieve spasms, griping pains, nervous headache, and such like, and are used, in two ways either by hot water—soaked toweling or by placing thin flannel cloths dipped in hot water and wrung out nearly dry in any cloth, so that the part may be steamed and a sedative effect produced.

Turkish Baths.

THEORY OF THE BATH.—The impression that a bath necessarily implies water is erroneous. The Turkish Bath consists primarily in the application of heated air to the surface of the body for the purpose of cleansing the skin, purifying the blood, and thereby giving relief from pain and disease. In the East, Hot Air Baths have been in use for centuries, both as a luxury and as a religious custom, by those who regard physical cleanliness as an aid to moral purification. It remained for the present age to adopt and apply the Eastern Bath as an invaluable remedial agent.

The regular Turkish Baths comprise a suit of four rooms, namely: the Frigidarium, with which is connected the dressing-rooms; the Tepidarium, or warm room; the Calidarium, or hot room; and the Lavatorium, or bathing-rooms. The bather enters the first; retires to the curtained recess, were he can privately prepare him for the bath; and then enters the Tepidarium, where he remains until the body becomes warm and be has accustomed himself to the temperature of the room, ordinarily about 100° Fahr.; after which he enters the Calidarium, the average temperature of which is 180°, and reclines at leisure on one of the marble couches. When the bather is perspiring freely, the attendant goes though a series of manipulations of the person, called Shampooing the object of which is to relax the muscles, and, at the same time, give greater freedom to the skin in relieving the body of its effete matter. This done, the bather enters the Lavatorium, and is there completely lathered with perfume soap, and rubbed with a brush or sponge, after which, he is subjected to the necessary ablutions. He is then wrapped in a dry sheet, and conducted to the cooling-room, where he reclines on one of the lounges until his skin is dry, when he resumes his ordinary attire. The skin is now " as soft as velvet, as smooth as marble, and as sleek as satin," and the sensations experienced delightful in the extreme.

EFFECTS OF THE BATH.—Its first physiological effect is to perfect the respiratory function of the skin—to give a living and healthy cuticle, instead of the weak, diseased, and dirty covering which the majority of people possess. The skin is thus fitted for imbibing the oxygen of the atmosphere, and giving off the carbon from the blood, two most important processes. When we consider that the skin is provided with no less then seven million pores, designed to assist the several excretive organs in discharging refuse matter from the system, some idea can be formed of the vast importance of keeping it in a perfectly healthy state. To a person liable to take cold from exposure to slight draughts, the feeling of defiance to cold, imparted by the Baths is one of their most striking results. Those engaged in manufacturing processes where a high degree of heat is employed, are found to be entirely free from colds. In no diseases are the effects more magical then in Rheumatism. In northern climates, the functions of the skin are, to a great extent, dormant, and its purpose as an outlet for refuse matters of the system almost nullified by inaction. The habitual use of these Baths remedies this state of things, giving, at the same time beauty, to the skin and health to the body. Mr. D. Urquhart, than whom, there is no better authority, says: Where the Bath is the practice of the people, there are no diseses of the skin.

PERSPIRATION NOT WEAKENING.—It is common to associate profuse perspiration with debility, and to imagine it to be weakening to the system. This is a mistake. Perspiration induced by passive means can not weaken, particularly when the bather partakes freely of water. Travelers in the East resort to the Bath for refreshment and invigoration. The porters at Constantinople, who are frequent bathers, will place a load of five hundred weight unaided on their backs. Farmers laboring in the hot sun of harvest days, are benefited rather than debilitated by abundant perspiration. In fact, the Bath is highly tonic, and the rule is to put weak people in often, as it is considered conducive to flesh and strength. Perspiration drains away no living tissue, but merely effete and poisonous matter which enervates instead of strengthens. If you perspire well you come out of the Bath stronger than you went in.

The Turkish Bath differs materially from the Russian or Vapor Bath. In the one case, the heated body is surrounded by *dry air*, which favors perspiration and the free absorption of oxygen from the atmosphere; whereas, on the other hand, the body is immersed in vapor, which being absorbed in place of the oxygen, thereby interferes with the process of evaporation, which nature provides for cooling the body. The same rule applies to warm water Baths with even greater force. The depressing effect of a hot, damp "muggy" day in summer, in contrast with the exhiliration of a fair clear day, is an apt illustration of the difference. Hot water can not be used with comfort much over 100° Fahr.; steam not over 112°, or possibly 120°; while hot air may be applied by the practised bather at as high a temperature as 200°, with but little inconvenience. In the Vapor Bath, the pulse is accelerated from forty to fifty beats a minute before perspiration is induced, while in the Turkish Bath there is but very little variation from the normal standard.

How important therefore it is to pay proper attention to some system of Bathing—even were it for no other purpose than that of cleansing the pores existing all over the surface of our bodies, for there are scattered millions of minute orifices, which open into the delicate convoluted tubes lying underneath the skin, and are called by anatomists sudoriferous glands. Each of these tubes when straightened, measures about a quarter of an inch; and as according to Erasmus Wilson, whose figures we follow, there are 3,528 of these tubes on every square inch of the palm of the hand, there must be no less then 882 inches of tubing on such a square inch. In some parts of the body the number of tubes is even greater; in most parts it is less. Erasmus Wilson estimates that there are 2 800 on every square inch on the average; and as the total number of such inches is 2 500, we arrive at the astounding result that spread over the surface of the body, there are not less than twenty-eight miles of tubing, by means of which liquid may be secreted, and given off as vapour, in insensible perspiration, or as water in sensible perspiration. In the ordinary circumstances of daily life the amount of fluid which is thus given off from the skin (and lungs) during the twenty-four hours varies from 1 2-3lb to 5lb.; under extraordinary circumstances the amount will of course rise enormously. Dr. Southwood Smith found that the workmen in the gasworks employed in making up the fires, and other occupations which subjected them to great heat, lost on an average 3lb 6ozs. in forty-five minutes; and when working for seventy minutes in an unusually hot place their loss was 5lb and 4lb. 14ozs.

The best time for taking this or any other Bath is that which will least interfere with the process of digestion; for instance, before a meal. Two hours should elapse after eating lightly, and at least three hours after dinner or a hearty meal. The time generally required for a Bath is one hour, though the processes may be shortened or prolonged at will.

The frequency with which the Bath should be taken depends upon the object in view. For invalids, the frequency must be regulated by a medical adviser who understands its effects and proper application.

Marine water is undoubtedly better for the bather than fresh, it exerts a more tonic influence, and its temperature is always more agreeable. The proper bathing season in this country is from the beginning of June to the end of September; the temperature of the water then ranges from 55° to 70° Fahrenheit. When it is colder than this, should bathing be ordered for medicinal or other purposes, resort should be had to *Medicated Baths* in which the water is impregnated with certain mineral, vegetable, and sometimes animal substances. Thus we have sulphur, chlorine and iron baths, aromatic and milk baths; which, if properly prepared and applied, may be productive of very beneficial effects. The *Aromatic Vapor Bath* is prepared by passing the vapor of boiling water through aromatic plants, from which the active principles are thus carried off. A good *Alkaline Bath* may be prepared thus:—Subcarbonate of potash 8 ounces; hot water about 20 gallons; employed as a revulsent in chilblains and sanguineous congestions.

In bathing children, it should be borne in mind, that the power of producing heat in warm-blooded animals is at its minimum at birth, and increases successively to adult age; hence, the water that feels but cool to the nurse's hand, may be absolutely cold to an infant. Some persons are fond of what they call hardening their children, by plunging them into cold water in winter; but this is a pernicious practice, and often produces disease of the lungs or of the digestive organs.

We all know how intimately health and cleanliness are connected and as a sanitary precaution merely, it would be well for our public authorities to afford every facility and inducement to the poorer classes to wash and bathe more frequently than they now do or can. There would be less danger from epidemic diseases, which commencing with them frequently spread through the whole community, if the bath and towel were in greater requisition among them.

CHAPTER VI.
Medical, Curative, and Useful.

It is as difficult to draw the dividing line between food and medicine as it is between the animal and vegetable kingdoms. Many hold the opinion and in our opinion wisely,—that food is both nutritive and therapeutic or curative—take water for example, the most importat internal and external of the whole materia medica. So in like manner with all our eatables and drinkables, they are all dual in their operations—enriching or depleting—as well as obstructive or curative—all good medicines may therefore be said to be nutritious, all good food medicinal.

The more naturally we live the better is the health we enjoy, and the less we think about the evils of dispepsia, the less cause we have to feel it. The main reason why dispeptics have so much cause of complaint about certain articles disagreing with their stomachs is because they stingily refuse them to that organ—as if to use a Hebrew saying "bricks could be made without straw;" formerly bricks were mixed with chopped straw in the manner now of hair in mortar, to prevent their falling to pieces when sun drying. *The stomach cannot do its work if it be not made out of the material it has to digest*—hence the way to digest is to obtain a healthy digester. Persons are found who gradually drop one article of food after another till they are reduced to a very sparse bill of fare and still complain of indigestion—but let them once keep on eating what appears to disagree with them, not in abundance but in ever changing variety, and they will forge a new stomach that will soon hardly refuse "Horse-nails."

Some food induces relaxation, diarrhœa and watery discharges, while other food generates mucous, giving rise to catarrhs, predisposing lung and throat difficulties and oppressions—but if all be eaten, they will be found self correcting, and nature will do the rest—and by day carry on her nightly work of digestion, under the influence of light, air, and exercise, and by night of gradual assimilation under the mantle of darkness, in the stillness of the air, and in the absence of exercise. The contest of the schools of medical learning have ever ended in extremes of opinion—and it is a noteworthy fact in these days of investigation and diffused knowledge that no two physicians will diagnoze and prescribe the same for the same difficulty—on the other hand the most curative attendance is found in unstudied common sense, matter of fact folks such as are found in the Florence Nightingale class of nurses, and in books of reference such as "THE MINE OF WEALTH" where the simple and unsophisticated truth is alone found. The Allopaths healing power is in medicines; the Hygienic physicians consider that all healing power is in the living system, and that there is nothing curative outside the vital organism.

Again the Allopath and the Homœpath are at extremes in regard to quantity, the one increases large doses the other diminishes small ones—the one drugs with opposites the other medicates with similaritie —again, water, milk, magnetism, vegetables, the Sun and a host of other units of cure have their exclusive advocates and practisers until every branch and leaf and flower and fruit of the great world's trunk of medication, is diverse in some feature or another. Still man lives, man thrives and man does as he likes *as long as he can:* when the inherent power is impaired through ignorance, another fountain of often greater ignorance is applied to, to re-establish the normal condition—and then in most cases the self-hood of the individual is surrendered to another, the directions given are *never* followed exactly, and the patient gradually succumbs to the Epitaph

Affliction sore, long time I bore,
Physicians were in vain, &c.

The time is coming however when books like THE MINE OF WEALTH will reach every sensible man in the world, and fill him with new ideas, ideas that will enable him to understand himself and his surroundings, as well as his own health and its connection with the common activities of every day life.

Consumption.

The popular terms, Consumption and Decline, are not always applied to the same diseases, being used to designate any of those ailments which are characterised by a wasting away of the substance of the body. Some people suppose, moreover, that all affections which have for symptoms a gradual diminution of muscular strength, *with cough*, must be cases of Consumption. There is a wide-spread conviction that all these cases are hopeless and incurable. It is our agreeable duty to show the errors of these popular prejudices. Having giving our attention, particularly to diseases of the chest, it is neither our intention to elevate false hopes, nor to speak more discouragingly than we are positively warranted by experience. We have no new remedy to recommend, nor any pet theory to establish: but we believe that a general ignorance of the *nature* of consumption exists, and that the want of information leads to the neglect of preventive measures, which have saved many from an early grave.

Firstly.—Let us consider what consumption is. True consumption consists in the deposit, by the blood-vessels in the lungs, of a substance which is incapable of being alive. To explain this by its reverse: —warts or moles are unnatural growths; they do not decay upon the body, but have blood circulated through them. When a wound is made in the skin, from the blood which flows there is poured out or deposited a substance called *lymph*, which fills the incision, and, if the case proceeds favourably, gradually assumes all the appearances of the parts in which the wound was made: in other words lymph becomes *organized* and *lives*. When the wound does not heal by this formation or organization of lymph, matter, or *pus*, is poured out: this fluid is of lower vitality than lymph, but is evidence of no deterioration in the blood, and is capable of being absorbed again by the vessels under peculiar circumstances. It performs an important part in the growth of wounds, where a large portion of flesh has been destroyed, and has to be filled up by granulation, or gradual growth. A substance of less vitality is TUBERCLE, the deposit of which is the cause of the disease properly called consumption. This substance can never be vitalized nor absorbed after it is once deposited; but sooner or later excites inflamation around every portion of it, just as a thorn, or a splinter, or any other foreign body would do if it were introduced into the flesh and allowed to remain therein.

Tubercle, or tuberculous matter, is found in various conditions, and different situations. It is not uncommonly deposited in the glands of the neck, and is then known as *scrofula*. In children it is occasionally deposited in the glands and tissues which surround the membranes of the bowels in the cavity of the abdomen—in these cases it is called *mesenteric disease*. Later in life the scene of its destructive influences is located in the upper portions of the lungs, and then it is recognised as *consumption*. It varies in character, from a hard grain like a millet seed (its primitive condition) to a cheesey-looking substance, in larger quantities. Occasionally, and rarely it is found in a dried state surrounded with a thick skin-like bag called a cyst. These details are given because the probability of a cure depends, in a great measure, upon the state in which the tubercles in the lungs happen to be. If they are in the first, or milary state, they may remain without producing inflamation for months or years; if in the second state, inflamation, the formation of matter (pus), and the ulceration of the lung is certain ; in the last, the tuberculous matter being prevented from irritating the tissue which surrounds it, may never produce any fatal effects ; the last state is, however, very rare.

To sum up then—consumption consists in a deposit of tuberculous matter in the lungs, which may *or may not* be so injured thereby as to destroy life. If the quantity of tuberculous matter is not large, and if the constitution is in such a state as to bear inflamation and ulceration of the lungs (whereby the irritating substance may be removed from their tissue), then is consumption curable ; but if, as is commonly the case, the tubercles have been allowed to be deposited in large quantities in both lungs, and great debility arises as both the cause and effect of the state of the lungs—then, alas! there is but little hope.

The usual history of fatal cases is as follows : tuberculous matter is deposited in the lungs as small grains ; a low kind of inflamation results around each nucleus, and more tuberculous matter is poured out. The tubercle then softens, and the effort of nature to expel the intruder results in ulceration. At this period a portion of the lung softens and comes away with the cough ; a blood-vessel is burst, and the constitution, thus weakened, is disposed to a fresh deposit of tuberculous matter. This round of deterioration of the blood, fresh deposit of tubercle, and fresh ulceration goes on, until the powers of the system are exhausted, and death takes place.

The second part of the subject brings the writer to the most important part of his remarks, the CAUSES of consumption. We have seen that tubercles have their origin in the blood, and that consumption is to be traced to a diseased state of that fluid ; which instead of depositing, as in healthy reparative inflamation, a substance capable of organization, pours out in the place thereof an effete matter, which is incapable of vitality or absorption. We find deposits at various ages in various parts. All these circumstances prove that local causes alone will not entirely account for the sad phenomenon. Whatever the causes be, they are evidently such as affect the constitution generally, and dispose the circulating fluid (when called in excess to any congested or irritated part) to deposit therein what would have been organizable lymph, if the blood had been in a healthy condition, but which in its impoverished condition is *tubercle*. To sum up, the immediate causes of tuberculous deposit are a peculiarly impoverished state of the blood, combined with a congestion or extra supply of blood, resembling a diffused slight inflammation in the part affected.

The former is evidently the most important, because if the constitutional ailment exists, a local congestion will soon give opportunity for its effects; whereas the latter *without* the former might cause so little derangement of the health as to be unnoticed. The question now arises—What is the *cause* of this condition of the blood? Upon our knowledge of this depends mainly the hope which we entertain of the success of preventive and curative measures, and this is the knowledge which it is most desirable should be generally diffused. By correctly understanding the true causes and nature of the disease, hundreds of persons who now fall victims to the nostrums of ignorant quacks, would learn that no mere drug has the power to check their disease; but that their hope of life depends upon a combination of sanitory measures, adopted early, and perseveringly pursued; and those measures directed to give the blood a higher vitality, at the same time that local congestion or irritations are prevented or removed.

The causes of consumption may therefore be classified as follows:

A.—GENERAL CAUSES, or influences which produce a diseased

condition of the blood : which fluid, upon a congestion of any organ, becomes liable to deposit tuberculous matter therein.

B.—SPECIAL CAUSES, or influences which produce congestion or inflamation in particular organs, which are most commonly the seat of tuberculous deposit.

A.—GENERAL CAUSES.

In estimating the various influences which produce the consumptive cachexia, it must not be forgotten that *age* and *sex* must always be considered when weighing the importance of any other predisposing causes; because it has been proved by statistics that females are more liable than males to fall victims to this melancholy complaint. Men are more liable between the ages of twenty-one and twenty-eight; while females are more exposed to this disease before the age of twenty. From fifteen to thirty years, however, in both sexes, is the period which seems unfortunately favourable to the development of tubercles in the lungs. After the age of thirty-five, deaths from consumption are comparatively rare. In giving a popular essay on this part of our subject, we at once feel called upon to remind our readers that *prevention* is better than *cure*; that consumption may be prevented in a large number of cases where it is threatened; but that cure, after the disease has become rooted is *very rarely* effected. Of the causes, those under this head are by far the most serious, because they are most difficult to remove.

1. *Hereditary disposition.*—Innumerable familiar cases prove to every observer the sad truth, that the liability to tuberculous disease, or consumption, is transmitted from parents to children. The peculiar state of the constitution called the consumptive *diathesis cachexia*, is observed to run through a whole family; the various branches of which die off when they attain a certain age. It may assume in some instances different forms in the persons attacked: as, for instance, in one it may appear as mesenteric disease; in another as scrofula; and in the elder branches as consumption. In

estimating the probability, therefore, of any individual being attacked by tubercles in the lungs, an important light is thrown upon it by the existence or absence of the tuberculous cachexia among his near relations.

2. *Insufficient exercise, air, and light.*—In persons not hereditarily predisposed, this is the most fertile cause of disease. It must not be supposed that mere muscular labour is all that is required. The tiring inordinately of one set of muscles has been proved to be particularly injurious: unless the whole of the muscular system is called into exercise, the general health is sure to suffer. Sedentary employments are often less injurious than those in which one set of muscles are unremittingly exerted. But the want of fresh air, and especially of light renders the lungs unable to perform their functions, however varied the employment may be. The laws of the constitution of man are unalterable on this head; and the want of exercise, air, and light are *certain*, ultimately, to produce disease and death.

3. *Insufficient food; Indigestion.*—The effect of either of these causes is deficient nutrition, the impoverishment of the blood, and the impairing of the general strength and tone of the system. This is so plainly favourable to the development of tuberculous disease, that no more need be said, except to point out the importance of early attention to indigestion in persons known to be predisposed to consumption. From the experience of the writer, he is inclined to believe that it is one of the earliest symptoms of the vitiated state of the constitution, if not the immediate cause of the attack in a large number of cases.

4. *The attacks of fever, dissipation, the use of intoxicating drinks, and the depressing passions, are all fertile sources of the tuberculous cachexia.* However much matter of-fact old people may sneer at what are called the romantic feelings of youth, and however lightly the disappointments and separations of early life may be treated by them,

it is not to be denied that the deep sadness which often results, is too commonly the originator of disease of fatal character, which developes itself long after the operation of its primary cause, and when the "first love" and their sorrows have lost their intensity.

5. *Compression of the chest and abdomen.*—This last of general causes is fortunately becoming daily less prevalent. It is the unnatural habit of binding up the body with belts or stays. The gradual promulgation of popular physiology is triumphing over fashion; and the directions of the minds of both sexes to art has taught them how entirely ignorant of the highest personal beauty those persons are who still advocate stays and tight lacing. It is therefore unnecessary to write more here.

B. SPECIAL CAUSE OPERATING LOCALLY.

1. *Exposure to cold.*—This influence, by driving the blood from the surface for a considerable time, of necessity overloads the vessels of the internal organs. As it is the duty of the skin to assist the lungs in the performance of the function of perspiration, the effect is to produce a congestion of the latter. Then passing from heated rooms to a cool air, or the reverse, will also be calculated to produce an inflamation of the membrane which lines the air tubes of the lungs: this inflamation readily seems to extend itself to the particular tissue of which the lungs are composed.

2. *Dusty atmosphere.*—Persons employed in workshops or places where there is much dust, are also liable to suffer from the inflamation of the air tubes, or *bronchia*, of the lungs. These persons have been found to be particularly liable to consumption.

From what is written, it will strike the reader that to prevent consumption, it is chiefly necessary to remove or counteract the causes. How this is to be effected we shall next proceed to explain, first giving a general outline, in popular language, of the earliest signs of the consumptive cachexia which are discoverable by the non-professional eye.

The earliest signs of the tuberculous or consumptive cachexia which are noticeable by the non-professional eye, are:—the tumid cracked lip; the red denuded eye; the florid complexion; soft skin and hair; and the precocious mind. Long before the ear of the physician can discover auscultation, or percussion, the evidence of tubercles in the lungs, the constitution of the patient takes the alarm. The pulse becomes much more rapid, and differs *very little* when the patient is sitting or standing (which is not the case in health); the respiration becomes hurried, and is accelerated with a slight excitement. There is, moreover, a peculiar susceptibility to cold or heat. In females, the countenance is often as pallid as wax, with a shade of lividity about the lips, and at the root of the finger nails. The circulation in the hands, feet, ears, and nose, is disposed to be sluggish; and the fingers are apt to lose their sensibility, or, in common phraseology, to " become dead." With these, other disturbances of the general health arise. There is a peculiar form of the nails of the fingers, which seems to be very often connected with the consumptive cachexia, and which may be best described by " bean shaped," the upper surface of the nail being *rounded* like a bean, or blister.

The writer wishes to be distinctly understood that no *one* or *two* of these symptoms, *taken alone*, are to be received as a positive proof that any individual is " in a consumption." They are taken generally as the early warnings of the approach of the disease, and, if heeded, will be the means of saving life by early attention. *These symptoms do not indicate that the case is beyond hope.* CONSUMPTION IS CURABLE IN THIS STAGE.

Later—if the disease is not prevented by remedial means—a hacking cough, with a dull pain in the chest, and a sense of oppression in the respiration, are complained of. The patient is unable to run up stairs with as great ease as before, and a sharp pain in the side follows unusual exercise. A copious perspiration is noticed in bed before sunrise, and a loss of flesh and strength is per ed. *At this stage no time or exertion is to be lost,* FOR THERE IS A CHANCE FOR THE PATIENT YET.

A step further—and there is no more ground for hope—except for advent to a brighter world! At this stage the treatment is directed only to alleviate, for cure is impossible; the care of the patient is wholly under the direction of the medical attendant and the nurse.

In the first part of this article, the writer alluded to the great ignorance which existed on the subject of consumption, and stated that it was a popular error to suppose the disease incurable. The want of information as to the early symptoms of the disease, and the consequent neglect of preventive and corrective means, have given a hopeless aspect to a large majority of cases, and afforded a fatal confirmation of the generally received opinion. With a view to warn before it is too late, to alarm before the time of hope is past, *irrevocably*, we have endeavoured, by a minute delineation of symptoms, to give to parents and relatives the means of discovering the approach of a disease which now carries off one-fifth of our population.

THE TREATMENT, for the sake of perspicuity, may be divided into three periods, corresponding to those sketched above:—

I. PREVENTIVE—applying to the period of the earliest and most doubtful indications.

II. ALTERNATIVE—applying to the period when there is little doubt of the accession of the disease.

III. ALLEVIATE—applying to the period when the disease has made fatal progress.

I. *Preventive.*—As far as possible remove all known causes. The patient must be rigidly particular in rules of regimen and diet, and food, sleep, and exercise, must be taken at regular hours. *Early rising is essential.* The dyspepsia, or any other malady of a weakening character, should be communicated to the medical attendant without delay. Sea air and bathing; the use of the shower-bath or, if these cannot be obtained, the habit of sponging the body with cold salt water every morning, are remedies of which it is impossible to speak to highly. Cheerfulness should be promoted, and solitude carefully prevented. The food should be of a light, nutritive character. Gymnastic exercises in company should be practised, and sedentary employment in ill-ventilated rooms avoided.

2. *Alterative.*—This portion of treatment, necessarily differing with the peculiarities of each individual, must be guided in a great measure by a medical man. The common mistake is, not to consult a medical man until it is too late. The writer cannot forbear at this point urging the employment of gentlemen who are known to be thoroughly acquainted with the use of the stethoscope, and with the applicability of auscultation and percussion to the discovery of early signs of disease in the chest. Iodine in various forms, the use of emetics, careful depletion by leeches, or the cupping glasses applied beneath the collar bones, blisters in the same situations, and stimulating liniments applied to the chest, are the principal remedial measures. Of the latter kind, the following liniment cannot be too highly commended;—Take of oil of turpentine, one ounce; acetic acid, one ounce, olive oil, two ounces; and the yolk of one egg. Mix. To be freely rubbed into the chest night and morning.

3. *Alleviative.*—The treatment under this head is chiefly that of the sick room. The means to be used by the physician need not be alluded to. The friends of the patient should take care that he is placed in a light, and well-ventilated room, which can be warmed without being close. The bed-linen should frequently be changed, and every exciting cause removed. The attendants should be kind and tender in manner and spirit, without any hastiness, or show of solicitude—teasing kindness is highly injudicious. Vinegar and water may be freely sprinkled about the room, and the hands of the

sufferer sponged with it. The directions of the medical adviser should be strictly complied with; if the patient objects, mild but firm remonstrance will generally gain the acquiescence. The bed-curtains should never be drawn at night; in the day they may be useful to screen the eyes, if they are dazzled by too strong light. The desire for particular articles of food may, as a general rule, be gratified in moderation; but the appetite and relish will very often depend upon the delicate cleanliness of the bearer, and the smallness of the quantity presented.

Before laying down the pen, the writer feels it his duty to sound a warning voice to those who form their conceptions of Consumption from novels or romantic stories. It is not a painless disease, but one of prolonged suffering and distress. The pictures of the fading lily, or the drooping rose, have been favorite metaphors to illustrate the *fancied* gliding to the grave by imperceptible gradations; and popular poetry has spoken of the dwindling away of the thread of life, fibre by fibre, without struggle, or shock, or suffering, till the gentle parting of the last filaments. To the young and romantic, such falsely colored pictures are perniciously attractive, and lead them to neglect and contemn the early remedial measures which ought to be actively adopted, whenever the slightest symptom of predisposition to tuberculous disease is detected.

DEVELOPMENT OF THE LUNGS.—Much has been said and written upon diet, eating and drinking, but scarcely a notice by any writer upon breathing or the manner of breathing. Multitudes, and especially ladies in easy circumstances, contract a vicious and destructive mode of breathing. They suppress their breathing and contract the habit of short quick breathing, not carrying the breath half way down the chest, and scarcely expanding the lower portion of the chest at all. Lacing the bottom of the chest also greatly increases this evil, and confirms a bad habit of breathing. Children that move about a great deal in the open air, and in no way laced, breathe deep and full in the bottom of the chest, and every part of it. So also with most out-door laborers, and persons who take a great deal of exercise in the open air, because the lungs give us the power of action, and the more exercise we take, especially out of doors, the larger the lungs become, and the less liable to disease. In all occupations that require standing, keep the person straight. If at table, let it be high, raised up nearly to the armpits, so as not to require you to stoop; you will find the employment much easier —not one half so fatiguing; whilst the form of the chest and symmetry of the figure will remain perfect. You have noticed that a vast many tall ladies stoop, while a great many short ones are straight. This arises, we think from the table at which they sit or work, or occupy themselves, or study, being of a medium height— for a short one. This should be carefully corrected and regarded, so that each lady may occupy herself at the table to suit her, and thus prevent the possibility or necessity of stooping. It will be as well not to remain too long in a sitting position, but to rise occasionally, and thus relieve the body from its bending position. The arms could be moved about from time to time.

CARE OF THE TEETH.—Few people know the importance of teeth, and still fewer take proper care of them. Only when persons grow old and find them wanting, or when they suffer from their decay, do they properly appreciate their value. It is remarkable, that while man has only one set of any other organs during his life-time, he has two distinct sets of teeth; and this fact may be admitted to show their great importance in the animal economy. Man properly has thirty-two teeth, which are fixed with great firmness to the jaws, which latter are moved by very powerful muscles, and the upper and lower rows of teeth are pressed towards each other with considerable force during the mastication of food. By these means, the substances eaten are broken, and macerated by the salivary juice which flows from the glands of the mouth during the presence of food. The subsequent digestion of food in the stomach much depends upon its perfect mastication; if the teeth have effectively done their work, and reduced the food to a soft mass, the gastric juice of the stomach more easily dissolves it, and blood is the more speedily and completely formed therefrom, and the body the better nourished. Many people who have good teeth suffer indigestion from neglecting to properly use them; and those who have them not are afflicted from their absence. To preserve the teeth, they should be regularly cleaned night and morning. Cleanliness in this respect much promotes personal elegance, and frees the breath from the disagreeable taint that would otherwise accompany it. The best tooth-powder is a little pulverised charcoal. Camphor, or camphorated chalk, acts chemically upon the enamel (i. e. the hard white coating of the teeth which protects the soft bone and nervous structures beneath), and destroys it. Neglect of the teeth is so common, and the employment of improper substances, as articles of diet so general, that comparatively few people have their teeth sound, and many suffer the excruciating pain termed toothache. This pain is so severe that we should do right to interpret it as a warning to take proper care of parts so important to the welfare of the body. Creosote, oil of tar, alcohol, opium, and other substances, are often employed as remedies for the tooth-ache. But these only aggravate the evil, by accelerating the decay, and often disordering the gums. The wisest course is, to seek prevention in cleanliness in the manner already pointed out, and by living upon simple and pure articles of diet. But when decay has taken its seat, the best remedy is to have the apertures filled with a substance which hardens therein, and thus supplies an artificial enamel to shield the nerve from irritation.

INFLUENCE OF TEMPER ON HEALTH.—Excessive labour, exposure to wet and cold, deprivation of sufficient quantities of necessary and wholesome food, habitual bad lodging, sloth, and intemperance, are all deadly enemies to human life; but they are none of them so bad as violent and ungoverned passions. Men and women have survived all these, and at last reached an extreme old age; but it may be safely doubted whether a single instance can be found of a man of violent and irascible temper, habitually subject to storms of ungovernable passion, who has arrived at a very advanced period of life. It is therefore, a matter of the highest importance to every one desirous to preserve "a sound mind in a sound body," so that the brittle vessel of life may glide down the stream of time smoothly and securely, instead of being continually tossed about amidst rocks and shoals which endanger its existence, to have a special care, amidst all the vicissitudes and trials of life, to maintain a quiet possession of his own spirit.

EXPOSURE TO THE SUN.—There are few points which seem less generally understood, or more clearly proved, than the fact that exposure to the sun, without creating free perspiration, will produce illness; and that the (same) exposure to the sun, with sufficient exercise, will not produce illness. Let any man sleep in the sun, he will awake perspiring and very ill—perhaps he will die. Let the same man dig in the sun for the same length of time, and he will perspire ten times as much, and be quite well. The fact is that not only the direct rays of the sun, but the heat of the atmosphere, produce abundance of bile, and powerful exercise alone will carry off that bile.

CHOLERA.—All diseases are first germinal—and are born—the birthplace of the germ of cholera is in the digestive canal—hence the ideas which imperfect science has attributed to what are called choleraic and non-choleraic habits of eating and drinking—the line is not yet defined in respect to dietetic treatment, and much harm is done by breeding apprehension about consuming fruit and vegetables—for cucumbers and the like, have removed as many predispositions to cholera as they have contributed to their development. The principle vehicle of germinal cholera is the air—it nurses, atmospheric impurities. The sources of its supply, are the exhalations from a porous soil impregnated with decaying vegetable matter, and the discharges of persons affected with the disease—but in all conditions of production, there may yet be wanting a power to attack, for it is proved that in the absence of dejection and fear, the most potent assault may be resisted, provided the contact be not so direct as to overpower these guards. That is to say, a continuance in a cholera-generating atmosphere or the non-removal and destruction of the fæcal discharge of patients.

Standing water collects on its surface whatever the atmosphere has to contribute, and when it is understood that dust is settling on it through the poisoned air continually it will be understood that none but freshly drawn water should be ever used in cholera times. It is a disease, of which it may be truly said, "Remove the cause and the effect will cease."

THE FEET.—To preserve the feet in a proper condition, they should be frequently soaked, and well washed in warm or tepid water. The nails of the toes should be pared to prevent their becoming inconveniently long, and from growing into the flesh. Many persons suffer severely from tender feet. This generally arises from the use of thin cotton or silk stockings, and tight boots or shoes, that are not sufficiently porous to permit of the escape of the perspiration. The best treatment is the immediate adoption of worsted stockings or socks, and light easy shoes of buckskin, goatskin, or some other equally soft kind of leather. It is highly necessary, for the preservation of health, to preserve the feet DRY; persons who are, therefore, exposed to the wet, or who are frequently passengers through the public streets in bad weather, should regard sound and good boots and shoes as the most essential portion of their clothing. In fact, in a hygienic point of view, a wet back should be less shunned than wet feet. Many persons frequently experience extreme coldness and numbness of the feet; the best remedies for such are exercise and friction. In these cases stockings of flannel or worsted alone should be worn, and should be kept on throughout the night if required. The peculiar and disagreeable odor which is evolved by the feet of some individuals in hot weather, may be removed by the observance of extreme cleanliness, and by occasionally soaking the feet in warm water, to which a small quantity of chloride of lime has been added.

RECEIPTS.

Asthma.—This disease is generally brought on (except where it is hereditary) by sudden exposure to heat and cold, to unwholesome air, fetid smells, by hard drinking, full meals, violent exercise, and by cold, damp, and foggy weather. Generally speaking its attacks are confined to the later period of life, and the violence of each fit seldom exceeds two or three hours in duration. Persons thus afflicted should avoid the above causes, keep themselves dry and warm, wear flannel, keep the bowels regular, and the stomach in order.

Asthma Draught.—Vinegar of squills half a drachm; ipecacuanha wine, fifteen drops; cinnamon water, one and a half ounces. Mix and take as a draught three times a day.

Asthma Mixture.—Milk of gum ammoniacum, three ounces; syrup of squills, two ounces; ipecacuanha wine, one ounce. Mix and take a small teaspoonful, three or four times a day as an expectorant.

2—A Tonic.—Infusion of cardavilla, three ounces; infusion of gentian, two ounces; simple syrup, one ounce. Mix and take two tablespoonsful three times a day.

Asthma Pills.—Compound iron pills, two drachms; extract of gentian, one drachm; Mix and divide into sixty pills and take two each night and morning.

Cure for Asthma.—Saturate some brown paper (that is to say the old fashioned tar brown) in acetic acid diluted, or vinegar, and dry it off. When the asthma is distressing, some of this may be burned; and the smoke breathed. This is a quick relief.

Astringent Pills, for Diarrhea.—Alum, six grains; extract of opium, one grain; powdered catechu, twenty grains. Make into six pills, and take one after each motion.

Wash for Weak Eyes.—Compound liquor of alum, half an ounce; rose water, five ounces; laudanum, sixty drops. Shake well before using—wash the eyes with it two or three times a day.

Cough Mixture.—Paregoric, ten ounces; tincture of castor, four ounces; laudanum, one ounce; tincture of cochineal, half an ounce; oil of aniseed dropped on a lump of sugar, fifteen drops. Mix and take a teaspoonful or more according to the severity of the attack, three times a day.

Compound Lead Cerate.—For burns, scalds, excoriations, &c.—Solution of diacetate of lead, three ounces; white wax, four ounces; olive oil, half a pint; camphor half a drachm. Prepare it by adding eight ounces of the oil to the melted wax, and as soon as it begins to cool, add the solution of lead, and continue the stirring until cold; then add the camphor dissolved in the remaining portions of the oil.

Disinfecting Agents.—Common copperas which costs but a few cents per pound, is perhaps one of the most efficient and economical disinfecting agents known. If two pounds of copperas be dissolved in ten quarts of water, and the solution poured into the gutters, sinks, cesspools, and other places where filth necessarily accumulates, its deodorizing power will become speedily and convincingly apparent. Every housekeeper should provide a quantity of the article, and keep it constantly on hand, to be used when wanted. The unpleasant odor emanating from the barn yard, and other places where manure is stored or kept during the hot weather, ordinarily experienced during the vernal and summer months, is speedily neutralized by a slight sprinkling of this solution, as well as the extremely unpleasant smell engendered by decaying animal and vegetable substances in cellars and outhouses, and which it is frequently found difficult to prevent. Copperas is also an excellent manure. It acts as an absorbent and fixer of the gaseous and volatile products of decomposition, and thus becomes an efficient medium of their transportation to the field where they are required to give energy to vegetable life. Sulphuric acid—another cheap article, which like copperas can be obtained of the druggists in any desirable quantity—is also a most desirable article for this purpose. If used in a diluted state and sprinkled over the floors of the stables and other buildings where animals are kept, it will in a short time disinfect the same of all nauseous and unpleasant odors, and render the atmosphere perfectly pure and sweet. Like copperas it is also a good manure. Another article of great efficiency is found by slacking quick lime to a thick, plastic consistency, with water saturated with salt. This is what may be properly called domestic chloride of lime, being in every respect similar to, if not strictly identical with, the chloride of lime found at the stores and shops, although it comes at less than one-twentieth the cost.

To restore the Color of the Hair.—Tincture acetate of iron, one ounce; water, one pint; glycerine, half an ounce; sulphuret potassium, five grains. Mix well and let the bottle remain uncovered to pass out the foul smell arising from the potassium. Afterwards add a few drops of bergamot or other essence. Rub a little of this daily into the hair, and it will not only restore it to its original color, but benefit the health.

Cure for Sore throat.—Dissolve some powdered borax in one ounce of glycerine and four ounces of hot water, and use as a gargle. It will cure the most inveterate sore throat.

Chornic Diarrhea.—Pulverised rhubarb, bicarbonate of soda tincture of camphor, each one drachm; essence of peppermint, two drachms; sulphate of morphia, ten grains; white sugar, four ounces; boiling water, one pint. Dose, a tablespoonful twice a day.

To remove unpleasant odors from the Person.—The unpleasant odor arising from perspiration can be removed effectually by putting about two tablespoonsful of the compound spirits of ammonia in a basin of water, and washing the face, hands and arms in it; it will leave the skin as clean, sweet, and fresh as one could wish. It is not only perfectly harmless and cheap, but more efficacious than any of the costly unguents and perfumes of the day now in use.

Disinfecting Powder.—Thoroughly mix one hundred pounds of finely pulverized quick lime, twenty pounds of dry charcoal powder, ten pounds of dry sawdust or peat, and half a pound of crude carbonic acid. The acid is to be first stirred into the sawdust, and then added to the other ingredients, and the powder distributed in infected places, thoroughly purifies them.

Water Purifier.—A teaspoonful of powdered alum thrown into a pailful of muddy or turbid water will precipitate the impurities to the bottom, leaving the water clear and all the better for drinking purposes on account of the alum.

Malignant Scarlet Fever and Sore Throat.—Mix two tablespoonsful of capsicums, with one teaspoonful of salt, infused for one hour in a pint of boiling liquid composed of equal parts of water and vinegar. Strain when cool. If the case is a very serious one take half an ounce for an adult every half hour. The same to be taken as a gargle.

Chronic Diarrhea may be permanently cured by a diet of pure cow's milk, or such articles as bread and milk—in which milk is mainly in use but for drink milk only must be taken. This must be faithfully followed out for three weeks.

Toothache cured instantaneously.—Dissolve one part of mastic in one part of ether. A yellow oily substance is the result, which is to be kept in a well stoppered bottle. Saturate a small piece of cotton of the size of the cavity in the tooth, and introduce it without painful pressure, so as to fill the cavity exactly. The ether evaporates while the rosin remains protecting the tooth from the action of air and food taken into the mouth.

To cure Hiccough or Hiccup.—This spasm is caused by flatulency, indigestion, and acidity. It may be relieved generally by a sudden fright or surprise, or any sudden application of cold, also by swallowing two or three mouthfuls of cold water, by eating a small piece of ice, taking a pinch of snuff, or anything that excites coughing.

Cure for Snake Bites.—Make a paste of ipecacuana and apply to the bite. This simple remedy has performed some wonderful cures not only of bites from venemous snakes, but also of stings of scorpions, centipedes, and various poisonous fish. Equally efficacious is it to bathe the wound with strong liquid ammonia, and then apply a linen cloth saturated with the same to the affected part.

Cure for Burns and Scalds.—Dissolve from twenty to forty grains of crystalized nitrate of silver in an ounce of water, and apply it to the burn or scald (over the whole surface) with a camel's hair brush. It immediately furnishes a complete protection to the inflamed surface, subdues the pain, arrests the serous discharge, and promotes a speedy cure.

Rheumatism.—A slight attack of rheumatism can be readily checked and cured by dissolving half an ounce of camphor in eight ounces of spirit of turpentine, and thoroughly rubbing the parts affected morning and evening with it, and covering with flannel. If the attack is a very severe one then take one ounce of gum gaiacum in powder and infuse it in a bottle of rum. Take half a gill at night as a perspirant, and keep well covered.

Remedy for Yellow Fever.—In the incipient stages of yellow fever, a teaspoonful of pulverized charcoal taken three times a day in a glass of water will effect a cure. And where it is prevailing as an epidemic, by taking the charcoal in the above manner it will act as a preventive.

To Destroy Stomach Worms.—Turpentine taken in doses from ten drops for a child of three years of age, to a dessert spoonful, according to the age of the person, taken in the morning fasting, next day an ordinary dose of rhubarb, the turpentine and rhubarb to be thus taken alternately for three days each will destroy stomach worms. During the time of taking the turpentine and rhubarb it is necessary to avoid liquids of all kind as much as possible, and also abstain from eating greasy food.

To Cure attacks of Cramp.—Persons when attacked with cramp, whether in the feet, legs, stomach, or any other part will obtain immediate relief by holding in the hand a stick of rolled brimstone, when it comes on. At such time the brimstone crackles and emits an offensive odor, which is not the case unless the cramp is present. If the attack is severe, the brimstone as soon as *touched* breaks into pieces; after the same piece has been used several times, it loses its power and a new piece must be resorted to. To lay it in the palm of the hand is sufficient. It does not relieve from pain by applying it to the *part* affected with cramp.

Excellent Fumigator.—A few spoonsful of fresh ground coffee spread and exposed on a plate, and burned with a red hot iron is a safe, and pleasant fumigator. It will immediately destroy any foul air or smell existing in the room and has a tendency to promote a healthy atmosphere for sick persons to inhale.

Cooling Drink.—Cream of tartar, two ounces; two lemons peeled and squeezed, white sugar, four ounces; place in a stone jug or vessel that will not crack and four or six quarts of boiling water. Let cool and bottle for use. Instead of sugar, three tablespoonsful of raspberry vinegar and six ounces of honey can be used—it gives a richer flavor. The above is excellent in case of fever.

Cure for Corns.—Roast a clove of garlic on a bright coal or in hot ashes; appply it to the corn and tie on with a piece of cloth just before going to bed. Renew the application two or three times in the twenty four hours washing the foot on removing the old garlic. After a few days steady application the thick skin which forms the horny coating of the corn will disappear, and the corn itself, no matter how inveterate will be softened to such a degree that it can be loosened and wholly removed with the finger nail.

Another.—Dr. Hall in his Journal of Health says—"Never let anything harder than your finger nail touch a corn. The worst kind are controllable as follows;—Soak the feet in quite warm water for half an hour before going to bed, then rub on the corn with your finger, for several minutes, some common sweet oil. Do this every night and morning. Bind on the corn during the day two or three thicknesses of buck skin, with a hole in the centre to receive the corn. In less than a week, in ordinary cases, if the corn does not fall out, you can pinch it out with your finger nail."

Cure for Tooth-ache.—Effectual where there is no rheumatism; impalpably powdered alum, two drachms; nitrous spirits of ether, seven drachms; mix well and apply to the tooth.

Cure for the Sting of a Bee.—Instant relief can be obtained by pressing on the place stung with the tube of a key. This extracts the sting and relieves the pain, and the application of common spirits of hartshorn will immediately remove it.

Tonic for Indigestion.—Twenty grains each of rhubarb, gentian, cartoriate of iron, and Spanish liquorice; pour on them a pint of boiling water, and take of the cold infusion two tablespoonsful three times a day.

Lime water.—Quick lime, one part; water, sixteen parts; mix, and after a short interval, shake well; then let stand to settle and decant the clear liquid. This article should be both made and kept in a close vessel.

Smelling Salts.—Subcarbonate of ammonia, eight parts; put it in coarse powder into the bottle, and pour on it oil of lavender one part, keep well stopped.

Blood Purifier.—Take of white sugar, rice and starch each eight ounces; ground sarsaparilla six ounces, ground senna, four ounces; finely pulverize the whole separately, then mix them well and take as a dose a tablespoonful three times a day.

Instant Relief Liniment.—No family should be without this preparation. It is invaluable in the removal of pains of any kind. It must be well rubbed in, and but a small quantity used at a time as it is very penetrating. Where the pain is internal in addition to the outward application from twenty to thirty drops can be taken on some sugar: Alcohol, ninty-five per cent, half a gallon; cayaput oil and essence of capsicum, each half an ounce; of cloves and oil of sassafras each half one ounce; oil of cedar, one drachm.—Mix well and keep well stoppered.

Purgative Pills.—Colocinth, eight grains; calomel, three grains; rhubarb eight grains;—make into three pills.

For Purging, Teething and Bowel Complaint in Children.—Calcined magnesia, one scruple; powdered rhubarb, thirty grains; carbonate of soda, fifteen gains; essence of mint, five drops; water two ounces. Mix well and always shake up before giving. Dose, a teaspoonful every two hours until relieved.

Hooping Cough.—Half a scruple of cochineal, one scruple salt of tartar, one gill of pure water; mix well together and sweeten with loaf sugar. A teaspoonful three times a day is a dose for a child.

To Make the Hair Grow.—This preparation has met with most flattering success where every thing else has failed:—Tincture cantharides, two ounces; proof spirit, two ounces; mix well, then cold drawn castor oil, two and a half ounces; sweet oil, two and a half ounces; best French brandy, two ounces; add a few drops of bergamot. Mix the whole well and apply to the head daily.

Golden Ointment, for Piles, Sores, &c.—Clear white lard one pound; brown beeswax, eight ounces; camphor, laudanum and areganum each one ounce; alcohol, five ounces. Melt the lard, beeswax and camphor and then add in the other ingredients whilst milk warm. Mix well and preserve in tin boxes. Apply three times a day.

Chilblain Ointment.—Ointment of nitrate of mercury, one ounce; camphor, one drachm; oil of turpentine, two drachms; oil of olives, four drachms; mix well together, and apply by gentle friction two or three times a day.

Cough Mixture.—Dose a teaspoonful in a little warm tea whenever the cough is troublesome. Tincture of tolu, a quarter of an ounce; paregoric elixir and tincture of squills, each half an ounce; syrup of white poppies, one ounce. Mix well.

2.—As a draught, to be taken in a little warm tea at night on going to bed—syrup of poppies, one dessert spoonful, of antimonial wine twenty drops;—this is for a single dose.

A Fistula Specific.—Sulphate zinc one ounce; sulphate copper one ounce; best, gunpowder one ounce; warm water one quart.

Eau de Cologne.—Oil of bergamot, one ounce; oil of cedar, one ounce; oil of orange peel one ounce; oil of lemon peel one ounce; oil of orange flowers one ounce; oil rosemary fifty drops; camphor, six grains; spirits of wine sixty degrees above proof, three quarts. Shake well about fifteen minutes and then let stand a fortnight without stirring; filter and put in eau de cologne bottles.

Fever and Ague Mixture.—Peruvian bark, two ounces; sal tartar or salts of wormwood (either) twenty grains; snake root, twelve drachms; alcohol, eight ounces; water, eight ounces. Digest for twenty-four hours, shaking occasionally. Dose from a tablespoonful to a wine-glassful three times a day.

Disinfecting Fluid.—Mix one half of a pound of chloride of lime, and one quarter of an ounce of sulphuric acid in one gallon of water. Shake well before using. This solution sprinkled about yards, or rooms of houses will remove all foul or putrid smells, and is an excellent preventive to the spread of cholera and other contagious diseases.

Cure for Drunkenness.—Sulphate of iron, five grains; magnesia, ten grains; peppermint water, eleven drachms; spirit of nutmeg, one drachm. Take a teaspoonful twice a day for a few weeks or months for inveterate topers and it will effect a perfect cure.

Fluor Albus.—Take twenty drops of muriated tincture of iron three times a day—after the third day increase the dose to twenty-five drops; wash the teeth well after taking otherwise the enamel will be injured. This will cure most severe cases by taking it as above and with regularity.

Remedy for Chilblains.—Boil some turnips, and mash them until reduced to a pulp; put them into a tub or large basin, and put the feet into them, also as hot as can be borne, for a short time before going to bed. persevere in doing this for a few nights, and the itching and irritation of the chilblains will be cured; of course this must be before the chilblains are broken.

For the Croup.—Saturated tartar of antimony two grains; calomel one grain. Mix in a marble mortar with ten grains of fine sugar.

Olive Ointment, for sore, weak or inflamed Eyes.— Fresh unsalted butter, three ounces; white wax, half an ounce. Melt them together on a plate and then add, red precipitate two and a half drachms; camphor, one drachm; zinc, one drachm; olive oil, twelve drops. Mix all well in together until quite cold. Put a small bit on the eyes on going to bed at night and place over it a bandage wetted with cold slippery elm water.

Cough Syrup, and for Sore Lungs.— Take the outside shaggy bark of the sweet Hickory tree (white hickory) and put in a large pot with plenty of water; boil from six to eight hours to extract and concentrate. Add white sugar whilst yet warm, just enough to make sweetly palatable. Dose, a wine glassful three or four times a day according to the severity of the attack.

Diarrhea Mixture.— Tincture of ginger, three ounces; essence anise, essence of peppermint, and paregoric each half an ounce. Mix well. Take a teaspoonful every half hour until relieved, and two or three doses afterwards.

2.— Smartweed, two parts; tansy one part; ginseng, one part; make into a strong tea and drink about one third or half a teacupful every half hour or hour according to the severity of the attack. Thousands have used this with beneficial effect.

3.— A strong tea made from the bark of the Cashu fruit tree. A half a tumbler every hour until relieved. The Indians of Central and South America use this in preference to all other other remedies. It is effectual.

To remove Warts.— Rub the warts at night going to bed with the following ointment—Nitrate mercurial ointment, one drachm; arsenical powder, one grain. It will effect a safe and speedy cure of them.

Severe Dysentry.— Four grains of Dover's powders every two hours until relieved. Give also one or more ounces of either Gum arabic, linseed or starch water, with a few drops of laudanum.

2.— Take a tumbler of cold water and thicken with flour to the consistency of cream, and drink it. Repeat several times during the day and as often as thirsty.

3.— Take a teacup half full of vinegar and dissolve in it as much salt as it will bear keeping the salt a little in excess. Add boiling water until the cup is two thirds full. Skim it and let cool, then bottle down for use. Dose, tablespoonful three times a day.

Suspended Animation.—In cases where a body is found in a suspended state, and life is seemingly extinct, the chief remedy consists in cupping the temples or opening the jugular vein, and so relieving the head of the blood which accumulates in its superficial veins in consequence of the ligature. Where the body is cold, from having been long suspended, friction, and the other means used for restoring the animal heat in drowned persons, should be likewise resorted to. Electricity or galvanism may also be of service.

For a swollen Face arising from Toothache.—Get a poppyhead, and boil it in about a pint of water, and bathe the face with it, as hot as you can bear it, twice a day; the swelling will go down in two or three days.

Chloride of Lime left standing in an open vessel will keep places and rooms sweet, that are liable to be disagreeable to the smell.

Healing Ointment for Wounds.—Take a quarter ounce of white wax, and a half an ounce of spermaceti, and put them in a small basin, with two ounces of almond oil. Place the basin beside the fire till the ingredients are dissolved; when cold the ointment is ready for use.

Remedy for Deafness.—Cleanse the ear out thoroughly by means of a pledget of lint or cotton with warm water; afterwards soak a piece of cotton in some glycerine, which insert in the ear; after a few applications you will find relief. Glycerine is the sugar of oil.

Cure for Cold Feet.—Almost any one may protect themselves from chilled feet in walking who insert horsehair with the soles of their stockings after the manner of running heels.

Low Spirits.—The best remdey is one teaspoonful of spirits of lavender, and drops of spirits of hartshorn in half a wine glassful of cold water.

Bilious Powder.—Potophelia, two grains; sectarine aloes, half a grain; cream of tartar a teaspoonful. Mix well. One dose.

Foul Stomach or derangement of the Liver.—Soda, rhubarb, and pulverized peppermint each one ounce. Mix well. Take a teaspoonful every morning for three successive mornings, repose for three and again repeat until relieved.

Boils.—Boils and their kindred symptoms of inflamation may be arrested by creosote—it is an effectual local remedy, but if a core has formed the only remedy is its riddance by the poultice.

Cancer.—The efficacy of figs in hastening the absorption of inflamatory particles in a cancerous sore is indisputable. Raw bruised ripe, cold cranberries are also an excellent application. A confirmed cancer may be taken out without using the knife by a plaster of arsenic covered with cobweb, and properly protected. Keep it on and time will take it out.

Chapped Hands.—Five grains of bismuth thoroughly incorporated with an ounce of simple cerate is a speedy cure.

Cure for Felons.—As soon as the parts begin to swell get the tincture of lobelia, and wrap the affected part with a cloth saturated thoroughly with the tincture, and the felon is dead.

Mixture to Restore the Appetite.—Gentian root sliced, quarter of an ounce; fresh orange and lemon peel, each one ounce; tincture of rhubarb one ounce; compound tincture of cardamons half an ounce; spirits of red lavender, quarter of an ounce; boiling water one pint. Pour the water on the gentian and peels, and macerate for two hours; strain, and add the other ingredients; and if it be wanted very clear, it may be filtered through blotting paper; lastly, add two ounces of lump sugar. Dose. A small wine-glassful early in the morning or shortly before dinner.

A cure for Blistered Feet.—Rub the feet, at going to bed, with spirits mixed with tallow, dropped from a lighted candle into the palm of the hand. On the following morning no blisters will exist.

A good Gargle for sore Throat.—Tincture of myrrh, two drachms; common water, four ounces; vinegar, half-an-ounce. Mix.

Remedy for a Sprain.—Take camphorated spirit, common vinegar, spirits of turpentine of each, one ounce.

Deafness from Deficient Secretion of Wax.—Take oil of turpentine, half a drachm; olive oil, two drachms. Mix. Two drops to be introduced into the ear at bed-time

Bleeding at the Nose.—To stop this malady, which is sometimes alarming, it is recommended by Dr. Negrier (who has extensively tried it) simply to elevate the patient's arm.—The explanation is based upon physiological grounds; the greater force required to propel the blood through the vessels of the arm when elevated, causes the pressure upon the vessels of the head to be diminished by the increased action which takes place in the course of the brachial arteries (the arteries of the arms). If the theory be sound, both arms should be elevated.

Cholera and Bowel Complaints.—Rhubarb powder half a drachm; calcined magnesia one dram; paregoric elixir one ounce; peppermint water half a pint. Mix and shake up, and take two tablespoonsful every three hours till relieved.—The following is a better prescription for the same purpose:—Take of chalk mixture eight ounces: aromatic confection one dram; compound tincture of camphor three drachms; oil of carraway three or four drops. Mix. Take two tablespoonfuls every three hours, or oftener, if the pain and purging is urgent. A teaspoonful is a dose for young children, and one tablespoonful for those of ten or twelve years of age.

Ear Ache.—Sometimes ear ache is connected with chronic ulceration in the internal and external part of the ear, when injections of warm water and soap are advisable. In this case, there is sometimes a constant fœtid discharge, for which the following mixture is recommended:—Take of ox-gall, three drachms: balsam of Peru, one drachm Mix. A drop or two to be put into the ear with a little cotton.

For Shortness of Breath, or Difficult Breathing. Vitrolated spirits of ether, one ounce; camphor twelve grains. Make a solution, of which take a teaspoonful during the paroxysm. This is usually found to afford instantaneous relief in difficulty of breathing, depending on internal disease, and other causes, where the patient, from a very quick and laborious breathing, is obliged to be in an erect posture.

Sedative Ointment.—The violent local irritation which often follows the application of blisters to the surface of children, is a serious objection to their use, and requires that particular care be taken to lessen the liability of sloughing, &c. Should, however, the ulcer be irritable, the following ointment thickly spread on lint will be found serviceable;—Lime water, oil of almonds, of each, half an ounce; mix well together, then add prepared lard one ounce.

Seidlitz Powders.—Two drachms of tartarised soda and two scruples of bicarbonate of soda for the blue packet, and thirty grains of tartaric acid for the white papers.

Rose Lip Salve.—Eight ounces sweet almond oil, four ounces prepared mutton suet, half an ounce white wax, two ounces spermaceti, twenty drops otto; steep a small quantity of alkanet root in the oil, and strain before using. Melt the suet, wax, and spermaceti together, then add the coloric oil and otto.

A Valuable Receipt for the Tic Doloreux.—Take half a pint of rose water, add two teaspoonful of white vinegar, to form a lotion. Apply it to the part affected three or four times a day. It requires fresh linen and lotion each application; this will, in two or three days, gradually take the pain away.

[At least three hundred "infallible cures" for the doloreux have been discovered. The disease arises from such various causes, that no remedy can be relied upon. Carbonate of iron cures one; quinine another; upon a third these remedies have no effect. The remedy here suggested is safe and simple.]

To Cure the Sting of a Wasp.—Apply oil of tartar, or solution of potash, to the part affected, and it will give you instant ease.

To prevent Infection from Typhus Fever.—Six drachms of powdered salt-petre, six ounces oil of vitrol; mix them in a tea-cup by adding one drachm of the oil at a time. The cup to be placed during the preparation on the hearth, and to be stirred with a tobacco-pipe. The cup to be placed in different parts of the room.

An excellent Remedy for Sprains.—Put the white of an egg into a saucer, keep stirring it with a piece of alum about the size of a walnut until it becomes a thick jelly; apply a portion of it on a a piece of lint or tow large enough to cover the sprain, changing it for a fresh one as often as it feels warm or dry; the limb is to be kept in an horizontal position by placing it on a chair.

For Rheumatism, Bruises, &c.—One raw egg well beaten, half a pint of vinegar, one ounce of spirits of turpentine, a quarter of an ounce of spirits of wine, a quarter of an ounce of camphor. These ingredients to be beaten well together, then put in a bottle and shaken for ten minutes, after which, to be corked down tightly to exclude the air. In half an hour it is fit for use. Directions;—To be well rubbed in, two, three, or four times a day. For rheumatism in the head, to be rubbed at the back of the neck and behind the ears. This liniment can be made at home for twenty five cents; if not made at home, the druggist should be told to follow the prescription exactly.

Antidote Against Poison.—Hundreds of lives might be saved by a knowledge of this single receipt. A large teaspoonful of mustard mixed in a tumbler of warm water, and swallowed as soon as possible, acts as an instant emetic, sufficiently powerful to remove all that is lodged in the stomach.

Pains, in the Stomach.—Sudden spasmodic pains in the stomach may be safely relieved by swallowing one or two small wine-glassesful of rum. Where inflamation exists, it should not be given.

Treatment of Bruises.—The best application for a bruise, be it large or small, is moist warmth; therefore a warm bread and water poultice, or hot moist flannels, should be put on, as they supply the skin so that it yields to the pressure of the blood beneath, and thereby the pain is lessened. If the bruises be severe, and in the neighborhood of a joint, it is well to apply some leeches on grown-up persons, but not on young children. The poulticing or fomenting should be continued so long as the pain and swelling remain; and it may be sometimes necessary to put on the leeches a second, or even a third time. If the bruise be a joint, the poulticing will often require to be continued longer, on account of the stiffness which usually remains for some time; and when left off it is well to wrap up the joint in a soap plaster. If the bruised part be on the knee or ankle, walking should not be attempted till it can be performed without pain. A "black eye," is generally no more than a bruise of the eyelids, spreading more or less over the face, according to the size of the instrument by which it is inflicted. The great number of persons who get a black eye deserve it, and so for as I am aware there is no remedy save warm bathing, which will hasten its removal, but it is often a very tedious business.

To correct Offensive Breath.—Nothing is so good as concentrated solution of choloride of soda. From six to ten drops of it in a wine-glassful of pure spring water, taken immediately after the operations of the morning are completed, will instantly sweeten the breath, by disinfecting the stomach, which, far from being injured will be benefited by the medicine. If necessary, this may be repeated in the middle of the day. In some cases the odor arising from carious teeth is combined with that of the stomach. If the mouth be well rinsed with a teaspoonful of the solution of the chloride in a tumbler of water, the bad odor of the teeth will be removed.

Antidote for Rattlesnake Poison.—The following is an infallible cure for the poison of a rattlesnake bite;—Four grains of the iodate potash: two grains of corrosive sublimate: five drachms of bromine; Mix together, and keep the mixture in a glass stoppered vial, well secured. Ten drops of this mixture, diluted with a teaspoonful of brandy, constitute a dose: the quantity to be repeated, if necessary, according to the exigencies of the case.

Diptheria.—A kind of throat disease, which has recently made its appearance in the United States and Europe, and proved very fatal. It consists in the formation of a false peculiar membrane, the origin of which is somewhat obscure; it attacks the tonsils, part of the tongue the pharynx, the epiglottis, the larynx, and the trachea: causing suffocation by stopping the air passage. It has occurred in localities where so malignant and fatal a form of disease could scarcely have been looked for: where the surrounding country was open and beautiful, and the soil dry, and the persons attacked were not among the most wretched and ill-fed. Its character is peculiarly treacherous and insidious, being first so slight as to be scarcely noticeable. By the time medical advice is sought, the peculiar exudation has reached the air passages, and death shortly ensues often by syncope, when the case appears to be progressing favorably. Hitherto, medical measures have been attended with but little success; the best is unquestionably the application of strong caustic to the throat at the earliest possible period; hydrochloric acid is recommended; this appears to stop the progress of the false membrane; but when this has reached the trachea, and bronchia there is little hope for the patient. It is believed by some that this disease is to the respiratory membrane what thrush is to the intestinal, having a confervid origin, and that the effect of the poison, when absorbed is in its elimination, to set up an æstnenic inflamation, like croup. Hence, the employment of counter irritation, leeches to the trachea, chlorine gargles, with the administration of port wine, quinine, and chlorine of potash, would seem to be the most rational mode of treatment, Some advocate the employment of emetics, and some tracheomy.

Disguising taste of Medicines.—Dr. Polli recommends a means, founded on the physiological fact that a strong impression on the nerves, whether of vision, hearing, or taste, renders that which follows less perceptible. Instead of applying to the mouth, therefore, agreeable substances after swallowing nauseous medicines, we should prepare it before, in order that the taste of the medicine may not be perceived. Aromatic substances, chewed just before, as orange or lemon peel, &c., effectually prevent castor oil, &c., being tasted. In preparing the mouth for bitters, licquorice is the only sweet that should be used, the others producing a peculiarly disagreeable compound taste.

Dental Neuralgia.—Acetate of morphia one and a half grains, acetic acid two drops, and eau de Cologne two drachms. A little of this mixture placed in the ear in cotton, in the ear of the same side as that in which the dental neuralgia prevails, is of remarkably efficacy.

Naptha in Ringworm.—Dr. Chappelle says he has found the following procedure the most successful of any that he has tried ;—The hairs are to be cut short, the creamy fluid let out of the pustules, and the crusts removed by linseed poultices. The denuded surface is then to be covered with a thin layer of oil of naphtha, over which a flannel compress is to be placed, the whole being secured by an oil-silk cap. The application is to be renewed twice a day, first well washing the parts with soap and water; and the surface of the scalp is to be carefully searched, in order to detect any small favous pustules that may have appeared. These must be pricked with a pin, the matter removed, and the surface covered with the oil. This evolution of pustules is successive, so that the hair must be kept short in the vicinity, that their advent may be watched. This application secures the rapid absorption of the pustules; but when the scalp is too tender to bear it, it should be mixed with other less irritating oils, of which the huile de cade (empyreumatic oil of juniper) is one of the best.

Variola ; or,

SMALL POX.—This disease comes on with the usual symptoms of inflammatory fever. About the third day, red spots, resembling flea bites, make their appearance on the face and head, and gradually extend over the whole body. About the fifth day small circular vesicles, depressed in the centre, surrounded by an areola, and containing a colorless fluid, being to form, when the feverish symptoms abate; about the the sixth day the throat becomes sore; about the eighth day the face is swollen, and about the eleventh day the pustules acquire the size of pea, and cease to enlarge, the matter which they contain becomes opaque and yellow, a dark central spot forms on each, the swelling of the face subsides, and secondary symptons of fever come on; the pustules become rough, break and scab over, and a dark spot remains for some days, often followed by permanent indentation. At the end of the sixteenth or eighteenth day, the symptoms usually disappear. In the confluent smallpox, the pustules caolesce, the eruption is irregular in its progress, and the inflammatory symptoms are more severe. The treatment of ordinary cases of smallpox resembles that mentioned above for chickenpox. When great irritability exists, small doses of morphia, opium, or camphor, may be administered, and obstinate vomiting arrested by effervescing saline draughts. The application on the third day of a mask formed of thick muslin, covered with mercurial ointment, and having holes cut out for the nostrils, eyes, and mouth, will effectually prevent "pitting." Gold leaf is also applied for the same purpose.

CHICKEN POX.—An eruptive skin disease, consisting of smooth vesicles of various sizes, which afterwards become white and straw colored, and about the fourth day break and scale off. In hot weather the discharge sometimes becomes purulent, and at others the eruption is attended with considerable fever. The treatment consists in the adoption of a light vegetable diet, and in the administration of mild aperients and cooling drinks.

COW POX.—This disease was proposed as a substitute and preventive of smallpox, Dr. Jenner in 1798. The success which has followed its artificial production has nearly led to the extinction of smallpox in England. The process of vaccination is similar to that of inocculation for the smallpox, before noticed. About the third day the puncture usually becomes red and elevated, and continues to enlarge and become vesicular, until at about the 8th or 9th day, it is at its height, and the vesicle is surrounded with a florid areola. About the 11th or 12th day these symptoms decline; the centre of the pustule becomes brown, and a dark scale gradually forms and separates, leaving the arm as heretofore. This disease seldom requires medical treatment; but should febrile symptoms come on, an aperient may be given.

CARE OF SLEEPING APARTMENTS.—It is of great importance that sleeping rooms should be frequently and thoroughly ventilated. There are many of the European practices, which in this particular, are superior to our own. In Italy, for example, it is the custom to take care that a separation of all the cloths that have been used during sleep be effected, and thus separately suspended from the windows, so as to get the benefit of free and full exposure to the purifying influence of the atmosphere. Many are the contrivances of modern ingenuity for the purpose of insuring an unobstructed circulation of air in rooms—but where there is a door, and a window, and a chimney-place, all these contriyances may be dispensed with. Let the windows of the bed room, however, be so constructed, as that they shall be capable of being drawn down as well as pushed up; and let it always be recollected, that no effectual ventilation can be accomplished without this plan of admitting condensed and purer, and giving exit to lighter and impurer atmospheric matter A good mode of airing bed-rooms, in which persons are constantly sleeping, is that of pumping them, as it is called; or waving the door backwards and forwards for some minutes together, so as by agitation to favor the universal diffusion of the admitted air.

AVOID EXTREMES OF HEAT AND COLD.—The extremes of hot and cold are unfavorable to constant industry, but much may be done by intellectual beings to obviate the tendencies of climate. A great deal of time is wasted in winter, in hovering over the fire and talking of the cold: in delaying to set about a piece of work, because it requires one to leave a warm room. But a little resolution will remedy all this. You can make yourselves as comfortable by taking your work or book, and sitting at a moderate distance from the fire, as by hanging idly over it; and if you run off briskly after what you need, the exercise will warm you better than the parlor fire.

ATTENTION TO HEALTH IN YOUTH. The most precarious period of life is said to vary from the ages of ten to twenty-one years, when the frame is most prone to deformity; but particularly from ten to fifteen, when the body is in its active state of growth. The most frequent cause of deformity at this most dangerous period is the over-exercise of the mind, to the neglect of the body, augmented in the female sex by the baneful use of stays. "Many are the children," says a physician, "who have been born healthy and robust, the pride and hope of fond parents, having the rosy hue of health upon the cheek, the sparkling eye and laughing mouth; happiness and enjoyment, the certain attendants upon robust health, plainly marked upon their countenances; the voice, the active romping motion of the body, confirm it; but wait a little while, until the approach of the assidious age, the period when the body is at its highest progress of upward growth, the muscular fibres being still lax, the bones comparatively soft; when the powers of the system are so severely tried, nature requiring to be supported by the most careful watching and utmost aid of science, in supplying and regulating the quality and quantity of air, food and exercise, so requisite at this period; whereas, instead of such judicious attention, we often find that the too fond parent, ever and wholly absorbed with the mental education of his offspring, to the entire neglect, and even sacrifice of his bodily frame, at this most dangerous stage of his life, often fancies that it is the best age for mental training and activity; consequently, taxes both the mind and body of the youth to the utmost, by forcing him to employ all the hours of the day in study."

RULES FOR A SICK ROOM:—1. A sick room should be kept very sweet and airy; there should never be a close smell in it; if the weather is warm enough, let the the door or window be open; if cold, let there be a small fire; the chimney should never be stopped up.

2. It should be made rather dark, by a blind over the window; but bed-curtains should not be drawn close.

3. It should be very clean; the floor should be wiped over with a damp cloth every day; all chamber-vessels should be removed as soon as used, and if there is any bad smell, a little *blacking liquid* should be put into them, and be sprinkled on the floor.

4. The medicine should be kept in one particular place; all bottles, cups, &c., that are done with, should be taken away at once.

5. The room should also be very quiet; there should be no talking or gossiping; one or two people at the most, besides the invalid, are quite enough to be there at a time; more people make it close and noisy, and disturb the sick. Neighbors should not be too anxious to see the sick person unless they can do some good.

6. The sick person's face and hands and feet should be often washed with warm water and soap, and the mouth be rinsed with vinegar and water; the hair should be cut rather short, and be combed every day.

7. Never give spirits unless ordered by the physician; sick people always feel weak, but yet such things given at a wrong time would only make them weaker.

Tea and its Adulterations.

A very considerable amount of skill and ingenuity are displayed, as we shall hereafter perceive, both at home and abroad, in the adulteration of tea, as well as in the manufacture of spurious articles in imitation of it.

We shall first treat of black tea and its adulterations. The chief adulterations to which black tea is subject, consist in the use of leaves other than those of tea; in the re-preparation of exhausted tea-leaves; and in the employment of substances, either for the purpose of imparting color and astringency to the infusion, or to glaze and face the surface of the dried leaves so that they present an improved appearance to the eye.

It has been repeatedly ascertained that the leaves of various American plants are sometimes used in our country in the adulteration of tea. The leaves of the following species have been detected, from time to time, in samples of American fabrication: beech, elm, horse-chestnut, plane, bastard-plane, fancy oak, willow, poplar, hawthorn, and sloe. The leaves in general are not used whole; but when dried are broken into small pieces, and usually mixed with a paste made of gum and catechu: afterwards they are ground and reduced to powder, which, when colored with rose-pink, is mixed with inferior descriptions of black tea, resembling in this state tea-dust.

Before the observer is in a position to detect the presence of foreign leaves in tea, he must first acquaint himself with the character of tea, and other leaves used to mix with tea. Thus, he must note well the size and form of the leaves, the conformation of the edges; but, especially, the arrangement and distribution of the bundles of woody fibre, veins as they are commonly termed.

By the microscope, it is in many cases even possible to distinguish the leaves of different plants when ground to a dust-like powder, so that they may be thus detected when substituted for tea-dust.

Catechu, or *Terra Japonica*, which consists principally of tannin, is sometimes had rescourse to, when exhausted tea-leaves are used, or when other leaves than those of tea are employed. It imparts increased astringency and color to infusions made from such leaves, and supplies the place of the tannin abstracted from them. The leaves of the sloe also contain a considerable quantity of tannin and are, therefore, astringent; and it is on this account that they, are so frequently employed in the adulteration of tea.

In this place may be noticed two articles occasionally met with and employed as substitutes for tea. The first of these is La Veno Bono;—

La Veno Bono consists of a coarse powder of a reddish-brown color, intermixed with small fragments of sumach leaf. To the taste, the powder is astringent and bitter, and, on analysis, is ascertained to be coarsely-powdered catechu. Now catechu, as already stated, consists principally of tannin, which, from its astringent action, would be extremely apt, when taken in the quantity in which it exists in *La Veno Bono* to produce constipation, with the manifold evils which result from such a condition.

The second article is *Chinese Botanical Powder;* or *Chinese Economist*.

This preparation appears to be got up in imitation of *La Veno Bono*, and is sold for the same purpose as that article, viz. to mix with tea.

It consists of a coarse powder of a reddish-brown color, and astringent taste, and is made up of a mixture of *catechu and wheat flour*, the latter ingredient being added to reduce the strength of the catechu.

The great difficulty experienced in the re-preparation of exhausted tea-leaves, is to cause them to resume the twisted form imparted by the Chinese method of rolling and drying the leaves. For this purpose, the leaves are steeped in a strong solution of gum; this in drying, occasions the contraction of the leaves, and causes them to assume, to a certain extent only, their original appearance; the solution at the time imparting a polished surface to the leaves. The forms of the greater number of the leaves after this preparation are still, however, very different from those of tea as originally prepared; the leaves are more broken and agglutinated into small flattened or rounded masses. This circumstance, together with the shining appearance of the leaves, are sufficient to enable the experienced eye to detect samples of tea manufactured from exhausted leaves, even when mixed with a proportion of unused tea.

It is not black tea only which is manufactured from exhausted tea-leaves, but also green tea, the leaves undergoing the same preparatory process of gumming and drying; and, although in the case of green tea the difficulty of detection apart from chemical analysis is increased, yet the accurate observation of the form of the leaves is, in many cases, sufficient for the discovery even of this fraud.

A second substance is *Sulphate of iron*. When a solution of sulphate of iron is brought in contact with a solution of tannin, (which contains a large amount of tannin), the liquid becomes deeply colored, indeed almost black. Of this fact the fabricators of spurious tea are well aware, for they avail themselves of it, and frequently add to the gum-water a proportion of sulphate of iron.

Again; *Rose-pink* is occasionally used by adulterators, to give a color and bloom to the surface of black tea fabricated from exhausted tea-leaves; it is not, however, very frequently had recourse to. Rose-pink consists of the coloring matter of logwood in combination with carbonate of lime.

Other substances frequently used for blooming the surface of the teas, both black and green, especially the latter, are *Soapstone*, *China-clay*, and *Talc*, or *Mica*, which impart a pearly lustre to the teas.

Again: *Indigo* is employed by the Chinese in dressing the surface of certain descriptions of black tea; although this article is more commonly used in the manufacture of spurious green teas; this is a vegetable substance, and is possessed of active medical properties.

The last substance detected as being occasionally employed, is *Turmeric* powder; this coloring matter, however, like the former, is much more commonly used for the painting of green teas.

We now come to treat of the adulteration of Green Tea.

Of the analyses of thirty-two samples of the various kinds of green teas, in the state in which they are imported, (these analyses including samples of the many varieties of *Twankay*, *Hyson*, *Gunpowder*, and *Imperial*), the following are the conclusions arrived at:
—First. That the whole of the thirty-two were adulterated. Second.

That five of the samples called Gunpowder, consisted of *Lie Tea*, that is, of tea-dust and sand, made up with rice-water. Third. That one of the samples was composed of paddy husk, and other substances. Fourth. That another sample was composed chiefly of *Lie Tea*, made up in parts with other leaves than those of tea. Fifth. That another sample consisted principally of *Lie Tea*. Sixth. That the whole of the samples were artificially glazed or colored. Seventh. That this glazing or coloring consisted of two, and, in some cases, three substances—a blue, a yellow, and a white. The blue coloring matter was present in all the samples; and in twenty-eight, it was ascertained to be Prussian blue, and in the other two indigo; the yellow was detected in seventeen samples, and consisted in all instances of *Turmeric powder;* the white was observed in twenty-nine samples, and was in general found to be *China-clay, or kaolin.* That a second yellow substance is occasionally employed by the Chinese, mixed with turmeric powder, is evident from the analysis of the yellow dye given in the last report. Eighth. That in no one of the samples was a single leaf possessed of a green color, not produced by artificial means, detected from strong fact, notwithstanding a certain amount of evidence to the contrary, we are almost led to conclude that there is really no such thing as a "genuine green tea" of the color ordinarily supposed to be characteristic of that kind of tea. The leaves, when deprived of their artificial coating, have invariably presented different shades of yellow, olive, brown, and even black.

In addition, the gunpowders, in most cases, were further adulterated by admixture with various proportions of green *Lie Tea*, some of them consisting even entirely of this almost worthless substance. But the adulterations of tea by the Chinese, are not limited to the painting of the surface of the leaves, and to the manufacture of *Lie Tea*; for there is no question but that the Chinese do even adulterate some inferior descriptions of green Gunpowder tea, with the leaves of plants other than those of tea.

Lie Tea may be very readily distinguished by the circumstance, that when the little pellets are moistened, they easily fall to pieces under the pressure of a knife, the presence of sand being revealed by the well-known gritty feeling.

CHAPTER VII.

Pyrotechny.

THE art of making fireworks. "The three prime materials of this art are, nitre, sulphur, and charcoal, along with filings of iron, steel, copper, zinc, resin, camphor, lycopodium, &c. Gunpowder is used either in grain, half-crushed, or finely ground, for different purposes. The longer the iron filings, the brighter the red and white spots they give; those being preferred which are made with a coarse file, and quite free from rust. Steel filings and cast-iron borings contain carbon, and afford a more brilliant fire, with wavy radiations. Copper filings give a greenish tint to flame; those of zinc, a fine blue color; the sulphuret of antimony gives a less greenish blue than zinc, but with much smoke; amber affords a yellow fire, as well as colophony, (rosin,) and common salt; but the last must be dry. Lampblack produces a very red color with gunpowder, and a pink one with nitre in excess; it serves for making golden showers." When lightly mixed with gunpowder and put into cases, it throws out small stars resembling the rowel of a spur; this composition has hence been called "spur fire." "The yellow sand, or glistening mica, communicates to fireworks golden radiations. Verdigris imparts a pale green; sulphate of copper and sal ammoniac give a palm-tree green. Camphor yields a very white flame and aromatic fumes, which mask the bad smell of other substances. Benzoin and storax are used also on account of their agreeable odor. Lycopodium burns with a rose color and a magnificent flame; but it is principally employed in theatres to represent lightning, or to charge the torch of a fury." Dict. of Arts, Manuf., and Mines.)—Our space will only permit a brief notice of the process of making, and the composition for rockets and colored fires.

RECEIPTS.

BLUE FIRE, No. 1—Nitre, two parts; sulphur, three parts; zinc, three parts; pulverized gunpowder, four parts. Mix with care.

2.—English blue ashes, twelve parts; sulphur, ten parts; chlorate of potash, twenty-four parts. Mix well.

BENGAL FLAMES.—Nitre, seven parts; sulphur, two parts, antimony, one part. Mix well and press the composition into earthen tubes or porringers and place a slow match on the surface to ignite when necessary.

BLUE FLAMES.—Gunpowder, one part; king's yellow, one part; sulphur vivium, two parts; crude antimony powdered, four parts; nitrate of potash, fourteen parts; mix well and sift through lawn.

COMMON WHITE FIRE.—Nitre, fifty parts; sulphur, fourteen parts; sulphuret of antimony, eight parts. Mix well.

DETONATING POWDER.—Rub two grains of chlorate of potash into powder in a mortar; add a grain of sulphur. Mix them well but very gently. By pressing anything forcibly upon this powder a loud explosion will follow.

FRENCH WHITE FIRE.—Nitre, sixteen parts; sulphur, eight parts; antimony, four parts; mix well.

GREEK FIRE.—Asphaltum, thirty parts; sulphur, twenty eight parts; nitre forty-two parts. Mix well.

GREEN FIRE, No. 1—Nitrate of baryta, twenty-six parts; sulphur, eleven parts; chlorate of potash, eleven parts. Mix well.

2.—Nitre, sixteen parts; sulphur, six parts; verdigris, six parts; antimony, six parts. Mix well.

RED FIRE, No. 1.—Sulphuret of antimony, four parts; chlorate of potash, five parts; flowers of sulphur, thirteen parts; nitrate of strontian, forty parts. Mix well.

2.—Nitrate of strontian calcined, seventy-five parts; sulphur, twenty parts; pulverized charcoal, three parts; sulphur of antimony, three parts; chlorate of potash, twenty parts. Mix well.

The strontian can be calcined in any iron or earthenware vessel, over a fire without flame, care being taken that no particle falls into the fire.

The chlorate of potash must always be prepared with great care. It must be rubbed slowly and in very small quantities, in a mortar, until the whole is reduced to a very fine powder; then mix it carefully with one of the other ingredients using a bit of card or pasteboard for the purpose; then add the other ingredients one by one mixing in the same manner until the whole is prepared. These precautions must be used in *every case* where the chlorate of potash is used.

THIS CLASS OF FIRES, are always put up in small cylindrical boxes made of thin pasteboard or thick drawing paper from three to four inches high. The bottom is closed with a round piece pasted carefully in and about an inch of finely powdered dry clay is first put in and then the ingredients for the fire up to the top, which is closed with another round piece similar to the one at the bottom. When required for use a small hole is perforated in the top with a round bit of wood, and therein is inserted a slow match, which is to be ignited when you wish to burn the fire. The slow match is made by dipping brown paper into a strong solution of nitre and rain water, letting the water dissolve all it possibly can of the nitre. Then dry the paper carefully and thoroughly in the sun. Another kind of slow match is made by dissolving gunpowder in water and steeping brown paper or pack thread in it and afterwards claying it as above. This is more dangerous however, as it ignites more easily and burns with greater rapidity.

YELLOW FIRE.—Nitre, sixteen parts; sulphur, eight parts; amber, eight parts. Mix well.

EXPLOSIVE VOLCANO.—Take a tin cylinder closed at the bottom, from one to three inches in diameter and pack in as close as possible as many ounces of gunpowder as you wish power to the explosion, placing on top a well forced in wad of slow match. Make a volcanic cone of gunpowder wetted and mixed to the proper consistency with saturated solution of nitre and water. [When well mixed the powder is barely damped through but adheres together in a lump.] Place your cylinder in the ground near to its top, and fill in with the wetted gunpowder, and place thereon the cone. Ignite with a slow match. If well made it will resemble the eruption of a volcano on a small scale with its accompanying explosion.

FOUNTAIN OF FIRE.—To six ounces of water in an earthen basin, add gradually one ounce of sulphuric acid, then three quarters of an ounce of granulated zinc, and a few pieces of phosphorus the size of a pea. Bubbles of gas will be immediately generated, which, on coming to the surface take fire, and in a short time make the entire surface of the liquid illuminated, whilst fire balls and jets of fire dart from the bottom with rapidity.

TO MELT A COIN IN A NUTSHELL.—Rub together three parts of nitre, one part sulphur and one of dry sawdust, and press down and half fill a walnut shell with it; place in it a small rolled up coin of either silver or copper, and then fill up the shell with the powder, pressing down tightly; ignite, and when it has burned out, the coin will be melted into a mass.

CRIMSON FIRE.—Chlorate of potash four and a half parts; nitrate of strontia, sixty-seven and a half parts; alder or willow charcoal five and three quarter parts; sulphur twenty and a half parts; mix and press lightly into pasteboard tubes and ignite with a slow match.

CRIMSON STARS.—Chlorate of potash, seventeen and a quarter parts; sulphur, eighteen parts; nitrate of strontia, fifty-five parts; charcoal, four and a half parts; sulphuret of antimony, five and a half parts; mix, load into tubes and prime with a slow match.

LILAC FIRES.—Lamp-black, realger and nitre, each one part; sulphur, two parts; chlorate of potash, five parts; fused nitrate of strontia, sixteen parts; mix well..

BRILLIANT STARS FOR ROCKETS.—Nitre, fifty two and a half parts; sulphur and block antimony, of each thirteen parts; powder well, mix, and make a stiff paste with one and a half parts of isinglass dissolved in vinegar, six and a half parts, and spirits of wine, thirteen parts; form into small pieces and whilst moist roll them in meal gunpowder.

WHITE STARS FOR ROCKETS.—Nitre, sixteen parts; sulphur, seven parts; gunpowder, four parts; make a paste and prepare as for Brilliant Stars.

GOLDEN RAIN.—Nitre and gunpowder, each sixteen parts; sulphur, ten parts; charcoal, four parts; lampblack, two parts; mix and pack into small tubes. Ignite with slow match.

CHAPTER VIII.

Miscellaneous.

IF variety is the spice of life, as nature and common sense seem to admit, such a work as the present would not be complete without, adding a spicy chapter of miscellanea that shall add instruction to the many subjects here embraced, in the form of a few which claim our attention but refuse classification. Many are the hints that may be given in this way, and many are the subjects that admit of no other way, of rendering them to the popular mind—we have therefore opened our storehouse of disconnected facts and give out of our abundance the following.

Duties of Young Ladies to their Associates.

The importance of virtuous associates on the youthful mind is universally admitted. The human heart was made for friendship. Still, in the selection of intimates among her own sex, a young lady needs to be cautious. Imperfections there will be, even in those cases where a rare combination of excellent qualities exists. Elevation of character, frankness of disposition, firmness of principle, sterling virtue, and a warm heart, are the characteristics to be sought in a friend. Congeniality of taste, pursuits, intellectual pleasures and religious principle, constitute other essential pre-requisites. "Judge before friendship; then confide till death."

When you have found those of congenial spirit, strive to be mutually and greatly beneficial to each other. Kindly point out each other's imperfections; share each other's joys and sorrows; exchange books, and make the knowledge of one common to both. When you meet, discuss not character, but useful and entertaining topics.—When absent, regularly correspond, making judicious criticisms where manifest defects of composition, or errors of sentiment require.

A young lady's sense of propriety will lead her as a matter of course to treat civilly those of the other sex with whom she comes in contact. As the receiving of special attentions from young men is not to be regarded as a duty, but it is to be left entirely optional, a few suggestions on this topic will suffice. Indeed, it is thought by the more judicious that all such attentions had better be discouraged till the lady has arrived at the age of twenty. The less the youthful mind dwells upon lovers and matrimony, the better. In deciding who are worthy of special regard remember that "Around the mind of every one is a sphere of its own quality, as odour surrounds a flower; and this quality is perceived in attraction and repulsion by all who are similar or dissimilar." To the first impressions of character, therefore a young lady may pay some regard. Then, if she has brothers, their opinions should have weight in the decision. Especially should parents be consulted in the matter.

EARLIEST INTELLECTUAL EDUCATION OF CHILDREN.—Cultivate, by exercise, the five senses of *seeing, hearing, touching, smelling, tasting.* Teach the child to observe forms, sizes, weights, colors, arrangements and numbers. Practice all a child's knowing faculties on objects,—feathers, ribbons, buttons, pictures of animals, &c. Practice distinct articulation. If at four years of age a child has any defect, it ought to be systematically taught to pronounce correctly. Let a child put its toy to another than the intended use, if it does not destroy it; this exercises invention. Encourage construction, and furnish the materials, leaving ingenuity to work. Accustom the child to find its own amusement. It is the most unprofitable slavery to be constantly finding amusement for it. Remember that children love stories,—the simpler the better: and delight to have them told again and again. Always give them a moral turn and character. Be sparing of the marvellous, exclude the terrible and horrible, and utterly proscribe all ghost and witch stories. Accustom children to reptiles, insects, &c.; and prevent the foolish fear of those creatures which is often found in adults, and leads to the constant and most unnecessary destruction of them. Induce a child to give attention, by presenting objects, and giving narratives which interest it. Do not repeat that it must give attention. Avoid employing female servants as nurses who possess coarse habits and sentiment, or whose mode of speaking is coarse or indelicate. No difference need at first be made between the rearing and training of male and female infants. Allow female children as they grow up, to amuse themselves with dolls, and in a similar manner encourage and regulate the amusements of the boys. Many of these observations may appear trivial, but in most cases they form the basis of character in after life. It is highly important that we should set a value on some apparent trifles, especially in the rearing of children; for it is by these means their attention is directed to more serious objects.

DIRECTIONS FOR CLEANING SILKS AND SATINS.—White silk or satin may be cleaned thus:—Dissolve some of the best curd soap in boiling water, and when the solution is as hot as the hand can bear, pass the silk through it thoroughly, handling it gently not to injure the texture. If there are any spots, these may be rubbed carefully till they disappear. The article must then be rinsed in lukewarm water, and dried by stretching it out with pins. If satin, the glossy or bright side must be well brushed with a clothes-brush the way of the nap, till it shines ; it may then be calendered ; or it may be finished by dipping a soft sponge in a little isinglass dissolved in boiling water, and rubbing the wrong side of the satin, which must then be pinned out, and again brushed and dried Plain silks do not require brushing.

If the satin is not much soiled, the brightness may be restored by strewing on it some French chalk in powder, and then brushing it off with a hard brush ; if once is not sufficient the process may be repeated. When the silk is large, it may be laid smooth upon a board, and a little soap spread over the dirtiest parts ; then, having made a lather with fine white soap, this may be passed over the silk on one side with a brush, and then upon the other side. It must then be put into hot water, and afterwards rinsed in cold water ; it must next be dried, and smoothed on the right side with an iron not hot, or calendered.

If the white silks are flowered, the best method is to clean them by sifting on them some crumbs of stale bread, which must be rubbed on with the hands, and then thoroughly shaken and brushed off. If a very little powdered blue be mixed with the crumbs, it will be advantageous for some shades of white.

To Preserve Orange or Lemon Peel.—Cut the oranges or lemons in half, take out the pulp, put the peelings in strong salt and water to soak for three days; repeat this soaking three times; then put them on a sieve to dry; take one pound of loaf sugar, a quart of pure water put in the peelings and boil, skimming until quite clear; let them simmer until they become transparent then take out and dry them before the fire. Boil loaf sugar with just sufficient water to dissolve it, and whilst boiling put in the peelings, stirring continually until all the sugar is candied around them, then put them to dry either before the fire or in an oven, and when perfectly dry, put by for use.

To make paper Impervious to Water.—The following preparation for waterproofing paper intended for packages exposed to the weather is said to be recommended by Professor Muschamp, of Wurtemberg: Take twenty-four ounces of alum, and four ounces of white soap, and dissolve them in two pounds of water; in another vessel, dissolve two ounces of gum arabic, and six ounces of glue in the same quantity of water as the former, and add the two solutions together, which is now to be kept warm, and the paper intended to be made waterproof dipped into it, passed between rollers and dried; or, without the use of rollers, the paper may be suspended until it is perfectly dripped, and then dried. The alum, soap, glue, and gum form a kind of artificial leather, which protects the surface of the paper from the action of the water, and also renders it somewhat fireproof. Merely to convert paper into artificial leather, this would be a rather complicated process compared with the dipping of the paper in diluted oil of vitrol, and then washing it immediately with water and drying; but the Professor's method may, perhaps, render paper more impervious to water.

Tomato Sauce.—Take twelve large tomatoes, peel and cut them into two parts, placing the cut part upwards, sprinkle salt upon them. Let stand twelve hours, then squeeze, strain and add three small bruised crackers, a little pepper and a clove or two. Boil twenty minutes, keeping it well skimmed, then let cool, strain and bottle.

Egyptian Cream for the Hair.—Into three quarts of sweet oil put a quarter of a pound of alkanet root cut into small pieces; let them boil together ten minutes, then add to them three ounces of oil of jasmine, and one ounce of oil of lavender; strain the ingredients through a coarse cloth, taking care not to squeeze it. If required it can now be made thicker by adding to it a small quantity of fine hair powder, smoothly rubbed down with a small portion of oil.

How to loosen Glass Stoppers.—With a feather rub a drop or two of salad oil round the stopper close to the mouth of the bottle or decanter, and place before the fire at the distance of about a foot or eighteen inches, in which position the heat will cause the oil to spread downward between the neck and stopper. When it has grown warm, gently strike the stopper on one side and on the other, with any light wooden instrument, then try it with the hand. If it will not yet move, place it again before the fire adding another drop or two of oil. After a while strike as before, and by persevering in this process, however tightly the stopper may be fastened, it will at length become loosened.

Essence of Ginger.—Well bruised unbladed Jamaica ginger, four ounces; rectified spirits of wine, one pint; digest for a fortnight, press, filter and bottle and add five drops essence of Cayenne.

To restore Milk.—When milk has become turned by heat, it can be made sweet again and perfectly restored by mixing with it a small quantity of carbonate of magnesia.

Curious Facts.—If a tallow candle be placed in a gun, and shot at a door, it will go through without sustaining any injury; and if a musket ball be fired into water, it will not only rebound, but will be flattened as if fired against a solid substance. A musket may be fired through a pane of glass, making the hole the size of the ball, without cracking the glass; if suspended by a thread, it will make no difference, and the thread will not even vibrate. Cork, if sunk two hundred feet deep in the ocean, will not rise, on account of the pressure of the water. In the Arctic region, when the thermometer is below zero, persons can converse more than a mile distant. Dr. Jamieson asserts that he heard every word of a sermon at the distance of two miles.

To make hard water soft.—Dissolve two tablespoonsful of fresh quick lime in two and a quarter gallons of water. Stir this well into a barrel of hard water and let stand twenty-seven hours. It will then be soft.

Razors and hot Water.—It was long supposed that the effect of dipping a razor into hot water was to remove from its edge a kind of resinous substance, which was thought to injure its sharpness. Such, however, is not the real effect. The fine edge is given to all blades of steel by tempering them that is, heating them and plunging them into cold water. Now it has been proved by experiment, that the heat of two hundred and twelve degrees is the exact point at which razor edges are admirably tempered; and as the heat of boiling is two hundred and twelve degrees, by dipping a razor into it you, as it were, again temper or give a new edge to the razor.

Treatment of Bed-Sores.—M. Lecre, Physician to the Hotel Dieu of Laon (France), recommends tannate of lead to prevent bed-sores. He prepares it in the following manner: Oak bark, one ounce : water, eight ounces; boil down to four ounces, strain, and add liquor of the diacetate of lead in sufficient quantity until no more precipitate is thrown down; collect the latter, and spread a thick coating of it with the finger on the parts threatened with gangrene; the whole to be covered with a fine piece of linen. No eschar forms with this application, except in rare cases, when the wound, on the falling off of the eschar is to be dressed with the same tannate of lead, to which turpentine may be added.

Quinsy.—Those who suffer from this distressing malady will be thankful to hear of a simple and efficacious mode of relief, namely, an onion poultice. Bake or roast three or four large onions, or half-a-dozen smaller ones, till soft. Peel them quickly, and beat them flat with a rolling pin or glass bottle. Then put them directly into a thin muslin bag that will reach from ear to ear, and about three inches deep. Apply it speedily, and as warm as possible to the throat. Keep it on day and night, changing it when the strength of the onions appear exhausted, and substituting fresh ones. Flannel must be worn round the neck after the poultice is removed.

Convenient Method of Tracing.—Frame a square of glass of any convenient size; leaving the back open, that the glass may be seen on either side; hang it so that it may turn on a swivel, of the fashion of a looking glass for the dressing table but let the supporters be taller. Fix the frame horizontally; laying the drawing covered with tracing paper over the glass. The rays of light which play underneath will be increased by the reflection of the paper, and afford a light particularly adapted for tracing with accuracy.

Cold Cream.—Sweet almond oil, seven pounds by weight, white wax, three and a quarter pound, spermaceti, three and a quarter pound, clarified mutton suet, one pound, rose water, seven pints, spirits of wine, one pint. Directions to mix the above:—Place the oil, wax, spermaceti, and suet in a large jar; cover it over tightly, then place it in a saucepan of boiling water, (having previously placed two or more pieces of fire-wood at the bottom of the saucepan, to allow the water to get underneath the jar, and to prevent its breaking) keep the water boiling round the jar till all the ingredients are dissolved; take it out of the water, and pour it into a large pan previously warmed and capable of holding twenty-one pints; then, with a wooden spatula, stir in the rose water, cold, as quickly as possible, (dividing it into three or four parts at most), the stirring in of which should not occupy above five minutes, as after a certain heat the water will not mix. When all the water is in, stir unremittingly for thirty minutes longer, to prevent its separating, then add the spirits of wine, and the scent, and it is finished. Keep it in a cold place, in a white glazed jar, and do not cut it with a steel knife, as it causes blackness at the parts of contact. Scent with otto of roses and essential oil of bergamot to fancy. For smaller quantities, make ounces instead pounds.

To Preserve Cabbage, &c.—Cut them so that they may have about two inches of stem left below the leaves, scoop out the pith as far down as a small knife will reach, then suspend them, by means of a cord, exactly perpendicular, but in an inverted position, and daily fill up the hollow part of the stem with clear cold water. It is said that by this method, cabbages, cauliflowers, broccoli, celery, &c., may be preserved for a considerable time in a cool place. An easy method of keeping a supply of green vegetables during a severe winter.

Substitute for Eggs.—In winter *Snow* can be used as an excellent substitute for eggs in puddings, pancakes, &c. Two large spoonsful will supply the place of one egg, and the article it is used in will be equally good. It should be fresh fallen snow or under layers if old. The exposed surface loses its ammonia by evaporation very soon after it has fallen, and it is the ammonia contained so largely in snow which imparts to it the rising power.

Swine.—To keep swine in health, give them free access to charcoal, cinders, and ashes. To cure them of almost any disease, give them *fasting* on three succeeding alternate days a teaspoonful of black sulphuret of antimony, mixed and moistened in a pint of good meal.

To take Impression of Leaves on silks, satins, paper, or any other Substance.—Prepare two rubbers of wash leather, made by tying up wool, or any other substance, in wash-leather: then prepare the colors which you wish the leaves to be, by rubbing up with cold drawn linseed oil the wished-for colors, as indigo for blue, chrome for yellow, &c. Get a number of leaves the size you want, then dip the rubbers into the paint, and rub them one over the other, so that there may not be too much of the composition on the rubber; place a leaf on one of the rubbers and damp it with the other; take the leaf off and apply it to the substance you wish stamped: on the leaf place a piece of paper, and rub it gently, and there will be a beautiful impression of all the veins of the leaf. A leaf can only be used once. The leaves should be all nearly the same size, or the patterns will not look uniform.

To Preserve Flowers in Winter.—Take the buds which are latest in blowing and ready to open, cut them off with a pair of scissors, leaving the stem about three inches long, cover the end of the stem with a little melted sealing wax, and when the buds are a little withered, wrap them separately up in paper, and place them in a dry book. When it is desired to have the flowers to blow, take out the buds over night, and cut off the sealed end, and put them into water in which a little saltpetre has been dissolved. In the morning the buds will be open and blown.

Wet Clothes.—Handle a wet hat as lightly as possible. Wipe it as dry as you can with a silk handkerchief; and when nearly dry, use a soft brush. If the fur stick together in any part, damp it lightly with a sponge dipped in beer or vinegar, and then brush it till dry. Put the stick or stretcher into a damp hat, to keep it in proper shape. When a coat gets wet, wipe it down the way of the nap with a sponge or silk handkerchief. Do not put wet boots or shoes near the fire.

To Clean Plate.—Take of cream of tartar, alum, and common salt, each an ounce, and boil in a gallon of water, throw the plate in and boil; when taken out and rubbed dry it will look beautiful, and will seldom if ever tarnish.

A Water Purifier.—According to the Scotsman, the solid refuse of shale used in the manufacture of paraffine oil is a perfect purifier of the filthiest water. This substance is at present thrown aside by paraffine manufacturers as valueless.

To Preserve Cider Sweet.—Take two pound of stoned and picked raisins, one pound of mustard seed, and a quarter of a pound of cinnamon in stick, well broken up, and add to an ordinary sized barrel of cider. Mix well for a few days, and it will then retain its sweetness for months.

Lavender Water.—To a pint of rectified spirits of wine, put one ounce of the essential oil of lavender, and two drachms of the essence of ambergris. Put the whole into a glass bottle and shake well. Keep well stoppered as it is very volatile.

A Good Hair Wash.—Melt a little white soap, cut in small pieces, in spirits of wine, by means of heat, in the proportion of half a pound of soap to three quarters of a pint of spirits of wine and two ounces of potash. Carefully stir while heating. Let settle; pour off the clear liquid when cold, adding a little perfume.

To Remove Freckles.—Dissolve one ounce of alum in an ounce of lemon juice and a pint of rose-water. Keep well stoppered. Use as a wash three times a day until they are removed.

Superior Black Ink.—Make a tolerably strong solution of nutgalls, let stand twenty-four hours and then add a few drops (according to the quantity being made) of vanadic acid or vanadite of ammonia. This ink will be found superior in its qualities to any of the manufactured inks of the day.

To Preserve Boots and make them Waterproof.—Take a pound each of tallow and resin and melt and mix them well over a fire, and apply it whilst hot to the boots with a painter's brush, until neither the soles or uppers will absorb any more. If a fine polish is desired, let the boots stand two or three days and rub them with a composition made of one ounce of wax dissolved with a teaspoonful each of turpentine and lampblack. It must be applied cold.

To Sharpen Razors and Penknives.—Immerse the blade for half an hour in water to which one twentieth of its weight of sulphuric or muriatic acid has been added. Upon taking the blade out wipe it carefully and a few hours afterwads set it on a strop. Any edge tools may be sharpened in the same way.

To Stupify Bees.—Subject the hives from which you wish to take the honey to the vapor of flax dipped in salts of nitre, which acts as a powerful narcotic, and deprives the bees temporarily of movement; but without destroying them.

Cheap substitute for Almonds.—Peach kernels bear a strong resemblance in properties, appearance and chemical nature to bitter almonds, for which they are frequently and without inconvenience substituted in the shops. Distillers use preparations of peach kernels in making liquors and bakers flavor cake with them.

To Dissolve Gold.—Use a mixture of one part nitre acid and two parts of muriatic acid. To be kept in well stoppered bottles and in a dark place.

Peeling Onions.—In peeling onions put a large needle in the mouth, half in and half out. The needle will attract the oily juice of the onion, and any number may be peeled with impunity.

Colored Sugar for Ornamenting.—Pound loaf sugar and sift it through a coarse sieve; lay the sugar on a plate or dish and pour into it a few drops of carmine or prepared cochineal, mixing it well in. Put it on a screen to dry stirring frequently when dry put in a canister for use.

To remove stains from Glass.—Concentrated nitric acid, two ounces; common acetic acid, one ounce; water six ounces. Soak the glass in this solution a few hours and then wash.

Transparent Soap.—Cut into thin shavings half a cake of windsor soap, or according to the quantity to be made, put into a bottle, and half fill with spirits of wine, and place it near the fire until the soap is melted. Then pour into moulds to cool and the preparation gives you transparent soap.

How to shave or remove hairs from any part of the body without a razor.—Rub in a mortar and mix well into a powder, quick lime, ten parts; starch, ten parts; hyposulphate of soda three parts. For use add a little water to enough of the powder to form a paste, which lay on the face or hairs for two or three minutes. Scrape off with a wooden knife or anything dull and the hairs will be removed.

Gum for Envelopes and Paper.—Gum arabic two ounces; isinglass dissolved in three pints, warm water, one ounce; loaf sugar, three ounces; boil down to a thin paste and apply with a soft brush.

To Dye Hats and Bonnets.—Chips, straw bonnets and hats may be dyed black by boiling them three or four hours in a strong liquor of logwood, adding a little green copperas occasionally. Let the articles remain in the liquor all night, then take out to dry in the air. If the black is not satisfactory, dye again after drying. Rub inside and out with a sponge moistened with oil. Then black.

To kill Cockroaches.—Take a teacupful of ground plaster of Paris, mixed with double the quantity of oatmeal, to which add a little sugar. Strew on the floor, or in the chinks where they frequent.

Artificial Teeth.—Since the introduction of artificial teeth, which has enabled many to continue the mastication of solid food to a period of life at which they otherwise must have swallowed it whole, longevity is on the increase. Whether the dentist is really to claim this fact as the triumph of his art, or whether it be due to a generally improved system of hygiene, we will not discuss; but as mastication is so absolutely necessary, even to the strong and healthy stomach, we may fairly suppose that some years are added to the lives of those who are thus enabled to save distress to the other digestive organs when by age they have naturally lost some of their power.

Properties of Charcoal.—Among the many properties of charcoal may be mentioned its power of destroying smell, taste and color; and as a proof of its possessing the first quality, if it be rubbed over putrid meat, the smell will be destroyed. If a piece of charcoal be thrown into water the putrid taste or flavor will be destroyed, and the water be rendered completely fresh. Sailors are aware of this; for when water is bad at sea, they are in the habit of throwing pieces of burnt biscuits into it to purify it. Color is materially influenced by charcoal, and in numbers of instances in a very irregular way. If you take a dirty black syrup, and filter it through burnt charcoal, the color will be removed. The charcoal of animal matter appears to be the best for this purpose. You may learn the influence of charcoal in destroying colors by filtering a bottle of port wine through it. In the filtration it will lose a great portion of this color and become tawny; repeat the process two or three times, and you have destroyed it altogether.

Coke as Fuel for domestic purposes.—The value of coke for general use in private houses is comparatively little known. When once introduced, and the proper manner of using it is understood, this kind of fuel becomes almost indispensable. The best kinds of soft coal to be kept burning, require attention and frequent application of the poker. A coke fire, with the addition of a little small coal, which, in any other way, would be scarcely consumable, being properly made, will burn for hours without further attention or trouble, and at one-third less cost than a fire sustained by coal only. In the kitchen, coke is also very valuable. It makes the clearest fire for broiling, and a capital one for roasting. In all cases, the coke should be broken tolerably small.

To Clean Furs.—The following will be found very useful upon the approach of winter;—Strip the fur articles of their stuffing and binding, and lay them as much as possible in a flat position. They must then be subjected to a very brisk brushing, with a stiff clothes brush: after this, any moth-eaten parts must be cut out, and be neatly replaced by new bits of fur to match. Sable, chinchilla squirrel, fitch, &c., should be treated as follows: Warm a quantity of new bran in a pan, taking care that it does not burn, to prevent which it must be actively stirred. When well warmed, rub it thoroughly into the fur with the hand. Repeat this two or three times; then shake the fur, and give it another sharp brushing until free from dust. White furs, ermine, &c., may be cleaned as follows: Lay the fur on a table, and rub it well with bran made moist with warm water; rub until quite dry, and afterwards with dry bran. The wet bran should be put on with flannel, and the dry with a piece of book-muslin. The light furs, in addition to the above, should be well rubbed with magnesia, or a piece of book-muslin, after the bran process. Furs are usually much improved by stretching, which may be managed as follows: To a pint of soft water add three ounces of salt, dissolve; with this solution sponge the inside of the skin (taking care not to wet the fur), until it becomes thoroughly saturated; then lay it carefully on a board with the fur side downwards, in its natural disposition; then stretch as much as it will bear, and to the required shape, and fasten with small tacks. The drying may be quickened by placing the skin about six or eight feet from the fire or stove.

To brush Clothes.—Have a wooden horse to put the clothes on, and a small cane to beat the dust out of them; also a board or table long enough for them to be put their whole length when brushing them. Have two brushes, one a hard bristle, the other soft; use the hardest for the great coats, and for the others when spotted with dirt. Fine cloth coats should never be brushed with too hard a brush; this will take off the nap, and make them look bare in a little time. Be careful in the choice of the cane; do not have it too large, and be particular not to hit it too hard; be careful also not to hit the buttons, for it will scratch, if not break them; therefore a small hand-whip is the best to beat with. If a coat be wet, and spotted with dirt, let it be quite dry before brushing it; then rub out the spots with the hands, taking care not to rumple it in so doing. Brush both sides properly, fold them together: then brush the inside, and last of all the collar.

Vinegar in Dropsy.—Dr. Beyer, a military practitioner at Breslau, treats almost all dropsies exclusively by vinegar, giving a spoonful of the fluid every hour, and, in intervals, water acidulated with it. Six ounces are consumed daily, and a complete cure may require from six, to nine pounds. The appetite is increased, rather than diminished, during this treatment; and at first three or four stools per day are produced, which argues success. When, after a time, the patient becomes disgusted by the vinegar, lemon juice may be substituted.

Treatment of sore Nipples.—M. Anselmier observes, that in employing the nipple shield we should take care that it is neither too large nor too firm, since deglutition becoming difficult when the jaws are wide apart, the child soon becomes tired and refuses to suck. Collodion is of great use in chaps, although the pain it causes at first is complained of. It is, however, most indicated as a preventive when as yet only pain is present, and the child sucks forcibly. The gentle compression it exerts upon the nipple limits the turgescence of the organ, and the inflammatory process. It is also an excellent application in superficial excoriations, protecting these from the action of the air and the saliva. In deeper chaps, it is not of the same use; and, although other substances, as solutions of nitrate of silver or sublimate, may be beneficially and safely employed, with due precaution, yet they cause great pain, and are opposed by various prejudices. Reserving such means for very obstinate cases, M. Anselmier prefers benzoin, reduced to a state of impalpable powder. This is dusted over every part of the chap, and the nipple is then covered with carded cotton. No pain is caused, and cicatrisation soon ensues, a shield being used meanwhile.

A Cause of Nervous Disorders.—Many inquiries have been made why nervous disorders are much more common among us than among our ancestors. Other causes may frequently concur; but the chief is, we lie longer in bed. Instead of rising at four, most of us, who are not obliged to work for our bread, lie till seven, eight, and nine. We need inquire no further; this sufficiently accounts for the large increase of these painful disorders. It may be observed that most of these arise, not barely from sleeping too long, put even from what we imagine to be harmless, the lying too long in bed. By soaking (as it is emphatically called) so long between warm sheets, the flesh is, as it were, parboiled, and becomes soft and flabby. The nerves, in the mean time, are quite unstrung, and all the train of melancholy symptoms, faintness, tremors, lowness of spirits, so called, come on, till life itself is a burden.

Dyspepsia.—INDIGESTION.—This complaint, of all others, is of the most common occurrence, and pervades every rank of society. The usual symptoms are want of appetite, and transient distensions of the stomach, frequent eructations, heartburn, stomachic pains, occasional vomiting, and frequently costiveness and diarrhœa. Sometimes the head is affected, and dimness of sight, double vision, muscæ volitantes, and slight vertigo, are experienced, along with a multitude of other symptoms, depending on a disarrangement of the functions of the nervous system. The causes of dyspepsia are numerous. In the higher ranks of society, it is a common consequence of over indulgence in the luxuries of the table, or of the want of proper exercise, both bodily and mental. In the studious, and those who lead a sedentary life, it is usually caused by excessive mental exertion or anxiety, or by the fatigues of business, and the want of sufficient bodily exertion and pure air. It frequently arises from inebriety, or a deficiency of proper food.

TREAT.—The treatment of dyspepsia depends less on medicine than on the adoption of regular habits of life. Moderation in eating, drinking, and the indulgence of the passions; early rising, due exercise and retiring to rest at an early hour, will do much to restore the tone both of the stomach and nerves. Excessive study and mental exertion should be avoided, and recourse should frequently be had to society, and amusements of a lively and interesting character. If the bowels are confined, mild aperients should be taken, and if diarrhœa be present, antacids and absorbents may be had recourse to with advantage. The stomach should be strengthened by the use of mild bitters, tonics, and stimulants, and sea-bathing, or the tepid bath may be taken when convenient. Where dyspepsia is a secondary or symptomatic disease, the cause should be sought into, and the treatment varied accordingly. Among the aperient medicines most suitable to dyspepsia, may be mentioned—Epsom salts, phosphate of soda, and Seidlitz powders, either of which should be taken largely diluted with water. An occasional dose of medicine producing a stronger effect, may also be recommended. Among antacids, are the bicarbonates and carbonates of potassa and soda, either of which may be taken in doses of half a teaspoonful dissolved in water, or if the spirits be low one or two teaspoonsful of spirits of sal volatile will be more appropriate, and in cases accompanied by diarrhœa, a little prepared chalk. As bitters, compound infusion of orange-peel, or gentian, is excellent. As tonics, small doses of bark, or disulphate of quinine, to which chalybeates may be added, if there be no disposition to fever or headache.

To preserve Potatoes.—The Scotch method of preserving eggs, by dipping them in boiling water (which destroys the living principle,) is too well known to need further notice. The preservation of potatoes, by similar treatment, is also a valuable and useful discovery. Large quantities may be cured at once, by putting them into a basket as large as the vessel containing the boiling water will admit, and then just dipping them for a minute or two at the utmost, the germ, which is so near the skin, is thus " killed," without injuring the potatoe. In this way several tons might be cured in a few hours. They should then be dried in a warm oven, and laid up in sacks or casks, secure from the frost, in a dry place. Another method of preserving this valuable root is, first to peel them, then to grate them down into a pulp, which is put into coarse cloths, and the water squeezed out by putting them into a common press, by which means they are formed into flat cakes: Those cakes are to be well dried, and preserved for use as required. This is an excellent and ingenious mode of preserving potatoes, although attended with too much trouble on the large scale. It is said, that a piece of lime put into the water into which potatoes are boiling, will render the heaviest, light and flowery.

Mildew on Linen, &c.—The mildew upon linen proceeds from their being put away damp from the wash, and it is a very difficult blemish to remove. When it has unfortunately occurred, you will find that soap rubbed on, and afterwards fine chalk scraped upon the spots, with a day's exposure to the sun, will remove it, if not at once, at least upon a repetition.

Fruit and red wine stains may be removed by a preparation of equal parts of slacked lime, potass, and soft soap, and by exposure to the sun while this preparation is upon the stain. Salt of lemon (*oxalate of potass*) will remove ink and iron mould.

When linen or muslins are scorched, in the getting up, without being actually burnt, a brown mark is left upon the spot, which may be removed by laying some of the following composition on it, before the article is again washed:—Slice six large onions, and express the juice, which must be added to a quart of vinegar, with one ounce of rasped soap, a quarter of a pound of fuller's earth, one ounce of lime, and one ounce of pearl-ash. Boil the whole, until the mixture becomes thick, and apply it to the scorched spot while it is hot.

To Clarify Honey.—Place the vessel containing the honey in hot water, and take the scum off as long as it rises, afterwards stop it close.

To Polish Mahogany Tables.—Grate very small a quarter of an ounce of white soap; put it into a new glazed earthen vessel with a pint of water, hold it over the fire till the soap is dissolved; then add the same quantity of white wax cut into small pieces and three ounces of common wax. As soon as the whole is incorporated it is fit for use. When used, clean the table well, dip a bit of flannel in the varnish when *warm*, and rub it on the table; let it stand a quarter of an hour, then apply a hard brush in all directions and finish with a bit of clean dry flannel. This will produce gloss like a mirror; and, to those who dislike the smell of turpentine or oil, will be found very useful.

Dangers of Green Paint.—The following important statement is by Dr. Alfred Taylor, one of the first medical chemists of the day:—Sitting down to breakfast one morning, he perceived on the crust of a piece of toast a number of green spots and streaks. His curiosity being excited, he examined these green spots in various ways; and at last on analyzing them, extracted a considerable amount of arsenic. The spots were, in fact, the green paint known by the name of Scheele's green, a brilliant color, and one, therefore, much used, but dangerous from the amount of arsenic—fifty per cent—which it contains. Dr. Taylor proceeded to the shop of the baker, a respectable tradesman, and the cause of the green spots on the loaf at once met his eye. The shop had been recently re-decorated; and, among other things, the shelves had been painted a brilliant Scheele's green. The hot loaves placed upon these painted shelves—perhaps not thoroughly dry—had caused portions of the paint to adhere to them. Five or six loaves in succession examined in the baker's shop were all found to have more or less of the green adhering to them; the baker himself, quite unaware of the poisonous nature of the color, thinking little about it. Dr. Taylor states that, on the first loaf examined by him, there was enough of the arsenic paint to have killed an infant. To be sure, it is not to be supposed that any individual, whether infant or adult, would consume the whole crust; but still there might have been sufficient of the poison taken in to cause very serious symptoms. There cannot be too much caution exercised in the use of this paint in any situation, and it ought never to be allowed in connexion with eatables of any sort. Nevertheless as Dr. Taylor remarks, "In England green sweetmeats are actually colored with it; and lemon acid, and other drops, are sometimes sold, wrapped in paper coarsely tinged or dyed green with this dangerous compound of arsenic. In foreign countries there are strong restrictions placed on the sale and use of this noxious pigment."

A Cement for Cellar Floors.—Persons wishing to line their cellars, and who do not wish to go to the expense of buying cement, can take coal ashes and mix with water to the thickness of mortar. This can be put on about four inches thick, after which let it lay twenty-four hours, then stamp it with a heavy block of wood three or four times a day, until it is perfectly hard. It is better than cement, as it will not crack or scale off, and the lumps of cinders contained in the ashes do no harm.

Razors.—The simplest method of sharpening a razor is said to be to place the blade for about a half hour in water, to which one twentieth of its weight of sulphuric or muriatic acid has previously been added. Upon taking the razor out, wipe it off lightly, and a few hours afterwards set it on a strop. The acid thus supplies the place of a whetstone, by corroding the entire surface uniformly so that nothing but a good polish is afterwards needed. It is stated that this process never injures good razors, whilst poor ones are often improved by it. This mode of sharpening may be used with advantage for any kind of edged tools.

To Destroy Rats.—The Museum of Natural History at Paris was dreadfully infested with rats; but thanks to M. Cloez, it is now free from the nuisance. The happy thought of pouring bisulphide of carbon into the holes occurred to this gentleman, and the vapor was fatal to all the rats which inhaled it. "That settled 'em."

Salt in Chimneys.—In building chimneys bricklayers should put a quanity of salt into the mortar with which the interstices of brick are to be laid. The effect will be that there will never be any accumulation of soot in the chimney, for the reason that the salt in the portion of mortar which is exposed absorbs moisture every damp day. The soot, thus becoming damp, falls down into the fire-place.

To Clean Steel Pens.—When the pen has been written with, and appears spoiled, place it over a light (a gaslight, for instance,) for a short time—say a quarter of a minute—then dip it in water, and it will again be in good condition to write with. Also, any new pen which is too hard to write with, will become softer with being heated in the same way.

Moths.—For destroying moths in carpets, a plan which has been found perfectly successful is:—Wet a piece of muslin (an old sheet will answer very well), spread upon the carpet, and iron rapidly with a hot smoothing iron. This not only destroys the moths in whatever stage they may be, but also cleans and freshens the carpet.

To clarify Sugar.—Take four pounds of sugar, and break it into pieces; put into a preserving-pan the white of an egg, and a glass of pure spring water; mix them well with a whisk, add another glass, still whipping, until two quarts, have been put in; when the pan is full of froth, throw in the sugar, and set it on the fire, being careful to skim it everytime the scum rises, which will be the case as the sugar boils up. After a few boilings, the sugar will rise so high as to run over the edges of the pan, to prevent which, throw on it a little cold water; this will lower it instantly, and give time for the skimming, for the scum should never be taken off whilst the sugar is bubling; the cold stills it, and that is the moment to scum it. Repeat this operation carefully three or four times, when a whitish light scum only will rise; then take the pan off, lay a napkin, slightly wetted, over a basin, and pour the sugar through it.

The scum thus taken off, put into a china basin; and when the sugar is clarified, wash the pan and skimmer with a glass of water, which put to the scum, and set it aside for more common purposes.

To make Blacking.—Three ounces of ivory black; two ounces of treacle; half an ounce of vitriol; half an ounce of sweet oil; quarter of a pint of vinegar, and three quarters of a pint of water. Mix the oil, treacle, and ivory black gradually to a paste; then add the vitriol, and by degrees, the vinegar and water. It will produce a beautiful polish,

To clean Marble.—Pound very finely a quarter of a pound of whitening and a small quantity of stone blue; dissolve in a little water one ounce of soda, and mix the above ingredients carefully together with a quarter of a pound of soft soap. Put the whole into an earthen pipkin, and boil it for a quarter of an hour on a slow fire, carefully stirring it. Then when quite hot, lay it with a brush upon the marble, and let it remain on half an hour. Wash it off with warm water, flannel, and a scrubbing-brush, and wipe it dry.

To remove Iron Moulds.—Spirit of salt, oxalic acid, salt of lemons, are the usual applications to extract some unsightly stains; and as they are all so much of the same nature, that, unless great caution be used in their applications, the article will drop into holes, it becomes every mistress of a family to consider whether such a risk should be left to a laundress, or whether *she* be not the more likely person to effect a perfect application, as she must or ought to have her own interests at heart, more strongly than a person wholly indifferent to her. The only caution requisite, is to rinse the article thoroughly after application.

Fire-proof and Water-proof Cement.—To a half a pint of milk, put an equal quantity of vinegar, in order to curdle it; then separate the curd from the whey, and mix the whey with the whites of five eggs beating the whole well together, when it is well mixed, add a little quick lime through a sieve, until it has acquired the consistence of a thick paste, with this cement broken vessels, and cracks of all kinds can be mended, it dries quickly and resists the action of fire and water.

To remove the smell of Paint.— Place tubs of water in the room and the water will absorb and retain the effluvium of the paint, repeat and you will not be troubled with the smell.

Oil for Furniture.—For polishing mahogany furniture, we would mention, and *recommend* the following—it is simply *cold drawn linseed oil*. The property of this oil differs from that of most other oleaginous fluids; essential oils, as those of cinnamon, cloves, &c., are pungent; that of others soft and lubricating, as olive, palm, gallipoli, neatsfoot. But linseed oil possesses more particularly a tendency to harden and become solid, on long exposure to the air. It is this peculiar quality that is taken advantage of in its application to furniture; and, which, with a little patience, and no hard rubbing, will produce a varnish far superior in durability, beauty, and usefulness to French polish, or any mixture for the purpose, which we have ever seen; and we believe that there is scarcely one which we do not know, and have not made trial of.

A very little linseed oil is to be poured into a saucer; then, with a small piece of clean rag smear the furniture with it. In a few minutes, wipe it off with an old duster kept for the purpose; and then rub the tables, &c, quite clean, with a second cloth. This simple, easy operation, performed regularly once a week, will *gradually* produce a polish that is unrivalled: for unless it were to be washed with *soap*, it will not injure; boiling water even might be poured over it with impunity; indeed, occasional washing with plain water, is an advantage to it. Unlike the easily spoiled varnishes of the shops, furniture that is rubbed with this oil is not so readily scratched; and, if it be, the next week's application will nearly obliterate the marks. Again, the pores of the wood being filled with the application, it becomes very hard, and is able to resist the attacks of insects. We have possessed articles of furniture thus polished so beautifully, that our simple plan has been conjectured to be a newly invented preparation—" yet unknown to fame." We are aware that this method of beautifying furniture is *well*, but not *generally* known.

Perfume for Note Paper.—Powdered starch one half ounce: otto of roses four drops; orris powder one half ounce; the above should be put into bags, and kept in the writing desk, with the paper desired to be perfumed, this is the article used by the Queen of England.

To make Walnut wood color.—A given quantity of cerute, half that quantity of ochre de rue, a little umber earth, red ochre, and yellow ochre de berri, compose this color proper for distemper varnish, and oil.

To render Leather waterproof.—Take of neats foot and linseed oil two quarts, boil them two hours, then add six ounces of Indian rubber, and let the whole boil, until the rubber is dissolved; apply with a soft brush a little at a time.

To give Plaster figures the appearance of Marble.—Dissolve one ounce of pure curd soap, grated in four ounces of water, in a greased earthen vessel; add one ounce of white wax cut in thin slices, when the whole is incorporated it is fit for use; having dried the figure before the fire, suspend it by a string and dip it in the mixture; when it has absorbed the varnish, dip it a second time, and that generally suffices; cover it carefully from the dust for a week then rub it gently with soft cotton wool, and you will have a brilliant shining gloss, exactly resembling polished marble.

Method for cooling Liquids.—An old fashioned yet a simple, receipt for cooling liquids is to wrap a wet cloth round the bottle, and expose it to the rays of the sun, this will soon have the desired effect.

Preserving Vinegar for Domestic purposes.—Cork it up in glass bottles, set them over the fire with cold water, and as much hay as will prevent them from knocking together; when the water nearly boils, take off the pan, and let the bottle remain in the hay a quarter of an hour, vinegar thus prepared never loses its virtue though kept many years, or occasionaly left uncovered and is peculiarly adapted for pickles.

Turkish Cream.—Two teaspoonsfuls of white sugar, one tea spoonful of raspberry jam, two whites of eggs, juice of one lemon; beat for one hour, and serve up sprinkled with fancy biscuits.

To soften old Putty.—Dip a small brush in a little nitric or muriatic acid, and go over the putty with it; let it rest awhile and it will become so soft that you can remove it with ease.

To clean the Chimneys of Lamps.—Put a teaspoonful of oil of vitriol, in a long deep pie dish, of luke warm water, let the lamp chimneys remain in this for a quarter of an hour; in wiping dry, all smoke and discolorations will disappear.

To make Ink for marking Steel.—Dissolve sulphate of copper, in water, add a little sulphuric acid use a pen for writing, immediately on application copper letters will be formed on the iron or steel; it may be made without the use of vitriol.

How to restore discolored Gloves.—Have ready a little new milk in one saucer, and a piece of brown soap in an other, and likewise a clean towel rolled three or four times, spread out the glove smooth upon the cloth, dip a piece of flannel in the milk, rub it well upon the soap, and with this rub the glove downwards, towards the fingers, holding it firmly with the left hand, continue this process until the glove is white, looks like a dingy yellow though clean; if colored till it looks dark and spoiled; lay it to dry and it wiil look equal to new, soft, glossy, smooth shaped, and elastic.

Cement for glazing an Aquarium.—Putty mixed with any kind of mastic; it is very important, however, that the water should not be put in the tank, until the cement is perfectly hardened.

To strengthen and improve the Voice.—Take of beeswax two drachms; Copaibia balsam, three drachms, powder of liquorice root four drachms; melt the Copaiba balsam with the wax, in a new earthen pipkin; when melted remove them from the fire, and while in a melted state, mix in the powder, make pills of three grains each, two of these pills to be taken occasionally three or four times a day this is an excellent remedy for clearing and strengthening the voice, and is used by most professional singers on the continent.

To remove Sunburn.—Milk of almonds made thus; take blanched bitter almonds one half ounce, soft water one half pint, make an emulsion by beating the almonds and water together, strain through a muslin cloth and it is made.

Receipt for joining glass.—Melt a little isinglass in the spirits of wine, and add a small quantity of water. Warm the mixture gently over a moderate fire, when mixed by thoroughly melting it will form glue perfectly transparent, and which will reunite glass so nicely and firmly, that the joining will scarcely be perceptible even to the most critical eye. Lime mixed with the white of an egg forms a very strong, cement for glass, porcelain, &c. but it must be done neatly, so when hard, the superfluous part cannot be easily smoothed or taken off.

Rosemary wash for the Hair.—Boil one pound of rosemary in two quarts of water, and add to the filtered liquor one ounce of spirit of lavender, and one ounce of salt of tartar.

To mix Oil with Water.—Salts of tartar, is the best and cheapest substance, thus uniting two qualifications, it will cause any oil to unite with water.

Lavender Water.—One quart of rectified spirits of wine; essential oil of lavender two ounces; essence or ambergris five drachms; put it all into a bottle, and shake it until it is incorporated.

To preserve Seaweeds.—Put each specimen in a plate full of water, it will then be easy to spread out and arrange the branches or fibres, then introduce a sheet of paper under the seaweed and carefully raise it out of the water, the specimen will be beautifully displayed upon the paper, by means of the gluten in the seaweed.

How to make cheap French Polish for Boots and Shoes.—Mix together two pints of vinegar, and one pint of soft water; stir into it, one quarter of a pound of glue broken into small pieces, half a pound of logwood chips, quarter ounce of soft soap, and a quarter of an ounce of isinglass, put it on the fire, and when it boils up, continue the boiling for ten minutes longer. Strain it, and bottle and cork it: when cold it is ready for use; before putting it on the boots and shoes, remove the dirt with a sponge and water, then put on the polish with a clean brush.

To remove Grease from the Collar of a Coat.—Obtain six cents worth of ammonia, and mix it in a pint of cold water then well sponge the collar or other parts, until the grease disappears, which it will quickly do.

To take Grease out of Carpets.—Scrape and pound together in equal proportions, magnesia in the lump, and fullers earth; having mixed these substances, pour on them a sufficient quantity of boiling water to make into a paste; lay this on as hot as possible upon the grease spots, in the carpet and let it dry. Next day when the composition is quite dry, brush it off and the grease spots will have disappeared.

To clean Plaster of Paris Busts.—Take a small piece of very clean whiting, and dissolve it in a little water, then lay it over the bust in the form of whitewash, a little isinglass added to the water, made warm previous to mixing with the whiting will prevent the white rubbing off when touched.

To give a fine color to Mahogany.—Let the article be washed perfectly clean with vinegar, first having taken out any ink stains there may be with spirits of salt. Use the following liquid:—into a pint of cold linseed oil, put six cents worth of alkanet root, and two cents worth of rose pink in an earthen vessel; let it remain all night, then stirring well, rub some of it all over the article with a linen rag; when it has lain some time, rub it bright with linen cloths.

To gild Ivory.—Put the ivory you intend to gild into a solution of sulphate of iron (copperas) and then into a solution of nitro-muriate of gold; on withdrawing it from the latter, it will be beautifully gilded.

Remedy for Dandruff.—Let the roots of the hair be well washed with the following solution every day; lime water, one pint; distilled vinegar, one fourth pint. Mix.

Preventative against Moths.—Strew camphor or pepper over the things you wish to preserve from moths.

To take Ink out of Muslin.—Dip the part stained with ink into cold water. Then fill a small basin with boiling water, and on the top place a pewter plate; lay the muslin on the plate, then salt of lemon or tartaric acid upon the spot, rubbing it with the broad of a spoon; the spot will then immediately disappear.

Tainted Meat.—The taint may be removed by covering it for a few hours with charcoal, or by putting a few pieces of charcoal into the water, in which the tainted meat is boiled.

Fire in the Chimney.—In case of fire in the chimney, it is an excellent plan, to put salt on the fire, as it acts chemically on the flaming soot above.

For Making the hair Curl.—Beat up the yolk of an egg with a pint of clean rain water or lime water, a pint distilled; vinegar, a quarter of a pint:—Mix; to be applied warm, and afterwards wash the head with warm water.

Invaluable Dentrifice.—Dissolve two ounces of borax in three pints of water; before getting cold, add one teaspoonful of myrrh, and one tablespoonful of camphor; bottle the mixture for use, one wine glass of the solution added to a half a pint of tepid water, is sufficient for each application, this solution applied daily, preserves and beautifies the teeth, arrests decay, and produces a healthy action of the gums.

How to Freshen Salt Fish.—Many persons who are in the habit of freshening mackerel or other salt fish, never dream that there is a right and a wrong way to do it. Any one who has seen the process of evaporation going on at the salt works knows that salt falls to the bottom. Just so it is in the pan where your mackerel or white fish lies soaking; and as it lies with the skin side down, the salt will fall to the skin, and remain there; when, if placed with the flesh side down, the salt falls to the bottom of the pan, and the fish comes out freshened as it should; in the other case it is nearly as salt as when put in.

To Relieve a Cough.—This is the season for colds; and colds are the forerunners of consumption. Attend seasonably to the first, if you would avoid the last. For years we have found the following preparation the best for the cure or relief of a cough we have ever tried:—Take two ounces flaxseed, two ounces stick liquorice, half a pound brown sugar, half a pound raisins, one quart cider. Boil the whole down to one pint; strain it off and put it aside for use. Whenever the cough is troublesome, take a tablespoonful at a time.

A New Treatment for Wounds.—A French surgeon has discovered a new method of treating wounds which is said to be very successful. A jet of air is poured upon the wound by means of an ordinary pair of bellows, which causes a film to form, by means of which the healing process is greatly facilitated.

External Application of Castor Oil.—It is said castor oil is much better to soften and redeem old leather, than any other oil known. When boots and shoes are greased with it, the oil will not at all interfere with the polishing afterwards, as in the case with lard, olive, or any other oil. In Harrisburg, the old leather hose of some of the fire companies were greased with it, and found to become almost as soft and flexible as new leather. Leather belts for transmitting motion in machinery will usually last three or five years, according to the wear and tear they are exposed to; when greased with castor oil they will last ten years or more, as they always remain flexible and do not crack. Besides this advantage, castor oil prevents slipping, so that a belt three inches wide, impregnated with it, will be equal to a belt four and a half inches wide without castor oil. It is necessary, however, to wait twenty-four hours till the oil has disappeared from the surface and penetrated the leather, otherwise the freshly greased surface will cause slipping. That rats and other vermin detest anything impregnated with castor oil and will not touch it, is another advantage.

The Use of Borax in Washing.—In Belgium and Holland, linen is prepared beautifully, because the washerwomen use refined borax, instead of soda, as a washing powder. One large handful of borax is used to every ten gallons of boiling water, and the saving in soap is said to be one-half. For laces and cambrics an extra quantity is used. Borax does not injure the linen and it softens the hardest water. A teaspoonful of borax added to an ordinary seized kettle of hard water, in which it is allowed to boil, will effectually soften the water.

Receipt Worth a Thousand Dollars.—Take one pound of sal-soda and a half a pound of unslacked lime, put them in a gallon of water and boil twenty minutes; let it stand till cool, then drain off and put in a strong jug or jar. Soak your dirty clothes over night, or until they are wet through, then wring them out and rub on plenty of soap, and in one boiler of clothes, well covered with water, add one tea-cupful of washing fluid. Boil half an hour briskly, then wash them thoroughly through one suds, rinse, and your clothes will look better than the old way of washing twice before boiling.—This is a valuable receipt, and I want every poor tired woman to try it. I think with a patent wash-tub to do the little rubbing, the washer-woman might take the old Bible and compose herself on a lounge, and let the washing do itself.

Good Vinegar.—Here is a receipt which will be worth consideration to our readers who are fond of making vinegar: It may not generally be known that an excellent article of vinegar may be made by taking the late stalks of rhubarb, and chopping them as one would for pies or sauce; then pour scalding water over the whole, and let it stand on the stove till well cooked; then strain off into a suitable vessel, add one gill of molasses to each quart of the juice: set it in a sunny place; stir occasionally, and in a few weeks one may have a stout article of vinegar.

Sweet Green Tomato Pickle.—Peel and slice two gallons of green tomatoes, five tablespoonsful of ground mustard seed, two gills of mustard seed, two tablespoonsful of ground cinnamon, one tablespoonful of cloves, one pound of brown sugar, three quarts of vinegar. Boil altogether until quite done. If you choose, you may use one spoonful ground and a portion of cinnamon bark. Celery tops improve the flavor. They are excellent.

Tomato Catsup, No. 1.—Wash and boil one bushel tomatoes. When soft, pass the whole through a colander, mashing the mass till it has ceased to drip. There will be about eleven quarts of juice. Put this in a china-lined kettle, and add four tablespoonsful of salt, one of allspice, three of ground mustard, a teaspoonful and a half of ground black pepper, one of cayenne.—Boil this two hours at least; if you wish it thick, three or four hours. Bottle, putting a little sweet oil on the top of each to exclude air. Seal and it is ready for use in two weeks—is better in two years.

2.—Take six pounds of tomatoes and sprinkle with salt; let them remain a day or two, then boil and press through a coarse sieve or colander. Put into the liquor half a pint of vinegar, cloves, pepper, ginger and cinnamon; boil them, one-third away; bottle tight. It should be shaken before being used.

To Test Gold or Silver.—Metals purporting to be gold or silver, may be easily tested by moistening the metal and rubbing lunar caustic on the wet part. If the metal is pure the mark will be faint, but if it is not pure the mark will be darker in proportion as the alloy is greater, until in the case of counterfeit or base metals the mark will be quite black.

Rust.—Every particle of rust on iron may be removed by first softening it with petroleum and then rubbing it well with coarse sand-paper. To paint iron, take lamp-black sufficient for two coats, and mix with equal quantities of Japan varnish and boiled linseed oil.

Antidote for Poison.—After many experiments by the officers of the Smithsonian Institute and other scientific gentlemen, a certain cure is said to have been found for snake bite. It is as follows: Ten grains iodide of potassum, and thirty grains iodine, to be dissolved in one ounce of water, to be kept in a bottle with a ground glass stopper, and to be applied externally—never internally. If possible, stop the circulation in the parts bitten by bandaging and use a stick or anything to tighten the bandage, and apply the solution to the bite with a piece of cotton, sponge, or anything that will hold the fluid, and then bind it to the wound and keep wet until the cure is effected. It is said that five drops of undiluted poison from the fangs of a rattlesnake, mixed with five drops of the above solution and inserted in a wound with a syringe, was as harmless as ten drops of water.

Incombustible Wash.—Slake some stone lime in a large tub or barrel, with boiling water; when slaked, pass six quarts of it through a fine sieve. It will then be in a state of fine flour. Now to six quarts of this lime add one quart of salt and one gallon of water; then boil the mixture and skim it clean. To every five gallons of this mixture add one pound of alum, half pound of copperas, by slow degrees, three quarters of a pound of potash, and four quarts of white sand, or hard wood-ashes sifted. This solution will admit of any colored matter, and may be applied with a brush. It is more durable than paint. It will stop small leaks in the roof, prevent the moss from growing over and rotting the wood, and renders it incombustible from sparks falling upon it. When laid upon brick work, it renders the brick impervious to rain or wet.

Choosing Carpets.—A carpet should be always chosen as a back-ground, upon which the other articles of furniture are to be placed, and should, from its sober colors and unattractive features, have a tendency rather to improve, by comparison, objects placed upon it than command for itself the notice of the spectator. It should vie with nothing, but rather give value to all objects coming in contact with it. Composed of sombre shades and tones, and treated essentially as a flat surface, it exerts a most valuable though subordinate influence upon all the other decorations of the day. Upon it the eye rests while surveying the more important furniture; and its presence, properly treated, supplies the necessary material for a satisfactory contrast with other portions of the decoration, which comparison in nowise detracts from its own peculiar degree of merit, but proves from this circumstance how valuable it is as contributing to the pleasing effect of the whole apartment.

To Imitate Rosewood.—Boil half a pound of logwood in three pints of water till it is of a very dark red, and half an ounce of salt of tartar. While boiling hot, stain the wood with two or three coats, taking care that it is nearly dry between each; then, with a stiff flat brush, such as painters use for graining, form streaks with a black stain, which, if carefully executed, will be very nearly the appearance of dark rosewood. Stain for mahogany: Put one pound of logwood in four quarts of water, and add a double handful of walnut peels. Boil it up again, take out the chips, add one pint of the best vinegar and it will be fit for use.

To Fill Cracks in Furniture.—Moisten a piece of recently burned lime with enough water to make it fall into powder; mix one part of thin slacked lime with two parts of rye flour and a sufficient quantity of boiled linseed oil to form it into a thick, plastic mass.

Frosted Limbs.—Frosted limbs are permanently relieved by one or two applications of a boiled lye of wood ashes, made so strong as to be quite slippery between the fingers. This lye should settle, be drained off, and have a large handful of common salt to each quart of lye mixed with it. It should be quite warm, and the limbs be submerged for one or two hours.

To obtain a beautiful, clear, white, complexion, and a brilliant appearance of the skin.—Prepare a wash of one ounce of benzoic acid in six ounces of water. This is harmless, but effectual. The greater part of the highly praised nostrums of the day contain more or less of that dangerous preparation—white lead.

Extract of Rose-leaf Geranium.—Dissolve three ounces of oil of Rose-geranium in one gallon of deodorized alcohol. By filtering alcohol through charcoal it becomes deodorized of the fusel smell.

Offensive Breath.—This is easily cured and the mouth entirely disinfected by washing the mouth with a solution of chlorinated lime. Finely pulverized charcoal is another disinfectant for the mouth, but not so efficient.

New process for removing Freckles.—Take finely powdered nitre, (saltpetre) and apply to the freckles, by the finger moistened with water and dipped in the powder. When perfectly done and judiciously repeated it will remove them effectually and without trouble.

Scent Powders.—To be used for scent bags, wardrobes, boxes, &c.—Corianders, orris root, rose leaves, and aromatic calamas, each four ounces; lavender flowers, eight ounces; rhodium wood, one drachm; musk, twenty grains. Mix and reduce to course powder.

To clean kid gloves.—Make a strong lather with curd soap and warm water, in which steep a small piece of new flannel. Place the glove on a flat, clean, and unyielding surface—such as the bottom of a dish, and having thoroughly soaped the flannel (when squeezed from the lather), rub the kid till all dirt be removed, cleaning and resoaping the flannel from time to time. Care must be taken to omit no part of the glove, by turning the fingers, &c. The gloves must be dried in the sun or before a moderate fire, and will present the appearance of old parchment. When quite dry, they must be gradually "pulled out," and, will look new. We have repeatedly tried the above with success.

To Protect Children from Burning.—Add one ounce of alum to the last water used to rinse children's dresses, and they will be rendered uninflamable, or so slightly combustible that they would take fire very slowly, if at all, and would not flame. This is a simple precaution, which may be adopted in families of children. Bed curtains, and linen in general, may also be treated in the same way.

Diminution of Smoke.—Smoke from the fires of private houses in winter, may be greatly lessened by lighting the fires from the top, whereby much of the smoke is consumed.

To Preserve Apples and Pears.—Take a large jar coated inside with cement and place a layer of fine sand on the bottom, select the best fruit, either apples or pears, and having wiped thoroughly dry, place a layer on the sand in the jar, taking care that the fruit does not touch; then alternate layers of sand and fruit until the jar is filled, covering the whole with a thick layer of the sand gently pressed down. Keep the jar in a dry place free from all moisture and the fruit will keep in fine condition for some months.

Economical Hair Wash.—Take one ounce of borax, half and ounce of camphor, powder these ingredients fine, and dissolve them in one quart of boiling water when cool, the solution will be ready for use; damp the hair frequently. This wash not only effectually cleanses and beautifies, but strengthens the hair, preserves the color, and prevents early baldness. The camphor will form into lumps, but the water will be sufficiently impregnated.

How to Renovate Black Cloth.—Boil half a pound of logwood and half an ounce of copperas chips in three pints of water until reduced to a quart; when cold add two ounces of alcohol; mix well and apply to the cloth with a hard brush; when dry brush with a soft brush.

Excellent Domestic Yeast.—One pound of good flour, a quarter of a pound of brown sugar, and two ounces of salt boiled together for one hour. While yet warm bottle and cork close. One pint of this will make eighteen pounds of bread.

How to do up Shirt Bosoms.—Dissolve two ounces of fine white gum arabic in a pitcher containing a pint or more of boiling water, according to the degree of strength required—cover and let stand twelve hours, then decant carefully from the dregs into a clean bottle, cork, and keep for use. A tablespoonful of this added to a pint of starch made in the usual manner will give to shirt bosoms, or any article of lawn (white or colored) a newness of appearance when nothing else can restore them.

To Melt Iron Instantly.—Bring iron to a white heat, and then apply a roll of sulphur to it. The iron will instantly melt.

Candles, Plain Hints About.—Candles improve by keeping a few months. Those made in winter are the best. The most economical, as well as the most convenient plan, is to purchase them by the box, keeping them alway in a cool dry place. If wax candles become discoloured or soiled, they may be restored by rubbing them over with a clean flannel slighty dipped in spirits of wine. Candles are sometimes difficult to light. They ignite instantly if, when preparing them for the evening, you dip the top in spirits of wine shortly before they are wanted. Light them always with a match, and do not hold them to the fire, as that will cause the tops to melt and drip. Always hold the match to the side of the wick, and not over the top. If you find the candles too small for the candlesticks, always wrap a small piece of white paper round the bottom end, not allowing the paper to appear above the socket. Cut the wicks to a convenient length for lighting (nearly close), for if the wick is too long at the top it will be very difficult to ignite, and will also bend down, and set the candles to running. Glass receivers, for the droppings for candles, are very convenient, as well as ornamental. The pieces of candles that are left each evening should be placed in a tin box kept for that purpose, and used for bed-lights.

Twelve Golden Maxims For Families.

I. HEALTH MUST BE REGARDED.—This demands the first attention, and unceasing regard. The laws of health must be observed, and those wise and efficient means must be uniformly employed, by which, in connexion with the Divine blessing, the health of the various members of the Family may be secured. It is deeply to be regretted that so many Families disregard the laws of health: we cannot wonder that illness so often prevails,—that death so prematurely ensues.

II. EDUCATION MUST BE EARLY ATTENDED TO.—The mind must be early cultivated: acquisitions, varied and important, must be continually gained. The faculties must be wisely and vigorously disciplined not only from the consideration of the happiness which will be secured, and the true respectability which will be attained; but from the conviction that, at the present period, a good sound education will be essential to the members of our Households in future life,—that they will be worth comparatively nothing without it.

III. AMIABLE TEMPERS MUST BE CHERISHED.—The kindly dispositions in our Families are not only desirable, but indispensible; there is no domestic happiness without them. One must be bland, courteous, and amiable, to another. The law of kindness must be the rule—governing, moulding, harmonizing the Family. There must be nothing hard, stern or unyielding; but mutual concessions, mutual tenderness, mutual love.

IV. INDUSTRIOUS HABITS MUST BE FORMED.—Nothing is more essential. Unless active habits are cultivated, and cultivated from principal, no progress can be made in anything that is valuable; no respectability, intellectual, social or moral, can be gained; no confidence on the part of others can be realized; no blessings from Heaven can be vouchsafed. Indolent apathetic Families, habitually sluggish, and indisposed to labour, are ignorant, unhappy, immoral. This may be regarded as an indisputable fact.

V. MUTUAL CONFIDENCE MUST BE REPOSED.—There must be no shyness of each other. There must be no jealousy, no undue caution, no distrust. If these feelings be manifested in the Family circle, there will be no comfort; there will be a canker-worm at the root of domestic happiness; and this want of confidence will increase, until every thing that is petulant and malicious will be discovered.

VI. A CONTINUAL DESIRE FOR DOMESTIC TRANQUILITY MUST BE CHERISHED.—What can be more desirable than peace in our dwellings? that peace which is the result of love,—which springs from mutual respect and forbearance,—which is associated with principle,—which is the consequence of the fear of God,—which is identified with filial and unwavering trust in him. A tranquil, happy home, is the very emblem of Heaven.

VII. THE PARENTAL CHARACTER MUST BE HIGHLY RESPECTED.—There will be no domestic blessing, without this. There will be no true dignity in the Family, without this. There will be no real prosperity at home, without this. Parents must occupy their appropriate place: they are the heads of Families, and they must be regarded as such. There must be no neglect; no disrespect must be shown them. There must be no contempt of their authority, no indisposition to render obedience. Children must value and honour their parents, else instead of having a blessing throughout life, they will be sure to have a curse.

VIII. DOMESTIC ORDER MUST BE MAINTAINED.—Where there is disorder, there is no tranquillity, no excellence, no advancement, no happiness. Order in Families is essential to their peace, elevation, and progress. In our households, every thing should be done at the best time, as well as the best manner. There should be rules to direct and govern, from which there should be no deviation, unless necessity compel. Disorderly habits, a constant want of arrangements, will entail nothing but loss and misery; and as the children grow up, these habits will be rendered fixed and permanent, so that they will become men and women, fathers and mothers without any love of rule or order.

IX. THE LOVE OF HOME MUST BE FOSTERED.—There is no affection, when it is cherished from an early period, and from principle, which is stronger: and sure we are, that there is no feeling which is more valuable and important. It is connected with a thousand endearments; it preserves from a thousand temptations; it is identified with the cultivation of the noblest priniciples, and purest emotions; and it is inseparable from peace and happiness. In such a world as ours, Home should be the refuge from danger; the spot where freedom is found from every care; the haven where tranquil waters are met with after the fiercest storm.

X. SYMPATHY UNDER DOMESTIC TRIALS MUST BE EXPRESSED.—There must be no cold no unfeeling heart displayed. Family difficulties will occur; Family changes will be experienced; Family sorrow will be endured; Family bereavements will be undergone and in these situations, there must be sympathetic and tender emotions cherished. The Parents must feel for the Children, and the Children for the Parents; Brothers must be kind and compassionate towards their Sisters in affliction; and Sisters must endeavour to alleviate the sorrow and burden of their Brothers. Thus will support be administered under the heaviest pressure; consolation be afforded during painful illnesses and protracted calamities, and the benediction of Heaven be graciously imparted.

XI. SINCERE PRAYER MUST BE PRESENTED FOR EACH OTHER.— Parents in this way especially must remember their children, and children their parents. It is the best kind of remembrance; the most beautiful expression of love. There should be in the Family circle the elevation of the heart to God, for his blessing. Mutual prayer will cement mutual love,—will alleviate mutual sorrows,—will sweeten mutual mercies,—will heighten and purify mutual joys. Where these elevated feelings are not cultivated, there is no happiness, no security.

XII. THE FAMILY MUST LOOK FORWARD TO A PURER, BRIGHTER, NOBLER, WORLD THAN THIS:— A world where there shall be no ignorance to darken, no error to mislead, no infirmities to lament, no enemies to assail, no cares to harass, no sickness to endure, no changes to experience; but where all will be perfect bliss unclouded light, unspotted purity, immortal tranquillity and joy.

Members of Families, in passing through life, should make it apparent, by their principles, by their habits, by their conversation, by their spirit, by their aims, that they are above the present transitory scene; and that they are intensely anxious to unite again in that world of peace, harmony, and love, where there will be nothing to defile or alloy, and where the thought of separation will be unknown.

Families! make the above maxims your governing principles, and we promise you domestic bliss. Wherever you may find discomfort abroad, you will be sure to realize happiness at Home

MINE OF WEALTH; AND,

Maxims for the Sedentary.

Eat no suppers, or at least let them be light; half a dozen oysters, or a cup of sago are the best. Brush the mouth and teeth well every morning, with a toothbrush and cold water. It would be well to do the same at night. Never allow the stomach to remain too long without food, nor stop the sensation of hunger by drink. If employed in study, always make an hour subservient to pleasure and exercise in the open air. Do not walk to fatigue, for that debilitates very much. Dancing is a most wholesome exercise both for the mind and body, but avoid excess in it. Nuts of all kinds are unwholsome. Always keep the feet from wet. Beware of damp beds, for these are destructive to health. Should you be caught in a rain shower change the damp clothing as quick as possible and rub the body dry.

How to Make a Will.

Take care that if written on several sheets of paper, they are all fastened together, and that the pages are numbered. Sign your name at the bottom of each sheet, and state at the end of your will of how many pages it consists. If there are any erasures or interlineations, put your initials in the margin opposite to them, and notice them in the attestation. The attestation should be already written at the end of the will. The two persons intended to be the witnesses should be called in, and told that you desire them to witness your will, and then you should sign your name in their presence, desiring them each to look at the signature. Your signature should follow your will, but should precede the signatures of the witnesses, for if you were to sign after they have signed, your will would be void. When therefore, you have signed they should sign their names and residences at the foot of the attestation. You will observe that, according to the attestation, neither of the witnesses although he has signed the attestation, should leave the room until the other witness has signed also. Remembering that they must both sign in your presence, and therefore you should not allow them to go into another room to sign, or even any recess, or any part of the same room, where it is possible that you might not see them sign. If therfore, you do not choose them to sign after you at the same table or desk, have a table placed close to you before they come into the room, so as to create no confusion, at which they can and ought to sign before leaving the room. If you were to send your servant, who happened to be one of your intended witnesses, out of the room even for a table, he must leave the room before you sign, if after your death, a question were to arise upon the fact of your having signed in the presence of both the witnesses present at the same time, the man would of course, admit that he left the room before you did sign, and then imagine what reliance would be placed upon the fact in cross-examination, and in the address to the jury.

Sympathetic Inks.

Secret Writing was known to the ancients but we have no direct evidence that it was used among them for secret intercourse during war, though there is every probability of it.

In modern times the subject has received from several of the early chemists considerable attention, which although it has not materially benefited science, has nevertheless afforded much amusement to its followers; we therefore offer some practical hints upon the subject.

SYMPATHETIC INKS which, from their property of being invisible when written with, and remaining so till they have undergone some process, formed the medium by which secret writing was carried on.

These inks are usually divided into three classes.—1. Those rendered visible by moistening the writing with another liquid, or by exposure to vapour. 2. Those rendered visible by sifting some finely powdered dark or highly-coloured substance over the writing. 3. Those rendered visible by heat.

FIRST CLASS.—The inks in this class require the aid of some liquid, or vapour, to render them visible thus.—

Inks made Solution of	become	When Washed out.
Green vitriol	black	Decoction or tincture of galls.
Perchloride of mercury	"	Hydrochlorate of tin.
Nitrate of copper	brown	Prussiate of Potash.
Solution of gold	purple	Muriate of tin.
Nitrate of Cobalt	blue	Oxalic acid.
Green vitrol	"	Prussiate of Potash.
Carbonate of iron	"	Prussiate of Potash.
Arseniate of Potash	green	Nitrate of copper.
Alum in lemon juice	grey	Water.
Nitrate of bismuth	yellow	Prussiate of Potash.
Muriate of Antimony	"	Decoction of tincture of galls.
Diacetate of Lead	"	Chromate of Potash.
Nitrate of mercury	crimson	Chromate of Potash.
Corrosive sublimate	scarlet	Iodide of Potash.
Rock alum	white	Water.

If the writing is to be rendered legible by exposure to a vapour write with a solution of nitrate of bismuth, or diacetate of lead, which becomes black when exposed to sulphuretted hydrogen.

SECOND CLASS.—This includes almost all glutinous expressed juices of plants, milk of animals, or any other viscid fluids, which, when dry are invisible, but by being inverted over steam, or being breathed on, and having some coloured powder sifted over the writing, become visible from the viscous nature of the ink attracting and retaining the powder. An illustration of this class is afforded by writing with milk, to be afterwards dusted with soot.

THIRD CLASS.—This class, from the beauty of the colours it includes, and the property most of the inks possess of the colour disappearing again when allowed to cool in a *moist* place, is capable of affording considerable amusement, by employing the inks as the colouring matter in certain portions of drawings; and it is to encourage this kind of amusement that we introduce the subject.

As some of the inks included in this class are only rendered visble by heat, without losing the colour again on cooling, we shall treat of these previous to describing the others:—

BLACK INK is produced by writing with a solution of sal amoniac, or diluted sulphuric acid; *brownish black*, by lemon juice; *brown*, by milk; *brownish yellow*, by juice of onions.

Nitre, alum, tartar, and sea salt, produce nearly the same effects, but not so decidedly.

Those inks which lose their colour on cooling, and resume it on the application of heat, are now to be considered. If a landscape, or view of mountain scenery for instance be drawn and painted as usual, omitting the colouring and outline of the foliage of the trees, the grass, thatch, water, reeds, parts of the sky, &c., or even figures of men, birds, or animals, and these parts be filled with the appropriate inks, the drawing will have the appearance of winter until heated, when the scene will be entirely changed to that of spring, or summer. A tulip, or other blub, may be drawn as usual, and the leaves and flowers finished with sympathetic inks; an empty plate may be made to appear full of fruit and leaves; a flower-pot, with a rose-tree without its leaves, will suddenly appear in full bloom and leaf; change of costume is as easy as scene, and, in fact, the subject is almost endless.

The various colours are produced by employing the inks mentioned below:—

ROSE COLOUR—By using a solution of oxide of cobalt in spirit of nitre.

GREEN—Solutions of the nitrate and chloride of cobalt and chloride of copper.

YELLOW—Muriate of copper.

BLUE—Muriate of cobalt, (if pure.)

Having said this much, we may leave the reader to experiment upon the subject. A little practice will soon render the artist proficient in the production of the interesting illusive effects alluded to.

Rules For Success in Business.

SELECT THE KIND OF BUSINESS SUITS YOUR NATURAL INCLINATIONS AND TEMPERAMENT.—Some men are naturally mechanics; others have a strong aversion to anything like machinery, and so on; one man has a natural taste for one occupation in life, and another for another.

I never could succeed as a merchant. We have tried it, unsuccessfully, several times. We never could be content with a fixed salary, for ours is a purely speculative disposition, while others are just the reverse; and therefore all should be careful to select those occupations that suit them best.

LET YOUR PLEDGED WORD EVER BE SACRED.—Never promise to do a thing without performing it with the most rigid promptness. Nothing is more valuable to a man in business than the name of always doing as he agrees, and that to the moment. A strict adherence to this rule gives a man the command of half the spare funds within the range of his acquaintance, and encircles him with a host of friends, who may be depended upon in any emergency.

WHAT EVER YOU DO, DO WITH ALL YOUR MIGHT.—Work at it if necessary, early and late, in season and out of season, not leaving a stone unturned, and never deferring for a single hour that which can just as well be done *now*. The old proverb is full of truth and meaning—"Whatever is worth doing at all, is worth doing well." Many a man acquires a fortune by doing his business *thoroughly*, while his neighbor remains poor for life, because he only *half* does his business. Ambition, energy, industry, and perseverance, are indispensable requisites for success in business.

SOBRIETY. USE NO DESCRIPTION OF INTOXICATING DRINKS.—As no man can succeed in business unless he has a brain to enable him to lay his plans, and *reason* to guide him in their execution, so, no matter how bountifully a man may be blessed with intelligence if his brain is muddled, and his judgment warped by intoxicating drinks, it is impossible for him to carry on business successfully. How many good opportunities have passed never to return, while a man was sipping a "social glass" with a friend! How many a bargain has been made under the influence of the wine-cup which temporarily makes its victim so *rich*! How many important chances have been put of until to-morrow, and thence for ever, because indulgence has thrown the system into a state of lassitude, neutralizing the energy so essential to success in business. The use of intoxicating drinks as a beverage is as much an infatuation as is the smoking of opium by the Chinese, and the former is quite as destructive to the success of the business man as the latter.

LET HOPE PREDOMINATE, BUT BE NOT TO VISIONARY.—Many persons are always kept poor because they are too *visionary*. Every project looks to them like certain success, and therefore they keep changing from one business to another, always in hot water, and always "under the harrow." The plan of "counting the chickens before they are hatched," is an error of ancient date, but it does not seem to improve by age.

DO NOT SCATTER YOUR POWERS.—Engage in one kind of business only, and stick to it faithfully until you succeed, or until you conclude to abandon it. A constant hammering on one nail will generally drive it home at last, so that it can be clinched. When a man's undivided attention is centered on one object, his mind will continually be suggesting improvements of value, which would escape him if his mind were occupied by a dozen different thoughts at once. Many a fortune has slipped through men's fingers by engaging in too many occupations at once.

ENGAGE PROPER EMPLOYEES.—Never employ a man of bad habits when one whose habits are good can be found to fill his situation. I have generally been extremely fortunate in having faithful, and competent persons to fill the responsible situations in my business; and a man can scarcely be too grateful for such a blessing

When you find a man unfit to fill his situation, either from incapacity peculiarity of character or disposition, dispense with his services, and do not drag out a miserable existence in the vain attempt to change his nature. "You cannot make a silk purse," &c. He has been created for some other sphere; let him find and fill it.

Do not Procrastinate.—There is no moment like the present; not only so, but, moreover, there is no other moment at all; that is, no instant force and energy but in the present. The man who will not execute his resolutions when they are fresh upon him can have no hope from them afterwards; they will be dissipated, lost, and perish in the hurry of the world, or sunk in the slough of indolence.

Industry.—There is no art or science that is too difficult for industry to attain to; it is the gift of tongues, and makes a man understood and valued in all countries, and by all nations; it is the philosopher's stone that turns all metals and even stones into gold, and suffers not want to break into its dwelling: it is the northwest passage that brings the merchant's ship as soon to him as he can desire—in a word, it conquers all enemies, and makes fortune herself pay contributions.

Fix your Mind.—Lay it down as a sound maxim :—Nothing can be accomplished without a fixed purpose—a concentration of mind and energy. Whatever you attempt to do, whether it be the writing of an essay, or whittling of a stick, let it be done as you can do it. It was this habit that made Franklin and Newton, and hundreds whose labors have been of incalculable service to mankind. Fix your mind closely and intently on what you undertake; in no other way can you have a reasonable hope of success. An energy that dies in a day is good for nothing; an hour's fixed attention will never avail. The inventions that bless mankind were not the result of a few moments' thought and investigation. If you then, have a desire to bless your species, or to get to yourself a glorious name, fix your mind upon something, and let it remain fixed.

www.ingramcontent.com/pod-product-compliance
Lightning Source LLC
Chambersburg PA
CBHW031747230426
43669CB00007B/520